Pugs For Dummies®

W9-BNT-244

Shopping for Pug Supplies

Before you bring your Pug home, have the following supplies on hand (see Chapter 5 for more information):

- A wire pet carrier for your Pug to ride safely in the car or to sleep inside the house.
- Bedding for the carrier to make it comfy. A clean old blanket will do just fine.
- Exercise pen or baby gates to keep your Pug puppy from getting into trouble.
- Collar and leashes to take your Pug on outings. Your dog should be on a leash every time you take him away from home.
- Identification to make sure that your Pug is returned to you if he ever gets separated from you.
- Two stainless steel bowls — one for food and one for water.
- Nail clippers for dogs or a cordless hobby grinder to keep your Pug's feet in good condition.
- Brush and comb to keep your Pug's coat looking healthy.
- Toothbrush and toothpaste to maintain good Pug dental health.
- Shampoo and conditioner to keep your Pug clean and smelling fresh.
- Premium food recommended by your breeder, veterinarian, or folks at a shelter or breed rescue group.
- Toys, toys, and more toys to keep your Pug happy and having fun.
- Clean-up scooper to pick up your yard.
- Pet odor remover or carpet cleaner to deal with those housetraining accidents.

Housetraining a Young Pug

If you want your new Pug pup to know where his personal bathroom is and how to use it as quickly as possible, you need to stay on his paws and keep him on a schedule every waking minute. Here are some hints to help you (for more tips, see Chapter 10):

In the morning, follow these steps:

1. **First thing, take your Pug outside and stay there several minutes and tell him, "Go potty, Puggy!" or "Hurry, Puggy, hurry!" until he does the deed.**

   When he's done, tell him that he's a great puppy.

2. **Give him breakfast.**

3. **Take your Pug back outside for potty again. When he's done, bring him indoors.**

4. **If you can't watch him, put him into his carrier.**

5. **Take your Pug outdoors every 20 minutes if you're home.**

In the afternoon, here's what to do:

1. **Feed Puggy lunch.**

2. **Take him outside.**

3. **Bring him back indoors and return him to his carrier if you're busy and can't watch him.**

4. **If you can watch him inside the house, notice whether he keeps walking around and sniffing the floor for a few minutes. If he does, take him back outside.**

Here's your Pug's evening schedule:

1. **As soon as you get home, take your Pug outside.**

2. **Bring him in for dinner.**

3. **Take him back outside.**

4. **Right before you're ready for bed, take Puggy outside again for the last time.**

5. **Tell him "night-night" and put him in his carrier for the night.**

Knowing When to Take Your Pug to the Vet Immediately

Can't decide whether your Pug has a health problem that needs immediate attention from your veterinarian? If you aren't sure, it's always a good idea to call your veterinarian, but here are some conditions that require attention as soon as possible (for more tips, check out Chapter 14):

- **Antifreeze ingestion:** If you think your dog has ingested antifreeze and shows these symptoms — convulsions or diarrhea, excessive urination, weakness or vomiting, or loss of coordination — take him to your veterinarian immediately.

- **Cardiac arrest:** If your Pug is unconscious, stops breathing, has dilated pupils or white gums, or if you can't detect a heartbeat, your Pug may be in cardiac arrest.

- **Coma:** If your dog has irregular breathing but doesn't respond and won't get up, he may be in a coma.

- **Drowning:** If your Pug stops breathing, tip your Pug's head down and thump the chest a few times to drain the water from the airways.

- **Overheating:** Too much exercise on a hot or humid day or being left in a hot car can cause overheating. Your Pug may collapse or have severe muscle cramps, vomiting, seizurelike tremors, or rapid breathing.

- **Penetrating chest wounds:** Your Pug needs immediate care if he has had an accident that leaves an opening in the chest wall.

- **Poisoning:** Signs of poisoning can include vomiting, bloody diarrhea, tremors, excessive salivation, and nosebleeds.

- **Seizures:** Your dog will experience uncontrollable shaking of the head, legs, or body and have a strange faraway look in his eyes.

- **Smoke inhalation and burns:** You can't often determine the severity of the damage from smoke inhalation and burns, so get emergency help as soon as possible.

- **Steady bleeding:** Hold a clean dishtowel against the wound until you can transport your dog to the vet.

- **Wheezing:** If your dog has trouble breathing and sounds like a person with severe asthma, get him to the vet as soon as possible.

Wiley, the Wiley Publishing logo, For Dummies, the Dummies Man logo, the For Dummies Bestselling Book Series logo and all related trade dress are trademarks or registered trademarks of John Wiley & Sons, Inc. and/or its affiliates. All other trademarks are property of their respective owners.

Copyright © 2004 Wiley Publishing, Inc.
All rights reserved.
Item 4076-9.
For more information about Wiley Publishing,
call 1-800-762-2974.

Pugs FOR DUMMIES®

by Elaine Waldorf Gewirtz

WILEY

Wiley Publishing, Inc.

Pugs For Dummies®
Published by
Wiley Publishing, Inc.
111 River St.
Hoboken, NJ 07030-5774
www.wiley.com

Copyright © 2004 by Wiley Publishing, Inc., Indianapolis, Indiana

Published simultaneously in Canada

No part of this publication may be reproduced, stored in a retrieval system, or transmitted in any form or by any means, electronic, mechanical, photocopying, recording, scanning, or otherwise, except as permitted under Sections 107 or 108 of the 1976 United States Copyright Act, without either the prior written permission of the Publisher, or authorization through payment of the appropriate per-copy fee to the Copyright Clearance Center, 222 Rosewood Drive, Danvers, MA 01923, 978-750-8400, fax 978-646-8600. Requests to the Publisher for permission should be addressed to the Legal Department, Wiley Publishing, Inc., 10475 Crosspoint Blvd., Indianapolis, IN 46256, 317-572-3447, fax 317-572-4447, or e-mail permcoordinator@wiley.com.

Trademarks: Wiley, the Wiley Publishing logo, For Dummies, the Dummies Man logo, A Reference for the Rest of Us!, The Dummies Way, Dummies Daily, The Fun and Easy Way, Dummies.com and related trade dress are trademarks or registered trademarks of John Wiley & Sons, Inc. and/or its affiliates in the United States and other countries, and may not be used without written permission. All other trademarks are the property of their respective owners. Wiley Publishing, Inc., is not associated with any product or vendor mentioned in this book.

GENERAL DISCLAIMER: THE PUBLISHER AND THE AUTHOR MAKE NO REPRESENTATIONS OR WARRANTIES WITH RESPECT TO THE ACCURACY OR COMPLETENESS OF THE CONTENTS OF THIS WORK AND SPECIFICALLY DISCLAIM ALL WARRANTIES, INCLUDING WITHOUT LIMITATION WARRANTIES OF FITNESS FOR A PARTICULAR PURPOSE. NO WARRANTY MAY BE CREATED OR EXTENDED BY SALES OR PROMOTIONAL MATERIALS. THE ADVICE AND STRATEGIES CONTAINED HEREIN MAY NOT BE SUITABLE FOR EVERY SITUATION. THIS WORK IS SOLD WITH THE UNDERSTANDING THAT THE PUBLISHER IS NOT ENGAGED IN RENDERING LEGAL, ACCOUNTING, OR OTHER PROFESSIONAL SERVICES. IF PROFESSIONAL ASSISTANCE IS REQUIRED, THE SERVICES OF A COMPETENT PROFESSIONAL PERSON SHOULD BE SOUGHT. NEITHER THE PUBLISHER NOR THE AUTHOR SHALL BE LIABLE FOR DAMAGES ARISING HEREFROM. THE FACT THAT AN ORGANIZATION OR WEBSITE IS REFERRED TO IN THIS WORK AS A CITATION AND/OR A POTENTIAL SOURCE OF FURTHER INFORMATION DOES NOT MEAN THAT THE AUTHOR OR THE PUBLISHER ENDORSES THE INFORMATION THE ORGANIZATION OR WEBSITE MAY PROVIDE OR RECOMMENDATIONS IT MAY MAKE. FURTHER, READERS SHOULD BE AWARE THAT INTERNET WEBSITES LISTED IN THIS WORK MAY HAVE CHANGED OR DISAPPEARED BETWEEN WHEN THIS WORK WAS WRITTEN AND WHEN IT WAS READ.

For general information on our other products and services or to obtain technical support, please contact our Customer Care Department within the U.S. at 800-762-2974, outside the U.S. at 317-572-3993, or fax 317-572-4002.

Wiley also publishes its books in a variety of electronic formats. Some content that appears in print may not be available in electronic books.

Library of Congress Control Number: 2003116371

ISBN: 0764540769

Manufactured in the United States of America

10 9 8 7 6 5 4 3 2

1B/RX/QS/QU/1N

WILEY   is a trademark of Wiley Publishing, Inc.

About the Author

Elaine Waldorf Gewirtz is the author of and contributor to books (*Your Yorkshire Terrier's Life, The Dog Sourcebook, Dogs: The Ultimate Care Guide, and Dogspeak*) and numerous magazine articles on dogs and their care, and is the winner of the ASPCA (American Society for the Prevention of Cruelty to Animals) Special Writing Award. She is also the editor of *The Spotter,* the Dalmatian Club of America's publication, which received the Dog Writers Association of America's Maxwell Award for Excellence, and writes the Dalmatian breed column for the *American Kennel Club Gazette.* For ten years, she was a reporter with Scripps Howard News.

A graduate of UCLA's Masters in Writing Program and California State University at Northridge, Gewirtz is a member of the Dog Writers Association of America and the Independent Writers of Southern California, and has lived with Pugs and other breeds all her life. Elaine has also bred, trained, and handled Dalmatians in the obedience and show rings; teaches conformation handling classes; and has judged puppy Sweepstakes at the Dalmatian Club of America's National Specialty.

She shares her home in Westlake Village, California, with her husband, Steve; their daughter and expert canine caretaker, Beth-Jo; and the dogs, who often come first. The couple also have three other grown children, Sameya, Sara, and Seth, who come to visit and spoil the dogs completely and thoroughly.

Dedication

This book is dedicated to my parents, Leo and Rosalie Waldorf, who gave me my first love of dogs and writing, and to my husband, Steve, and our now-adult children — Sameya; Sara and her fiancé, Ryan Miller; Seth; and Beth-Jo, — for their constant support, love, and understanding.

Thanks also to good friend Cyndy Wood for her constant supply of spoiling, to expert professional handler Bruce Schultz, and to Camp Schultz pro assistants Tara Tuthill and Casandra Clark for being able to look into a dog's eyes and know exactly what he is thinking. You have taught me a great deal.

And, of course, to Buster, Lolly, Vicky, Bob, Jimmy, Will, Jill, and Sassy, who have sat beneath my computer waiting patiently for inspiration to strike so I will take them for a walk.

Author's Acknowledgments

I'm so glad to have the opportunity to thank so many people who helped me create this book. In a way, they're a lot like the very Pugs I worked to describe: even-tempered, playful, with hearts of gold, willing to help and to share whenever asked. First and foremost, thanks to the *Pugs For Dummies* staff for keeping the book on track and for their endless patience and expertise: Acquisitions Editor Tracy Boggier, Project Editor Allyson Grove, Copy Editor Tina Sims, and Beth Adelman, for her support.

Special thanks go to Judi Crowe, Pug breeder and photographer extraordinaire, who was always willing to answer all my questions (and there were many) any time of day (or night!). The breed is lucky to have people like Judi. I was also very fortunate to have esteemed Pug breeder and veterinarian Christine Dresser, DVM, serve as the technical editor for the manuscript. Thank you, Dr. Dresser, for being so kind to my writing!

I also want to thank the Pug Dog Club of America for lending information via its Web site (www.pdca.org), Margery Shriver for providing me with the club's excellent Illustrated Standard of the breed, the people at Kansas State University College of Veterinary Medicine for their knowledge, and Paul Krebaum for freely giving his skunk remedy to the world of dogs.

Thanks, too, to Pug breeders Tony Nunes and her family, who helped enormously with photographs; Karen Rivera for connecting me to some special rescue Pug puppies of Lois Wermer's; Blanche Roberts; and John Morgan. Sherrie Woodbury of Little Angels Pug Rescue was another great source, as was Meg Callea's photography.

Then there are the numerous breeders and owners whom I met along the way at dog shows, out walking in neighborhoods, and at Pug gatherings — thanks to them for sharing their love of Pugs with me. And thanks, of course, to the Pugs themselves for all they give to us. I know I've been Pugged now for sure.

Publisher's Acknowledgments

We're proud of this book; please send us your comments through our Dummies online registration form located at www.dummies.com/register/.

Some of the people who helped bring this book to market include the following:

Acquisitions, Editorial, and Media Development

Project Editor: Allyson Grove

Acquisitions Editor: Tracy Boggier

Senior Copy Editor: Tina Sims

Assistant Editor: Holly Gastineau-Grimes

Technical Editor: Christine Dresser, DVM

Editorial Manager: Michelle Hacker

Editorial Assistant: Elizabeth Rea

Cover Photos: © Francine Fleischer/CORBIS

Cartoons: Rich Tennant, www.the5thwave.com

Production

Project Coordinators: Adrienne Martinez, Erin Smith

Layout and Graphics: Andrea Dahl, Michael Kruzil, Heather Ryan, Jacque Schneider

Proofreaders: Carl William Pierce, Charles Spencer, TECHBOOKS Production Services

Indexer: TECHBOOKS Production Services

Special Help: Laura K. Miller

Publishing and Editorial for Consumer Dummies

Diane Graves Steele, Vice President and Publisher, Consumer Dummies

Joyce Pepple, Acquisitions Director, Consumer Dummies

Kristin A. Cocks, Product Development Director, Consumer Dummies

Michael Spring, Vice President and Publisher, Travel

Brice Gosnell, Associate Publisher, Travel

Kelly Regan, Editorial Director, Travel

Publishing for Technology Dummies

Andy Cummings, Vice President and Publisher, Dummies Technology/General User

Composition Services

Gerry Fahey, Vice President of Production Services

Debbie Stailey, Director of Composition Services

Contents At A Glance

Table Of Contents

Part IV: Raising a Healthy and Active Pug 181

Chapter 13: Getting Good Medical Care for Your Pug 183

Chapter 14: Dealing with Signs of Sickness 199

Introduction

*W*hat is it about Pugs that draws people's attention? Is it their friendly nature? Could it be their roly-poly shape, their big googly eyes, or all those crinkly wrinkles on their forehead? Pugs are pretty good lap sitters, too, and excel in the art of relaxation and getting plenty of zzz's, but sometimes they can be pretty pugnacious when it comes to getting what they want.

If you ask me, it's a combination of all these things, which is what drew our family to the breed while I was growing up. My mother was a true dog lover, so we always had a few different breeds in residence over the years, but one or two Pugs usually reigned supreme in our household. In the neighborhood where we lived, we were known as the Pug family, and we couldn't have been any prouder. Our dogs were willing make-believe participants on rainy days and refused to be left out of our outdoor shenanigans (as long as it was cool outside). Mostly they looked forward to greeting their fans like royalty during walks around the block. All in all, we couldn't have asked for better playmates.

For example, Boots, our black Pug, was my constant companion who tolerated homemade costumes, including the headgear. I'm not sure he was entirely happy when we made him wear a dress though — after all, he's a manly Pug — but at least he didn't rebel. Give Boots a cookie when the stage show was over, and he'd wear anything the next time!

Fawn Debbie, on the other hand, wanted no part of playacting and preferred hanging out in the kitchen waiting for goodies to fall her way. Her other hobby was waiting for the letter carrier and then eating the mail as it shot through our mail slot. We never told her that some of the envelopes weren't real U.S. Postal Service deliveries because we didn't want to disappoint her. She was convinced she had an important job in our household, and we wanted to oblige. After all, who were we not to please a Pug?

We were so Pug smitten that if we went on an errand and saw someone walking a Pug on the street, my Dad just had to pull the car over and see the dog up close and exchange Pug info with the owner.

Today, I'm glad to see that other people are just as happy to see Pugs as we were. There are Pug clubs throughout the country, and you see the breed just about everywhere you look, including television. But having Pugs star in films from *Milo and Otis* to the *Men In Black* series really launched their Hollywood careers and helped make them one of the most popular breeds. But just because they look all cute and cuddly on the big screen isn't a good enough reason to run out and get one.

Instead, you want to find out as much as you can about the breed before you get involved. That's where I come in. Consider this book your guide to all things Pug. Whether you have a Pug now or are thinking about getting your first or second, this book helps you know everything there is to know about the dog that's a lot in a little package.

About This Book

Pugs For Dummies tells you everything you need to know about what these cute little members of the Toy breed are really like in terms of personality and temperament. But that's just the beginning of the story. In addition, I explain what you should know before choosing a good Pug and what you need to do to take care of your Pug from the very first day he enters your life. This includes buying the right supplies, figuring out the mysteries of house-training, getting involved in showing or training, and dealing with the various health issues that affect Pugs.

Here's a book that can be your number one Pug reference, even after you've made it through the first few months of Pug life. When you have a dog, things always crop up that you want to know more about, such as what to do if you want to take your Pug on a long trip, what kinds of recreational activities you and Puggy can get involved in, or what to say if someone wants you to breed your darling.

I didn't leave anything Pug-related out, but you don't have to read everything all at once. In fact, I purposely arranged the topics in the book so that you can just turn at random to whatever chapter interests you at the time. Then later on, you can go back for more info as you want to read it.

Conventions Used in This Book

To help you more easily find some information in this book, I use the following conventions:

- *Italic* is used for emphasis and to highlight new words or terms that are defined.
- **Boldfaced** text is used to indicate the keywords in bulleted lists or the action part of numbered steps.
- `Monofont` is used for Web addresses.

What You're Not to Read

I've made it so easy for you to find out about Pugs that you don't have to read everything in this book all in one sitting to get the vital info.

Feel free to skip all the sections marked with a Technical Stuff icon (I talk about icons later in this Introduction) if you want to. Sidebars (text shaded in gray boxes) are skippable, too. This information is plenty interesting, I think, but if you miss it, no worries. You still discover all of the do's and don'ts about getting, raising, and enjoying a Pug.

Foolish Assumptions

I don't really assume too much about you, the reader. Well, maybe just that you love or want to fall in love with a Pug. I do know that you're eager to do all the right Pug-related things and can't wait to get started on being a Pug person.

The truth is that this book is chock-full of information to make your relationship with a Pug a wonderful one — no matter whether you have one right now, have a whole litter, or haven't even laid eyes on one (but are developing a keen interest in the breed). If you're already a devoted Pug fan, you're bound to find this book very useful. That's because I give you tons of tips and suggestions for life with Pugs, including the latest information to keep your Pug in tip-top shape for many years to come.

How This Book Is Organized

Pugs For Dummies has five parts, each dealing with a different topic. Feel free to bounce around the parts and even the chapters. Each is independent and lets you quickly go in and out of the book as the need arises to find out about your Pug. Here's a quick look at how I've organized the parts.

Part 1: Adding Pug Paws to Your Life

I begin by explaining what a Pug is and asking whether this is the right Toy dog for you. Personally, I can't imagine living without a dog that thinks he's a clown, but you may not want an entertainer around the house. I discuss what the ideal Pug is all about so that you can decide what kind of Pug you want. Can't decide between getting a puppy or a mature dog? I include facts about both age ranges and help you determine what's best for your situation. You have some color and quality choices to make, as well, and I explore these options for you to contemplate. I also give you suggestions on how to find the best Pug, whether the source is a reputable breeder, a shelter, or a rescue organization.

Part II: Living with Puggy

Before your Pug comes home, you need to stock up on supplies, such as bedding, collars, food and water bowls, and toys, and this part goes into detail about what exactly to buy. This is the fun part of getting a new dog, but you don't have to get everything all at the same time. I give you some hints about what things you need right away and what items you may want to add later on.

I also tell you what to expect on the day he comes home; how to create a safe environment for him; how to introduce him to your family, friends, and other pets; what and how much to feed him; and how often and what type of exercise he needs.

When you look at a Pug, it's easy to think, "Hmm, short-hair equals low maintenance." Well, not exactly. To keep your Pug looking and feeling spiffy, you need to know a few basic grooming secrets, which I also provide in this part.

Part III: Training Your Pug

Having a well-behaved Pug takes effort, but it's worth it. Pugs can be pretty impish at times and don't always take no for an answer, even after you've made it very clear what you want them to do. In some cases, you have to get a little creative when it comes to getting the message across, but after Puggy knows you're in charge, he's glad to make you happy.

This part offers a primer on all the training you'll be doing. I discuss housetraining, crate-training, teaching basic commands like Sit and Stay, meeting strangers, and traveling safely. All this upfront work results in a Pug who's a joy to be around.

Part IV: Raising a Healthy and Active Pug

Keeping your Pug safe and healthy helps ensure that you have your little canine friend for a long time. In this part, I explain the importance of regular checkups and vaccinations, the way to give medications and take your Pug's temperature, and the various types of identification.

This part also discusses some things you hope you never have to deal with — inherited diseases, parasites, and emergencies — but in case you do, you can know what to expect. I also talk about letting your Pug serve as a therapy dog, participate in Junior Showmanship, or earn his Canine Good Citizen award. You also find out some details about dog shows.

Part V: The Part of Tens

Here are some top-ten lists that every *For Dummies* book is famous for. This part gives you reasons not to breed your Pug, simple guidelines for living with a Pug, and sources of more information about Pugs.

Icons Used in This Book

What's an icon, and why are they all over the book? Icons are graphics I use to give you a quick clue as to what you're about to read. You can find them in the margins. They're designed to help you locate a quick tip, remember something very important, find out what your Pug loves, or be extra aware of something dangerous to your Pug. I also include some technical information that expands on what you're already discovering.

These icons easily identify special hints on training and caring for your Pug. As you can see as you flip through the book, I use this icon more than the others.

I forgot what this is for. Just kidding! This icon calls your attention to helpful information that you should commit to memory. Be sure to refer to these for special info that can help you and your Pug have a fun, healthy, and safe relationship.

I thought it would be very helpful to tell you things that I think your Pug will love, so I use this icon. Pug owners are always looking for ways to make their dogs happy, so smile and enjoy.

Watch out! This icon highlights potential dangers or problems that you want to pay special attention to. The information here also can help you prevent any health emergencies and other boo-boos in caring for your Pug.

You don't need to read the tech talk identified by this icon, but if you're curious, go right ahead. These icons often define terms or explain dog facts that aren't crucial to your basic understanding of how to raise a Pug.

Where to Go from Here

It's a big book, and you don't know where to begin? Don't worry. You don't have to start at the very beginning to find out everything you need to know about your Pug. Each chapter doesn't depend on the others for information. You can pick the book up at any time, peruse the Table of Contents for the subject you're looking for, and just turn to those pages. Or you can just open it up anywhere and start reading.

If you want to know all about a Pug, it's a good idea to read Chapters 1, 2, and 3 to become educated about the breed. Then, before you actually pick up your new Pug, I suggest that you read Chapter 5 about what supplies you need before Puggy comes home. And if you're curious about Pug health issues and what problems your Pug may end up having, check out Chapters 13 and 14.

Of course, if you're the type who likes to start at page 1 and go straight through to the last page, you can do that, too. Whatever works for you can get you all the Pug facts in this book that you'll ever need. Wherever you start, enjoy the journey you'll be taking with your Pug. I want you to have a great time, and I wish you the same happy Puggy memories that I have.

Part I
Adding Pug Paws
to Your Life

The 5th Wave
By Rich Tennant

"Your loyalty and devotion are legendary.
However, let me remind you that you are
under oath."

In this part . . .

Sharing your life with a dog is certainly an adventure, and this part reveals what having a Pug is all about. First, I explain what a Pug looks like (square, stocky, and cute!), and help you discover the wonders of his personality (he's a clown for sure!). I also tell you where you can go to find the ideal dog that's right for your lifestyle. Then, when you get there, I talk about how you can pick out the perfect Pug.

Chapter 1

Getting the Lowdown on Pugs

Welcome to the curly tail-wagging world of Pugs! Life with a Pug is a fun-loving, big-eyed experience, that's for sure. The Pug is a dog that wants nothing more than to fill your life with hilarious hijinks, lots of snorty kisses, and oodles of good company. In this chapter, I help you decide whether this cheery little fellow is the right breed for you. I also discuss what it means to add a Pug to your household.

Defining Pugs

The largest member of the Toy family, the Pug is one of the most popular breeds around. It's hard to go anywhere without seeing a Pug because people are totally in love with this dog. Why all the hoopla about this short little fellow? Well, it's easy to see why he's so popular. Here's a dog with his own ready-made slogan, *multum in parvo,* which means, "a big dog in a little body." Basically, a Pug has a lot going on in a small space.

First comes his compact yet very sturdy frame that's built to last. There's nothing fragile about Puggy, who weighs around 20 pounds and stands between 10 and 12 inches tall. Next, there's his expression with its big-eyed appeal. Two bright, glistening black globes watch your every move. Add in his pushed-in nose, big grin, and curious pattern of wrinkles crossing his face, and you have a pugtacular-looking little dog.

Last, but certainly the frosting on the canine cake, is the Pug's easy-going manner. Silly, yet serious when he needs to be, the Pug oozes personality, and plenty of charm and character is packed into his frame. He can be a lap dog one minute and an eager playmate the next. Mostly he loves hanging around his owners and doesn't want to be left out of anything.

Pugs are definitely a breed apart from other kinds of dogs and aren't your typical kind of fussy little dog. They're interested in pleasing you and aren't very demanding. They're sometimes a little too big to cuddle like a very small dog, but they're sturdy enough to play a fast game of catch and chase the birds in the yard. See Chapter 2 for more about the whole Pug picture and Chapter 3 for an official description (also called the *breed standard*) of the Pug.

Deciding Whether a Pug Is Right for You

No doubt about it, getting a Pug, or any dog, is a big decision. That's because a dog is a 24/7 responsibility. What seems like a good idea now is really a 12- to 15-year investment of your time, money, and freedom. Think you're prepared to take on this duty? Read the next few sections to help you decide.

Evaluating your lifestyle

Sure, the idea of having a Pug may sound exciting. Maybe you've always wanted to have a dog, but this is the first time you're able to think about getting one of your own. Perhaps you've just gotten your first big job in a new city and can now afford to take care of a dog, have the room to keep one, and the time to enjoy one. Should you rush out and get one? Maybe yes and maybe no.

A Pug is definitely great company and makes the best listener when you've had a hard day at the office and want to spout off about your boss. Likewise, if you live alone, a dog can offer good protection by barking when a stranger comes to the door. Many people actually say they feel safer with a dog in the house.

Although these are all good reasons for you to get a dog, you need to consider a few more things before rushing out to buy kibble. If you're the only one Puggy lives with, remember that he's been alone all day and is just bursting with energy when you come home. He wants to do things even though all you may want to do is veg out on the sofa. That means you need to plan ahead to spend some quality exercise time with Puggy if you want to have a happy dog when you come home. Maybe you want to check out some doggy activities that you can both do together, such as visiting hospital patients or taking obedience or agility classes. (See Chapter 15 for more specifics about visiting hospitals or taking classes with your Pug.)

In some cities, you can even find reputable doggy day-care facilities that provide activities for your pet while you're away. You may want to consider this option if you work long hours. These facilities range in price depending upon the services offered and the city — anywhere from ten to twenty-five dollars a day. Many facilities offer affordable packages that can be combined with overnight lodging, if you need to board your Pug.

Also, you can hire a dog walker to come in during the day and take your Pug for a walk while you're gone. Fees for these services range, and people aren't always available in every city, so you have to contact your veterinarian or ask other dog owners to locate reliable dog walkers.

Like to go away for the weekends? Unless you like to camp or go places that welcome dogs, you have to leave Puggy behind. You also need to get a pet sitter to take care of him, or you need to take him to a kennel. Besides the expense of dog care, you also have to look at your Pug's sad expression when you leave him. Doing so isn't easy, but just reassure him that you'll be back soon and that you'll miss him while you're away.

Sharing your space

Having a ranch or a large home with acres of safe grounds may be ideal for a Pug or any dog (or me!) to live in, but that's not everyone's living arrangement. Pugs don't need much room, but even small dogs need space to stretch their legs. If you live in an apartment, or a small condo or house without a fenced yard, Puggy can still feel right at home. Sometimes though, a small space can get pretty crowded with one Pug and a thousand toys!

And come rainy days, your small dog may get cabin fever when he doesn't get as much outdoor exercise as he'd really like. You can play fetch and keep Puggy entertained in a small hallway for only so long. Having a small house without a yard may also mean taking him out on a leash all the time to go to the bathroom, which may be more time-consuming than you first expected. Do you have the patience and the energy? If you do, by all means, get a Pug. If not, you may want to think twice about it.

For more information about how much room your Pug needs, see Chapter 8.

Accepting that your house isn't going to be spotless

If you like an immaculate home, a Pug or any other dog may not be for you. Sure, you can train Puggy to wipe his wet feet off on a mat before he comes into the house, but what happens when he has an upset tummy and regurgitates his breakfast on the new carpet? Your Pug will also have housetraining accidents, even after you think that he has figured out the bathroom routine. Are you going to be really upset, or can you clean the boo-boo up quickly and take it in stride? If you have a dog, count on picking up messes now and then. It happens.

Shedding — lots of it — is another inevitable fact of Pug ownership. Although most dogs shed to some extent, Pugs are major shedders. Accept the fact that you have tiny fawn or black hairs decorating your household. Besides, they add character to your décor! Although you can't stop Puggy from shedding completely, you can keep him clean and well-groomed, which cuts down on hair loss. See Chapter 9 for more Pug grooming basics.

When you think about it, cleaning up a few loose hairs around the house is a small price to pay for having such a loyal companion. Messes can always be cleaned up, but life with a Pug is special and meant to be magical.

Maintaining household harmony

Although you may think that a Pug is the only dog for you, other people who live in your home may have other ideas. How will they feel if you bring a Pug into the house without their approval? Sure, other family members can learn to love Puggy, but some people don't go with the flow. You don't want to have to continually stick up for your little guy. Plus, when you go away, you have to ask someone at home to pitch in and help out by feeding or walking your Pug. A happy dog household works best when everyone is on the same doggy page and likes your Pug.

 Assuming that everyone agrees about the dog, plan on having a few group discussions about the training methods that everyone wants to use and can stick by. I talk about how to teach your Pug some good manners in Chapters 10 and 11.

Another point you want to clear up with your family members deals with food. If you think that Puggy shouldn't be given table scraps, it helps if the whole household agrees. Everyone needs to agree on what your Pug eats on a regular basis so he doesn't get too heavy or eat something that doesn't agree with him. The last thing you want is to have a well-meaning member of the household inadvertently give him something that makes him sick. See Chapter 7 for more information about feeding your Pug properly.

Although Pugs do well with children, some children don't do well with small dogs. Youngsters can be afraid for no apparent reason. I remember a time when a lovely young family came over to our home for a visit with their 18-month-old son. We were looking forward to watching the child play with Boots, our black Pug. Well, the toddler took one look at Boots and began screaming. Boots never even went near him, but the child wouldn't stop yelling, despite our cajoling. I was never so glad to see guests leave.

One way to avoid this same kind of situation is to take your child with you when you're visiting Pug litters or contemplating adopting an older dog. This way, you can make sure that they can both get along before you bring the dog home.

Even if your Pug and your child get along famously, always keep an eye on both of them whenever they're together and never leave them unattended. Your child is learning how to play positively with your Pug and needs some guidance from you. For more information, see Chapter 6.

One last point to consider is other animals in the house (and I don't mean that pesky bird that sometimes gets into your attic!). If you already have an elderly dog or cat with health issues, he may not appreciate a young rambunctious puppy jumping all over him. Then again, a first dog in good health may like having a new Pug playmate. Pugs are eager to get along with any other dogs, cats, or small critters already in the home. I talk about this issue in more detail in Chapter 6.

Adding Up the Dollars and Cents: The Cost of Pug Ownership

Think about all the unconditional love that your Pug can give you. Can you really put a price on how much that's worth? Maybe, maybe not. But along with the joy comes financial responsibility. The companionship that a dog brings can sometimes be a luxury item if your budget is already stretched too thin.

If you're thinking about acquiring a new puppy or adopting an older Pug, make sure that your dog expenses can fit within your budget. Otherwise, you may end up resenting everything Puggy needs. Remember that when you take on a Pug, you're making a commitment to take care of him for the rest of his life.

If you're buying a puppy from a reputable breeder for several hundred dollars, you may think the purchase price is the most expensive part of owning a dog, but that's not the case. In fact, the purchase price is a drop in the bucket. Over the course of 12 to 15 years of a dog's lifetime, the average pet owner can easily spend $15,000 to $20,000.

A Pug comes with a long list of essentials, including the following:

- Baby gates
- Bedding and a pet carrier
- Bitter spray to deter chewing
- Bowls for water and food
- Carpet cleaner or stain remover
- Collars and leash
- Fencing and gates to secure the yard
- Food and, if necessary, food supplements
- Grooming products, such as ear- and wrinkle-cleaning products, shampoo, conditioner, brush, comb, toothbrush, toothpaste, and nail clippers or a nail grinder
- Grooming services
- Medications, such as flea control products and heartworm prevention
- Pet hair removers for furniture and clothing
- Pet insurance
- Pet sitter
- Registration and identification
- Toys
- Training classes for puppies and adults
- Travel harness
- Treats

✔ Veterinary expenses, including teeth cleaning and possible emergency care

✔ Waste scooper

Of course, you don't have to go overboard by supplying your dog with lots of expensive toys, fancy collars, and leashes, but you shouldn't skimp on his health. For example, make sure he has routine visits to the veterinarian for yearly checkups, teeth cleanings, and hopefully just minor problems, such as ear infections or a bad cough. See Chapter 13 for the lowdown on finding a good vet and ensuring that he or she keeps your dog in the best possible health.

REMEMBER

Speaking of the best possible health, it helps to know what vaccines your Pug will need so you can plan ahead for it in your budget. I cover that topic in Chapter 13.

One more health-related recommendation is to feed your Pug the same quality dog food at each meal. Feeding your dog whatever food is on sale at the supermarket isn't a good choice because it most likely doesn't have all the nutrition that Puggy needs. Some low-cost food manufacturers don't always use the same ingredients each time they manufacture and package their meals, so it's not always the same recipe your dog is accustomed to eating. Unlike people, dogs need to eat the same meal every time. When you do make meal changes, you have to do those changes gradually with a little of the new food combined with the old. See Chapter 7 for more details about a proper Pug diet.

Committing to Socializing and Training

Gosh, having a dog just looked so (warning: pun alert) doggone easy when you visited your friend who has a Pug. When it was time for his Pug to relieve himself, he just went to the door by himself and patiently waited to be let out, or maybe he just hopped through the doggy door when the need arose. Your friend didn't have to do anything but scoop up the mess outside when he got around to it. Simple enough, right? The reality is that your friend probably spent several weeks or even months training his new Pug all about the bathroom basics.

And no doubt he had to contend with more than a few accidents along the way. So what you have to determine is whether you're up for the challenge. New dog owners need plenty of patience — not to mention a sense of humor — when it comes to housetraining. Check out Chapter 10 for my tips to make the process as painless as possible.

And when it comes to overall training, you may think that Pugs don't need much because they look so well behaved on someone else's leash and seem so easygoing in public. However, this roly-poly, good-time-fellow appearance can be deceiving. Certainly, Pugs are easy to work with, yet they still need some measure of socialization and training, as do all dogs. Unfortunately, they weren't born knowing that a street is a dangerous place to run into and that the mail isn't just another thing to chew up.

So my advice is to plan on setting aside some time to take Puggy to puppy or adult obedience classes. You can also show your dog some behavior basics, such as Sit, Stay, Down, and Come at home, and I talk about this do-it-yourself training in Chapter 11.

You also need to introduce your Pug to the neighborhood and the overall world around him. You can do this by taking him with you when you go out for a walk or a jog near your home or even when you run errands. For example, maybe you have no intention of going to the outdoor shopping center, but if going there with your Pug gives him a chance to meet some new faces and therefore build his self-confidence, it's worth it. In fact, getting out and about not only helps your Pug become more socialized but also allows him to get some much-needed exercise (see Chapter 8 for more about exercising your dog).

Think about all that's involved in making your Pug the light of your life before you bring one home. That light will still need a connection to keep shining.

Signing Up for a Lifelong Tour of Pug Duty

When you make the decision to have a Pug, you're signing up for a lifelong responsibility. He's your dog whether you like what he's doing or you don't, but it's up to you to make the experience and time you have with him a positive one. The good news is that dog help is almost always available when you need it. By reading this book, you're already taking the first step to making your Pug's life with you a good one. Keep up the good work! Puggy deserves it.

Pugsters on the big screen

Pugs have been popular characters in both television and movies. You even see them in television commercials and print advertisements. And why shouldn't they be? Pugs are cute and personable, and they can have that serious actor look that all directors work hard to find. The following are a few famous movies in which Pugs appear. Some have larger roles than others, so don't blink during some of these movies, or you may miss the Pug's appearance:

- ✔ *The Adventures of Milo & Otis*
- ✔ *Best in Show*
- ✔ *Big Momma's House*
- ✔ *Cats & Dogs*
- ✔ *Dune*
- ✔ *The Gathering Storm*
- ✔ *The Great Gatsby*
- ✔ *The Great Race*
- ✔ *Heavenly Creatures*
- ✔ *Mansfield Park*
- ✔ *Men in Black* and *Men in Black II*
- ✔ *Men of Honor*
- ✔ *Monkey Bone*
- ✔ *Pie In The Sky: The Brigid Berlin Story*
- ✔ *Pocahontas*
- ✔ *Police Academy*
- ✔ *Pugsley, aka Manhattan Dog Story*
- ✔ *The Runaway Bride*
- ✔ *The Summer House*
- ✔ *Tom Jones*
- ✔ *The Truth About Charlie*

Chapter 2

Picturing the Pug Package

In This Chapter

▶ Getting a handle on the Pug's physical appearance

▶ Peeking at the Pug's personality

The world is full of lots of little dogs, but with her roly-poly body and big googly eyes, a Pug stands out from all the rest. Her good looks and curious curly tail turn heads wherever she goes. Puggy is a lot of dog in a small but sturdy shape. In fact, Pugs are the largest dogs in the Toy family.

The thing is that Puggy doesn't think of herself as a pint-size pooch; she acts just like a big dog. She's all about being confident and waddling, er, I mean standing tall. And although every breed has some genetic weaknesses, the Pug's are centered on the head and legs. In this chapter, I talk about Puggy's overall appearance and personality.

Appearance Is Everything: Checking Out the Pug's Physique

Although cars, appliances, and clothing styles are constantly changing and look different from year to year, Pugs look pretty much the same today as they did almost 200 years ago. That's because breeders take great care to make sure they're producing another generation that looks and acts exactly like other Pugs. They use the American Kennel Club (AKC) standard as their guide (see Chapter 3) to maintain the breed.

Although you're probably not breeding your own Pug (Chapter 18 tells you why you don't want to breed), you can use the AKC standard to appreciate what your dog looks like and to understand what makes Puggy a special fellow and so different from any other breed or mixed breed.

How the Pug got its name

The Pug started out with a few different names, but the breed name used today came from two different places. One origin is the Latin word *pugnus,* which means "fist," a word that describes the closed-hand shape of a Pug's head. Another origin is the name used for marmoset monkeys centuries ago (a popular pet of the 17th and 18th centuries), which were known as Pugs.

After you come face to big round face with a Pug, you know a Pug forever because this breed is easy to recognize. She's that curious-looking Toy dog with a square, stocky body; short legs; and a small tail that curls up and over her back. Other physical traits are a big head, tiny ears, and those jet-black oversize eyes that watch you wherever you go.

Oh yes, and don't forget all those wrinkles. (Check out the color insert for more on the Pug's physical features and unique characteristics.)

Size matters

The largest member of the Toy family, Pugs are typically 10 to 12 inches tall. They're also 10 to 12 inches long, if you measure from the front of the chest to the rear, so in proportion they're a square and stocky dog.

Their bodies shouldn't be longer than their height. Pugs are compact and well proportioned, and breeders like to refer to them as *multum in parvo,* which is a Latin phrase meaning that there's a great deal in a little package. This phrase also refers to the breed's big, generous, loving heart.

Weighty issues

At their healthiest weight, Pugs tip the scales between 14 and 18 pounds. If they get too heavy, health problems can develop, although many males who are show dogs weigh 20 to 24 pounds without any problems. The show dogs are usually exercised and conditioned to be able to handle that extra weight comfortably.

Because Pugs love food and eating, they can easily gain too much weight. In no time at all, they can look just like a portable footstool, which isn't healthy.

To get an idea of how big your Pug should be, check out Figure 2-1, which shows two Pugs. The Pug on the left weighs what she's supposed to weigh, and the Pug on the right is very overweight. You can tell the difference because the Pug on the right is very wide and has no extra fold of skin at the top of her body. In comparison, the Pug on the left has a shapely abdomen and wrinkles at the top of her body.

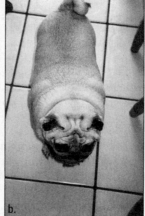

Figure 2-1:
Average weight Pug (left); very overweight Pug (right).

Left: ©Judi Crowe; Right: ©Elaine Gewirtz

To keep your Pug at a constant, healthy weight, control her food portions, don't feed her table scraps, and make sure she gets enough exercise. See Chapter 7 for more information about diet and Chapter 8 for details about exercise.

A Pug's frame

To support her short, stocky body, a Pug needs to have enough bone to keep her strong and healthy. Her back is level and strong, too, and is the Pug's framing structure.

Wonderful wrinkles

Unlike with people, the more wrinkles a Pug's face has, the better. They give Puggy that unique look that has fascinated people for centuries. Pugs have a prominent *nose roll,* or thick wrinkle just above the nose, and another between the eyes. The rest of the wrinkles are on their muzzle.

Wrinkles require some care on your part, though. You have to clean them out on a regular basis with a small piece of cotton soaked in some warm water. If not, dirt particles become trapped inside the wrinkle, which causes an odor that most people don't like. I talk more about caring for and cleaning wrinkles in Chapter 9.

A Pug's common sense (s)

When you look at a Pug's head, you can't help but notice how distinctive it is. It's round and wrinkled with a wide jaw and small ears set on top like little rosebuds (see Figure 2-2). But Puggy's head is more than just a pretty face. It does things. Her facial features enable her senses of sight, sound, smell, and taste to be highly developed.

Figure 2-2: A beautiful Pug head showing good expression.

© Judi Crowe

From China with love: Looking at the first Pugs

Although you can trace the history of many breeds back to a specific country, it's not known for certain where exactly the Pug came from. Many people believe that it's China, and descriptions about the Pug date back before 400 B.C.

Pugs were once treated as treasured house pets of the nobility, and dogs who closely resembled Pugs were often given as exotic gifts to Japanese rulers and later to Russian ambassadors. When traders first came to China, they often took back Pugs to their own countries.

For instance, Puggy's ears are very sharp, and she can hear about four times better than humans can. Open a can of dog food in another room and see how fast your Pug makes a beeline for the kitchen — and the food! She's also very sensitive to high-pitched sounds that many humans never hear. And what about those big protruding Pug eyes? They can see movement farther away than people can, but they do have trouble seeing things up close. In dim light, they can pick out objects but can't tell the difference between colors.

Because a Pug's eyes bulge outward and her nose isn't long enough to offer any protection, Pugs are prone to eye injuries. Take extra care to remove any sharp objects inside your home and prune outdoor plants with sharp or thorny ends that may accidentally scratch Puggy's eyes. Because she's so low to the ground, her face is very vulnerable.

Although a long nose and a great sense of smell can be assets for other breeds, Puggy's flat nose isn't all bad. Sure, she can't smell as well as other dogs, but she's surely never going to miss any bits of food you leave lying around. As for their sense of taste, Pugs actually have fewer taste buds than humans do, so they're willing to sniff out and sample anything and everything that even remotely resembles a food item.

Take special precautions with spoiled food items or anything dangerous, such as things with small bones, that Puggy may think of tasting. She has no sense of danger where food is concerned, and she can easily hurt herself or become sick by eating things she shouldn't.

Tail watchin': One curl or two?

Puggy's tail is a curious thing. Unlike tails on other breeds, the Pug's tail is unique because it's a tight and high-set model that curls up and over her back just enough to fascinate everyone. Some Pugs even have a double-curly tail, which goes around and then around again in a tight corkscrew shape.

The tail doesn't start out curly. When she's a puppy, the Pug's tail is usually straight. It takes a few months before it begins to curl up and then go over her back. If an adult dog becomes scared or loses confidence, the curl quickly unfurls and straightens out. Hopefully, that's only temporary because as soon as a Pug becomes sure of herself again, the tail pops right back up.

Figure 2-3 shows three Pugs with three different tails.

Figure 2-3: Three different Pug tails are all normal: straight puppy tail (top left), curly tail (top right), and double curly tail (bottom).

Top left: ©Elaine Gewirtz; Top right: ©Judi Crowe; Bottom: ©Judi Crowe

Fitting Personality Plus into a Pug

Although Pugs love to be taken care of, they also like to pay attention to their owners. They have loving and affectionate personalities, which means they're perfect companions for anyone who likes to get affection from his or her pooch. They're ideal lap warmers and very loyal to their families.

Putting a big dog into a little body

Pugs have a big idea about themselves and think that they're the prime movers and shakers in their households. They probably are because most owners end up catering to their Pug's needs. A Pug is determined to get what she wants, but only if she doesn't have to go too far from the couch.

Getting a heavenly house dog

Pugs are easy to get along with and don't require that much space to keep. As long as they have their toys, a comfortable bed to sleep on (yours), and enough food to keep them satisfied, Pugs are great to live with. They also like having you around and are happiest when you're nearby. No matter what you're doing, they're usually quite happy to be doing the exact same thing (see Figure 2-4).

Figure 2-4:
This Pug is sitting in his favorite spot and couldn't be happier.

©Tony Nunes

Curious George Pug: Always nosy

Leave an interesting object out where Puggy can see it, and soon it's gone. Pugs like to investigate things and get up close and very personal with your belongings. Although their sense of smell isn't as well developed as other breeds, a Pug still likes to test it out. In fact, she wants to sniff things until they're very wet and soggy. For example, if you leave a check sitting on the coffee table, in no time at all, it's separated into tiny wads of paper.

However, you need to be careful because this curiosity can kill a Pug. To prevent your Pug from injuring herself (or worse), don't leave poisonous substances or sharp objects around that your Pug may be tempted to investigate. If an object looks interesting or has any kind of a food aroma, it's probably going to be Pug history.

Clowning around: Pugs just wanna have fun

Pugs are clowns, and if you laugh even once at something they do, they gladly keep repeating the act to get you to laugh again and again. Fun is their middle name, and it's hard for a Pug to walk into a room without sizing up what she can get away with.

If you have two Pugs at home, count on them to make a toy out of anything. They love to play and find things to tug at and chew up (see Figure 2-5).

Figure 2-5:
These Pugs are entertaining the family with their playful antics.

©Judi Crowe

Having a busy calendar: Pugs like stimulation

As much as a Pug likes to be a lap dog, she also enjoys seeing and doing new things and discovering new adventures. As with any dog who's always confined to the house, Pugs can easily get bored. Finding activities you can both enjoy keeps your Pug happy about life and less motivated to want to eat.

Provide new and interesting toys for your Pug to maintain her interest around the house. Taking her along on safe outings can also please her. See Chapter 12 for more on heading outdoors with your Pug.

Finding another jogging partner: Pugs and intense exercise don't mix

If you're a jogger, don't even think that your Pug wants to accompany you on long-distance runs. Although her spirit may be in the activity, her body isn't, and she stops running or walking when she feels like it.

Never walk a Pug farther than you're willing to carry her. Sometimes she may just sit down on an outing and refuse to go anywhere.

When planning to do some outdoor exercise with your Pug, check the temperature first. Pugs aren't hot weather, outdoorsy types and definitely need to stay cool during workouts. See Chapter 8 for more about exercising with your Pug and avoiding high temperatures.

Now, some Pugs do like to swim and hike, and they're perfectly able to do so if they're properly conditioned. Swimming Pugs aren't that common, but they've been known to actually like the water (see Figure 2-6). If a Pug learns to like the water, swimming is a great activity for her — especially because you don't have to worry about her getting too hot. A pool is always cool!

Figure 2-6: This Pug loves to swim!

©Judi Crowe

Getting out to socialize: Pugs love people

Pugs are really people dogs. They crave a lot of human companionship and affection and want to be around you all the time. Expect a Pug to follow you from room to room and to want to go out for a car ride with you whenever you leave home.

Pugs are also naturally attracted to children — maybe because they're nearly the same size!

When children understand dogs and respect them, they can make great companions for each other. Be sure to always supervise children when they're playing with your Pug and don't leave them alone unattended. See Chapter 6 for more information about Pugs and kids.

Paying attention: Pugs like to be noticed

If a Pug thinks that you're neglecting her, you can count on her to come up with something creative to get your attention.

Leave it to a Pug to do anything to get you to look at her. She can wind up in the oddest places just to see your reaction. Although Pugs don't leap buildings in a single bound, they do like to do some jumping, and if they can figure out how to slowly creep up to the couch or a favorite chair, they're going to do it (see Figure 2-7).

Figure 2-7:
This Pug has his owner's attention by sitting on the kitchen chair!

©Judi Crowe

Accepting the big snore: Pugs and snoring go together

Pugs are no different than any other breed with a short muzzle — make that a very short muzzle — and pushed-in nose. They make a variety of noises while they nap or sleep. Find a comfy pillow at home, and you most likely see a Pug off in dreamland and letting the world know all about it. She makes just about every nasal sound you can think of, from a low snort to some good solid pump-up-the-volume breathing.

I'm ready for my close-up: Pugs in art

Since the 17th century, Pugs have been the subjects of paintings. They didn't appear as the sole subject in portraits, but they were part of the scene the artist was portraying. By the late 1600s and early 1700s, Pugs began showing up in British artwork alongside royalty. If a Pug was in a painting during William III's reign as King of England, it meant support for the King. The dogs were symbols of the wealthy and later a secret symbol during the mid-1700s. Pugs took the place of a secret handshake by the Freemasons by becoming a visual handshake when a painting with a Pug was given to someone else, usually another Freemason who

went underground. Early paintings of Pugs give an accurate picture of what the dog really looked like during this time. Both black and fawn Pugs were equally represented in art. (See Chapter 3 for more on the different colors of Pugs.)

Later in the Victorian era, Pugs and dogs in general became the sole subject in art. People wanted paintings of their dogs as companions. Artists were even commissioned to paint pure-bred Pugs who were good examples of the breed. Queen Victoria, who owned a black Pug, captured him, as well as all her favorite dogs, in portrait paintings.

If you're a Pug lover, you probably get so used to their sounds that you don't even hear this snooze alarm. Other people, however, may not think of it as music to their ears, so it's a good thing they can always get earplugs. But as long as Puggy's breathing is regular, the snore is a perfectly healthy sound.

Chapter 3

Deciding What Kind of Pug You Want

In This Chapter

▶ Describing the ideal Pug, AKC style

▶ Debating between a puppy or an adult

▶ Picking black or fawn

▶ Deciding between a show dog or pet quality

*I*f you have your heart set on a Pug, you probably should spend some time brushing up on your choices (puppy or adult, fawn or black, show dog or pet) before you actually bring home the Pug who you want for your own. After all, you do want yours to be the most perfect dog ever, don't you? Sure, you want companionship and a healthy, good-natured puppy, but you also want your Pug puppy to look like a Pug. You're selecting this breed precisely because you're drawn to the Pug's unique appearance.

As you're getting ready to select your new puppy, you need to know what features, in particular, make a Pug unique. In this chapter, I describe what the ideal Pug should look like. And if you're having trouble deciding whether you want a puppy or an adult, or what color Pug you prefer, I can help you with that, too. Finally, I give you some pointers on owning show dogs who may garner you fame (in the dog world at least) versus pet-quality Pugs who can undoubtedly become great stars of your household.

Getting the Scoop on the Official AKC Breed Standard

Believe it or not, the Pug doesn't look the way he does by accident. He's the result of several generations of careful planning by many conscientious breeders who have been following the same design.

Why the Pug is in the Toy group

The American Kennel Club assigns every breed to one of seven different groups. Each group of dogs shares a similar history for the jobs they performed for their owners — Sporting, Working, Herding, Terrier, Hound, Non-sporting, and Toy. The Pug belongs to the Toy group because he's smaller than dogs in the other groups, yet he's the biggest dog in that category. Originally, the Pug was bred to be a lap dog, so ideally Pugs should weigh between 14 and 18 pounds. If they get much bigger than that, your lap is pretty full.

The design for the perfect Pug was first formulated by Pug lovers in England in 1885 and reaffirmed in 1931 by members of the Pug Dog Club of America. Recognized by the American Kennel Club (AKC), the *design,* or *breed standard,* describes exactly how the Pug should look and act.

This standard includes the dog's ideal structure, personality, gait, and general overall appearance. When breeders match sires (fathers) and dams (mothers) together, they hope that the puppies they produce come as close as possible to the ideal breed standard.

Figure 3-1 shows how breeders and veterinarians describe parts of a Pug's body. You may want to refer to this figure as you read the following list, which explains the main physical characteristics of a Pug.

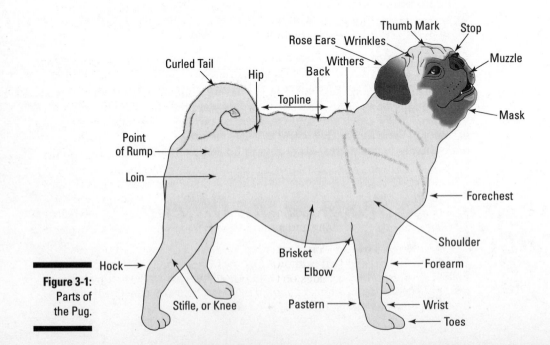

Figure 3-1:
Parts of
the Pug.

✔ **General appearance:** From any angle, the Pug has a square shape. Measure his height from the ground to his shoulders, and the measurement should be about equal to what his length is from the front of his chest to his rear.

✔ **Head/face:** To meet the standard, the shape of a Pug's head should be round when you see him from the side and square when you look at him face to face. The bottom of his black velvet ears should fall to his eye level. His large, round, dark eyes have a soft expression. Although he looks sweet, the Pug should also look animated and excited during playtime.

A Pug's snout, or muzzle, is very broad. When his mouth is closed, you shouldn't see his teeth or tongue. All those marvelous wrinkles around Puggy's face fold over his black nose and add character to his expression.

✔ **Neck, topline, and chest:** To support his big round head, the Pug's neck should be strong and thick. What's a topline? If you were to draw an imaginary line from the top of a Pug's shoulders down his back to where his tail begins, breeders refer to that area as a *topline*. It should be straight and level, without dipping in the middle, and it shouldn't slope downward or upward. The Pug's chest should be wide and full.

✔ **Body:** If you stand in front of your Pug, you should see straight, sturdy, short little legs connected to broad shoulders and chest. A Pug is not a Bulldog, so don't expect to see feet that turn outward. The Pug's chest should extend over the front legs. The Pug's rear legs should look strong and be parallel to each other from the back.

✔ **Coat:** The Pug's coat should be fine, smooth, short, and glossy (never hard or coarse). Both fawn and black Pugs have the same coat type, which is soft when you touch it.

✔ **Color and markings:** Pugs come in two basic colors — black and fawn — although the standard mentions a silver color that has become rare in the United States. The silver coat has been described as the color of moonlight, while the true fawn Pug's coat is sunlike. Sometimes the silver Pug is confused with a smutty fawn-color Pug, but there's a distinct color difference between the two.

Black Pugs should be a shiny, jet-black color. If there is any white on the black Pug, it's called a *mismark*. Fawn Pugs may have a white mark on their coats, too, but it blends well into the lighter coat and doesn't show up as easily. Fawn Pugs are more popular than the black dogs, and the contrast between the black muzzle and the fawn Pug may be one reason. The contrast is striking and should be very distinct.

Another interesting Puggy marking is a darkened spot centered on Puggy's forehead that is known as a *thumbmark* or a *diamond*. This area is formed by the wrinkles on the forehead but looks like a thumbprint.

✔ **Gait:** His legs should swing forward easily, with each leg moving in a straight line. Neither one should be flinging outward, and the path of one leg shouldn't cross over the path of the other one.

Going away from you, the Pug's legs should move in a parallel pattern along the same line as the front legs without any motion flinging outward. When Puggy speeds up to a trot, his legs should move toward a center line.

✔ **Personality:** Pugs are even-tempered and stable, and they love to have a good time. They can also be dignified, yet very charming, when the situation requires it — they seem to be able to tell when it's necessary to act mature instead of silly. Puggy is intelligent and curious, yet ready for a game.

Although the breed standard calls for the Pug to be steady and charming, his average behavior ranges anywhere from very active to least active. So, when you're choosing a Pug, remember that the typical Pug personality is anything within that range. Not all Pugs are couch potatoes or high energy. Somewhere in that broad temperament spectrum is the perfect Pug for you.

Determining Whether a Puppy or an Adult Dog Is Right for You

If you're choosing between a Pug puppy and a mature adult, and you want to be practical, think about how much training each one needs. On the other hand, if you're going for the cute appeal, few people can resist a puppy. Of course, each age group has its pros and cons, depending on your lifestyle and what you enjoy doing with your dog. Pick the Pug you're the most comfortable with, and you can't go wrong. Keep in mind that whichever one you choose becomes a full-time commitment.

Preferring a puppy

A Pug puppy enters your life like a sponge, waiting to soak up all the time, love, and training you can give him (see Figure 3-2). In fact, you start at square one, so expect to teach your new puppy just about every life skill. You have to let him know what he can and can't chew on. You have to housetrain him, teach him to walk on a leash, and coax him into sleeping through the night. In addition, you must lay down some other basic household ground rules from the first day you have him. Count on being pretty busy.

Figure 3-2:
With his eager, sweet expression, this puppy is ready for a good time but may need some training.

©Elaine Gewirtz

Puppies have two activity cycles — full speed or sound asleep — and someone must keep an eye on them during both of these periods. You can expect to have to keep constant watch on the puppy for several weeks or even months until the dog is acclimated to your household rules. New puppies don't know the difference between your good shoes and their toys. It's not their fault if they ruin your things — it's yours if no one's on guard.

A puppy also needs an extra meal sometime during the middle of the day, at least for the first few months of his life, and he frequently has to get out of the house for bathroom breaks. So, if you're working overtime or planning to be away from home a lot during the puppy stage, you may want to rethink choosing to get a puppy.

Although a Pug can't do much damage to objects above his head, he can still find lots of mischief to get into at his level — chair legs, wood molding, your best shoes, and the edge of the rug can all pique your Pug's curiosity. So be prepared to safeguard those areas with a bitter-tasting spray made specifically to discourage dogs from chewing. Or you can simply put them out of Puggy's reach, if possible. Now's the time to get organized by putting your best shoes away on closet shelves or getting rid of old magazines. See Chapter 5 for more on preparing your home for your new pet's arrival.

You need to make a few more visits to the veterinarian for routine vaccinations during those first months. Unfortunately, you also need to consider the possibility that you may have to pay for a medical emergency. Of course, you hope that nothing happens to your new puppy, but there's no guarantee.

Puppies are just starting out in life, and they can get into the oddest places and situations, some of which may be dangerous. (See Chapter 13 for more about making regular visits to the vet.)

Count on making shopping trips too for toys, bigger collars, and basic dog equipment, such as feeding dishes, leashes, and a wire pet carrier, if you don't already have those things. The price of purchasing these items can be costly and may not fit into your budget at the time you're looking to add a Pug to your life. If these expenses may overstretch your budget, think about waiting to get a Pug until you can comfortably manage it. You can find other Pugs available down the road.

Despite the work involved, a Pug puppy is definitely entertaining, and you can have a lot of fun watching him grow up and mature into a well-behaved, confident little character. If you think that you may miss out on something important by getting an older dog, then a puppy is definitely the way to go.

Noting the merits of a mature dog

Getting an older Pug has its advantages, too. An adult dog makes a wonderful companion because often he's already had basic training and has a better attention span than a new puppy.

After you get over the initial period of adjustment, an adult Pug bonds with you just as closely as a puppy can. He probably already knows how to walk nicely on the leash without pulling or tugging and isn't alarmed by strange sounds, such as sirens blaring or babies crying. On the other hand, an older dog may have acquired a bad habit or two along the way, but after you realize where the training gaps are, you can begin correcting the behavior.

It's definitely not true that you can't teach an old dog new tricks. A dog can be taught to do just about anything at just about any age. Doing so just may take you a little longer.

What Color Is Your Pug? Deciding between Black and Fawn

A fawn Pug and a black Pug may look like completely different dogs (see Figure 3-3), but both have the same great personality and the same Pug bodies. There's no difference in health, life span, or activity level, and dogs of either color give the same amount of kisses, too.

Figure 3-3:
A fawn Pug
and a black
Pug equally
enjoy their
morning
exercise.

©Judi Crowe

One color isn't better or worse than the other in a Pug. Choosing a black over a fawn Pug is just a matter of personal preference. You may prefer the crisp look of the distinctive black mask contrasting with the fawn body, or you may want to go with the solid look of an all-black Pug. They're both just as healthy and full of fun. But, with a black Pug, you don't have to worry about him showing the dirt as much!

Although some Pug owners think that the black Pug is smarter and more independent than a fawn, other Pug owners think the opposite is true. There are really no differences in character between the two, although both the colors can be born to a fawn mother and a fawn father.

There will always be Pug color rivalry between owners, but it's all in good fun. See the color insert for more on the different Pug colors.

Choosing between a Show-Quality or a Pet Pug

Conscientious, reputable breeders spend the same amount of time, energy, and devotion to produce show-quality Pugs as they do their pet Pugs. Both receive the same amount of care and love while they're being raised, and the parents of both should be the same excellent, healthy examples of the breed. So why would you choose either a show-quality or a pet-quality Pug? Like choosing between a black or a fawn Pug, it's a matter of personal preference, plus how much time and money you're willing to spend on your dog.

Westminster Kennel Club, here I come! Show-quality Pugs

Dog shows were originally created to designate breeding stock. When a dog won a dog show, it meant he could be used to father a litter or give birth to puppies. The tradition continues, even though not every champion gets the chance to be bred today. Breeders make sure that their breeding stocks have undergone and passed medical testing to make sure they don't have or carry genetic diseases. Some of these tests can't be given until the dog is 2 or 3 years of age, after they have competed in dog shows. Show-quality dogs can't be spayed or neutered until after they've completed their championship or been bred.

If you're interested in acquiring a show-quality Pug (see Figure 3-4), first visit dog shows in your area (see Chapter 16) to meet show breeders and to see their dogs in the ring. You can also contact the Pug Dog Club of America for names of breeders. They can refer you to reputable show breeders in your area. For more information about the club, see Chapter 19. The club can also provide information about the differences between a show and a pet Pug.

Figure 3-4:
A Pug champion has presence and stands proudly.

©Judi Crowe

Study the breed standard that I talk about in the section "Getting the Scoop on the Official AKC Breed Standard," earlier in this chapter, so that you can get a good idea of what a show Pug looks like before you visit breeders. Then, when you begin visiting breeders, you can tell the breeder that you're interested in purchasing a Pug you can show in conformation. She can show you which puppies have the best conformation and attitude, which make them the best show prospects.

Be sure to discuss the breeder's terms for selling you a show-quality dog. Why is that important? Some breeders require more money upfront or the promise of puppies down the line. Likewise, other breeders don't sell their show-quality puppies without the new owner promising to show the dog at dog shows.

The best idea is to get all the arrangements in a written contract so that both parties understand what's involved and what's expected.

Although show- and pet-quality Pugs are both lovable creatures and make wonderful companions, having a show dog is important to many people. They like competing with their dogs and having a superior specimen of the breed as a companion.

Show me . . . the backyard: Pet-quality Pugs

If dog shows aren't your thing, don't worry. Plenty of pet-quality Pugs may not meet the standards of the show ring, but they still make lovable, wonderful companions. They think they're pretty special, too. They can compete in performance competitions, such as obedience or agility, and are calm visitors to patients in nursing homes or hospitals. For more information about getting started in competitive activities and therapy, see Chapter 15.

Chapter 4

Finding and Selecting the Perfect Pug

- -

In This Chapter

▶ Shopping for a Pug

▶ Picking the puppy

▶ Making sure you have all the info to take care of your new Pug

- -

*W*hen you've decided that a Pug is for you, it's time to find that special dog. You can look for your Pug soul mate in a variety of places — some locations are better than others, of course. Although choosing your puppy is fun, you want to watch for a few key things before rushing into your decision.

In fact, you need to talk details with the seller, and in this chapter, I discuss the pros and cons regarding all the locations selling Pugs. I also tell you how to pick the best puppy and help you make sure you know as much as possible about where your puppy comes from.

Determining Where to Look for the Pug You Want

It seems easy. Want a Pug? Go to the Pug store. Not so. Happily, there's no such thing. Puppies aren't cans of peas you can stock on a supermarket shelf. Conscientious breeders take great care to plan litters in advance and never know exactly when their puppies can be available to go to their new homes. It depends on Mother Nature.

The first thing you need to have when you're looking for a Pug is patience. Your new dog will be with you for many years, so if you have to wait a few weeks or months for the right Pug, it's worth it.

You can find Pugs in pet stores, through breed rescue groups, shelters, and from reputable breeders. Regardless of where you get your Pug, there are general standards for choosing a quality Pug. You're looking for a healthy Pug with a good temperament — a good representative of the breed.

Buying pet shop boys (and girls)

Although I don't recommend buying a Pug from a pet store rather than from a breeder, there are a few advantages to doing so. You can do it on the spur of the moment, no one interviews you, and you can charge your purchase on a credit card. Unfortunately, these reasons aren't good enough to buy at a pet store because there are more disadvantages, such as:

- You don't see where the puppy was raised.
- You can't meet the puppy's parents or other relatives.
- Pet shop employees probably don't know much about the puppy's personality or about Pugs, in general.
- You pay more than you would if you bought from a breeder.

Before buying a Pug, you want to know as much information about her background as possible. This way, you have a sense of whether she was brought up in healthy conditions, whether the puppy's parents are good examples of the breed and are friendly and healthy, and how much the puppy has been socialized. These things are very important. Too little human attention when puppies are very young produces nervous and shy temperaments, and a dirty environment can make your Pug difficult to housetrain because pups become accustomed to defecating and urinating in the same area.

When you buy from a reputable breeder, you know these things. You also have a chance to talk to the person who bred the litter and find out if a Pug is a good match for you and your family. When you buy from a pet store, you likely won't have the opportunity to do so.

Adopting from rescue groups or shelters

If you know you want an adult Pug rather than a puppy, consider adopting one from a Pug rescue group or a shelter. (Sometimes these places have puppies, too.) These nonprofit organizations provide foster homes for lost, abandoned Pugs or for those Pugs whose owners must give them up for one reason or another. However, these groups can keep only so many dogs at a time, so they're only too happy to have someone rescue them.

Rescue organizations often have a very dedicated group of volunteers who use their own facilities and resources to take in the dogs they save. They often evaluate a new Pug when they acquire her to gauge her temperament and make sure she's not overly aggressive. They also keep her or find a foster home where people can care for her until a permanent home can be found. In addition, rescue Pugs are often seen by a veterinarian who administers any vaccines they may be missing.

A shelter, on the other hand, takes in all breeds and mixed-breed dogs and puts them up for adoption after a shelter worker has determined that their health and temperament are okay. Unfortunately, because many shelters are overcrowded as it is, they can keep a dog for only a short period of time. After that, they may euthanize her if no one adopts her.

Your chances of finding a purebred, pet-quality Pug — either a puppy or an adult — are greatest with a breed rescue group. Pug owners who can no longer take care of their dogs usually contact a rescue group in the hopes that another Pug owner wants their dogs.

Of course, the best thing about adopting a Pug from a foster home or shelter is knowing that you're possibly saving a Pug's life and giving her a loving, stable, and permanent home to live in.

A negative aspect of adopting a Pug from a rescue group or a shelter is that you don't always know about the Pug's background, including her medical history and any behavior problems. Likewise, you may find out after adopting a Pug from a rescue group that someone gave her up for a reason. Maybe she didn't get along with another dog in the family or wasn't good about going to the bathroom outdoors.

Checking out the agency

If you hear about a Pug rescue group, try finding out more about it before agreeing to adopt one of its dogs. Contact local breed clubs, your veterinarian, or the Humane Society to find out whether any complaints have been made against the group.

You can also visit a shelter or rescue group's facilities yourself to see whether the dogs' areas are kept clean and to see whether the dogs available for adoption are friendly and outgoing.

Finding out whether you and Puggy have a bond

If you see a Pug you think you want to adopt, get to know her personality and her background as follows:

✔ Ask whether you can take her out of the small cage and spend some time with her in a larger room or outdoors. Look for a Pug who's friendly and outgoing and seems genuinely glad to see a stranger. That's a good sign that she may have a stable temperament after she comes to your home. You want a Pug whose personality is somewhere between outgoing and slightly cautious. Such a dog can adjust to almost any household.

✔ Ask shelter or rescue personnel how old the Pug you're considering adopting is and if they've observed anything about her behavior that may be too quirky for what you're looking for. Many dogs are easily frightened when they first arrive at a shelter, but don't adopt a Pug whose tail is down and who seems fearful. This Pug may never have been around anyone but her former owner.

✔ Ask whether she has any medical problems that require medication or special procedures and whether she requires any special grooming, such as having to be bathed with a certain type of shampoo.

✔ Find out what kind of food they're feeding the Pug you want to adopt. If she has any special dietary needs that are too expensive for your budget, you may not want to add her to your household.

In addition to letting you get to know the Pug, a breed rescue group also interviews you to make sure that you're the best home for the dog it has available. This is the same screening that breeders do. For more information about the questions you may be asked when getting a Pug, see the "Buying from a breeder" section, later in this chapter.

A word about cost and home visits

The group may also want to visit your home to make sure that you have adequate fencing. After the adoption is completed, you can expect a follow-up call from the group to find out if everything is going well. The group may or may not want to make another house call to see for themselves.

Expect to pay a donation of $100 to $200 to adopt a rescue dog, but it's probably a lot less than buying a puppy from a reputable breeder. The group uses this fee to help defray the cost of spaying and neutering the Pug and for any vaccines that need to be given before she goes home with you. Or you may be required to spay or neuter the Pug if the group hasn't already done it.

Shelters don't require a home visit, although they do ask you a few questions to make sure you can provide housing and food for the Pug. You also have to pay around $75 to $125 to adopt a Pug, and that money may or may not cover the cost of spaying or neutering the Pug, depending upon the individual shelter.

Buying from a breeder

When you buy a puppy or an older Pug from a conscientious, reputable breeder, you know what you're getting. This person raises only Pugs, is a member of the Pug Dog Club of America and perhaps also a local Pug club, and shows her own dogs at dog shows.

Whether she has a large kennel of Pugs or just a few dogs in her home, the best breeder has devoted several years to the welfare of the breed and has paid attention to the latest developments in Pug research and health.

Avoid the first-time breeder, if possible. The exception to this is first-time breeders who have a reputable show breeder working with them. Puppies from an inexperienced breeder who doesn't have a mentor don't benefit from the expertise that a seasoned breeder has. Likewise, avoid the breeder who relies on selling pups for a livelihood or even for part-time income. Sure, dog breeding is an expensive hobby, but a breeder shouldn't be skimping on things a puppy needs for healthy development, such as regular veterinary care, stimulating play objects, and time and patience from the breeder.

Locating reputable breeders

You can find a reputable breeder in many different ways:

- ✔ Ask your veterinarian for names of breeders he recommends.
- ✔ Ask your friends who have dogs if they know breeders to recommend.
- ✔ Ask members of your local kennel club. Some club members may breed Pugs or know of others who do. The club may also have a breeder referral list.
- ✔ Ask the American Kennel Club for names you can contact. You can access its breeder referral list on its Web site (www.akc.org).
- ✔ Ask your local Pug club for names of breeders you can contact.
- ✔ Ask breeders at a dog show. Breeders are always glad to talk to potential Pug owners, usually right after they're done showing. You may even see some Pugs at the show that you like who may be siring some puppies or later giving birth to some.

Interviewing breeders

To help you narrow down your choices for the best breeder, here are some questions you can ask:

- ✔ **How long have you been breeding dogs? How often do you breed a litter? Is this a business or a hobby?** A breeder with a few litters under her paws has experience and know what to expect the puppies to be doing at various stages.

- ✔ **Why did you breed this litter?** A dedicated breeder has a well thought-out plan, is eager to preserve the health and well-being of the breed, and uses the dog's pedigree (his ancestry or family tree) to bring pairs together to complement the breeding.

- ✔ **Why do you like this breed?** Here you're hoping to hear about her passion for the dogs she's spending all her time with.

- ✔ **Is this breed right for me?** The breeder may see something in your interaction with the dog that you may have overlooked that may not work out. Maybe you're continually brushing off tiny Pug hairs from your good clothing. Once you get a Pug puppy home, loose dog hair becomes a way of life, and you should be comfortable with it.

- ✔ **What health issues do your Pugs have?** Hopefully the breeder is honest with you and explains some information you may have missed while researching the breed.

- ✔ **Where do you raise your puppies?** You're looking here for newborns to be inside the house where the temperature and natural elements can be regulated. They should be in a well-lit, stimulating environment that's kept clean at all times.

- ✔ **Can I meet the parents or at least the dam, if she's available?** Take a look at the parents, and you have a good idea what your puppy may grow up to look like.

- ✔ **What is your health guarantee like?** See the section "Getting a health guarantee," later in the chapter, for more information.

- ✔ **Do you have the puppy's pedigree and registration?** See the sections "Reading a pedigree" and "Registering your Pug with the AKC," later in the chapter, for details.

- ✔ **How much training does the puppy require?** Know going in the door how much training time you need to spend with your puppy.

- ✔ **Are you available for long-term help with training or behavior questions or problems?** Hopefully the answer is *yes*. (If the answer is no, I'd suggest you look elsewhere for another puppy.) You should feel very comfortable with this person and be able to ask her anything about your Pug throughout her lifetime. Your breeder should be a great source of information and guidance for all the years you have the dog. She should never be too busy to talk with you and supply you with literature and training hints about the breed.

- ✔ **What happens if I can't keep this dog?** Nearly all reputable breeders want the dog returned to them if there's a problem.

Through your line of questioning, you should begin to form an opinion about this person and whether or not you like her. Chances are that, if you like the breeder, you'll probably like the puppies, too.

Allowing the breeders to interview you

Any reputable breeder you talk to wants to ask you several questions about why you're interested in getting a Pug and how much you already know about them. It's okay. The question-and-answer session is a good thing. The breeders just want to make sure that they're making the best placements they can for their young charges. After all, they've cared for and worried about them for weeks, so they want to be sure they're doing the best job they can for their puppies.

Here are some questions a breeder might ask you:

- **Why do you want a Pug?** The breeder is hoping that you aren't interested in the breed just because you saw one in the movies or on television.

- **Have you had dogs before, and if so, what happened to them?** A reputable breeder who's spent months planning for and taking care of a litter is reassured if the person has some experience caring for this breed before.

- **Who will be mostly caring for the puppy?** Hopefully you're the one who can be the pup's main caretaker, and you're not thinking the kids or hired workers are going to be taking care of the dog.

- **Are there any children in the home, and if so, what are their ages?** Many breeders don't sell puppies to couples with children. Toddlers can get rough with Pugs and hurt their eyes. Some children also tease dogs or play too roughly with them.

- **Where will you keep the dog?** No breeder likes the idea of her puppies spending all their time outdoors or in a garage.

- **What is your yard situation?** Pugs can get a lot of natural exercise if they have a big, safe space where they can play. The breeder also wants to know whether you like to walk and take along a dog with you when you go. Your answer to that question lets the breeder know whether the Pug can have a chance to get out a little and not spend her whole life inside the house.

- **Is this puppy for you?** Breeders don't like providing gifts for other people because they don't have a chance to make sure that the person can provide a good home for the Pug and really wants a Pug. Maybe the individual isn't right for a Pug, or the lifestyle isn't conducive to raising a healthy, happy puppy.

When the breeder knows what you want, she can try to match you up with the right puppy. Or maybe she discovers that you're just not ready for one of her pets because the answers you've supplied to the previous questions aren't what she had in mind for the perfect Pug owner.

The breeder just wants to make sure that her puppy spends the rest of her life with you, happy and healthy.

Pick of the Litter: Selecting the Best Puppy for You

Choosing a puppy is a very personal decision. Everyone likes different puppies for different reasons, but your choice should be the one that *you* like the best. One person may prefer a puppy that keeps jumping into her lap and giving lots of kisses. Someone else may want the prettiest pooch or the most active, fun-loving fellow.

Still, the best puppy is the healthiest one, with a stable, outgoing temperament. If possible, make a few visits to see the puppies so that you can learn firsthand about their personality and how they interact with other Pug puppies.

Here are some other suggestions to help you find the right Pug:

- ✔ Spend at least ten minutes with each puppy you choose to evaluate.

- ✔ Sit on the floor so that you can pick the pups up easily and closely observe them at eye level.

- ✔ Take the puppy to another room so that you can tell something about her personality away from the rest of the puppies, her mother, and the breeder.

- ✔ Observe how the puppy reacts to this new situation. Hopefully she takes it in stride and doesn't become fearful or shy.

- ✔ See whether the puppy naturally follows you if you walk from one area to the next. If she does, this is a good sign because it means that the puppy likes to be around people.

- ✔ Offer different toys to see how certain puppies react and to get an idea about what kinds of toys you want to shop for before the puppy comes home. Does she like soft furry toys? Rubber balls? Noisemakers? What about household items, such as milk cartons and empty plastic water bottles? The only way you can find out is by giving the puppy these different toys.

Likewise, try playing a quick game of fetch with the puppy. Although Pugs aren't big retrievers, they still like a good game of fetch now and then, and going after the toy tells you she's interested in playing.

✔ Hold the puppy in your arms. Does she wiggle to free herself immediately or does she enjoy being held and cuddled? If you have a small child at home, the puppy's behavior in this situation is important because this is what children do with puppies.

Watching for signs of a healthy Pug puppy

When you visit a breeder, shelter, or rescue group, here are some things you want to see when trying to pick out a healthy puppy (see Figure 4-1):

✔ **A clean, shiny, smooth coat:** You shouldn't see any skin rashes or eruptions.

✔ **Bright, clear, open eyes:** The eyes shouldn't have any discharge or be bloodshot. The puppies shouldn't be squinting or rubbing at their eyes.

✔ **Sturdy legs and feet:** The dogs should not be limping.

✔ **Normal activity level:** The dogs should be playful and happy, not weak or lethargic.

✔ **Outgoing personality:** The puppies shouldn't be off alone the whole time you visit. Instead, they should be eager to come and greet you.

✔ **Normal weight:** The dogs shouldn't be too skinny, and the ribs shouldn't be showing. On the other hand, they shouldn't have a potbelly, either.

Figure 4-1:
A healthy puppy waiting to be adopted.

©Judi Crowe

Here are some indications that the puppy you're considering may have some health problems:

- **Watery or bloody diarrhea:** The dog should have firm stools and regular urination. If you watch the puppy long enough, sooner or later she's going to have to do her business, so you can see for yourself.

- **Vomiting:** If a puppy upchucks one time, it's not a serious problem, but if you see it happen again or even a third time, then I'd be a little suspicious that she has a health problem.

- **Gagging or coughing:** Persistent cough or intermittent gagging can mean that the dog has kennel cough or another respiratory problem that the vet needs to see (or hear).

- **Licking the urinary tract opening:** This may indicate that that the dog has a urinary tract infection and needs medical attention.

- **Thick, colored mucus drainage:** This isn't normal, and a puppy with this condition needs to see a veterinarian right away.

If you see any of these conditions, think about looking elsewhere for a puppy. Although they're not life threatening, you can probably find another Pug who doesn't have these problems.

Observing the puppies and meeting the parents

At the breeder's, you should be able to view the whole litter. Doing so gives you an idea of what all the puppies look and act like.

Sometimes breeders don't want visitors to see the conditions the puppies are raised in and bring out only one or two puppies at a time for you to see. If this happens, ask why you can see only one or two. In fact, ask the breeder to show you where the puppies and the whole litter spend their time. You want to see a clean, well-lit, and stimulating environment with healthy puppies.

If you're looking for a puppy at a shelter or a breed rescue organization, sometimes there's a litter you can choose a puppy from. If not, try looking at a few different puppies at different shelter or rescue organizations, if they're available. This way, you can compare one to another, wherever they're located. Sometimes there's only one puppy available through adoption, but maybe the mother is also there or the pedigree came along with the puppy.

Keeping your eye on just one isn't always easy

If the Pug puppies are either all fawn or all black (see Figure 4-2), you may not be able to keep your eye on the one puppy you're especially interested in all the time. Picking out the puppy of your dreams can be difficult when one looks so much just like the others.

To help distinguish one puppy from another, many breeders tie different colored ribbons around their puppies' necks soon after they're born. These ribbon collars help the breeders to easily identify their Pug babies when they need to check to see how they're doing as they grow. Then, once they know their puppies, most breeders remove the IDs so the puppies can't get tangled up in one another's ribbons and possibly hurt one another.

If you have trouble keeping your eye on certain puppies that you're especially interested in, ask the breeder to take the puppies that you know you're definitely not interested in out of the area, or ask the breeder to put colored ribbons on the Pugs you're considering.

Meeting the parents

When choosing a puppy from a breeder, try to see the dog's mother and father (if he's on the premises). You can see a grown-up version of your puppy and try to imagine what the pup may look and act like when she's an adult.

If the mother or father is a shy dog, chances are that the puppy will grow up to be the same way. When meeting the parents, you're hoping to see healthy, outgoing Pugs who enjoy meeting strangers.

Figure 4-2:
Everyone in this litter of black Pugs is ready for a good time, and they all look alike.

©Elaine Gewirtz

Reading a pedigree

A *pedigree* is a dog's family tree, and every dog has one, whether it's written down on paper or not. A pedigree lists the pup's sire (father) and dam (mother) and those dogs' ancestors. It doesn't mean that the puppy is registered with the AKC — it just shows who belongs in the family. Breeders like to keep this information written down and often give it to a new puppy owner.

What's a purebred Pug? It's a dog whose ancestors are all Pugs — parents, grandparents, and great-grandparents, as far back as records show. Besides sire and dam, some other terms you may encounter when looking at a pedigree are as follows: *Grandsires* and *grand dams* are the puppies' grandparents. The *paternal grandsire* and *grand dam* are the father's grandparents, and the *maternal grandsire* and *grand dam* are the mother's grandparents.

Perhaps the breeder has photos or videos of the grandparents and other relatives. You may enjoy seeing them and finding similarities to how your puppy looks, so be sure to ask the breeder if he has any photos of the rest of the family that you can see. No doubt the breeder loves getting the chance to boast about the famous family photo album.

You can also learn a great deal about a puppy's ancestors from a pedigree. In front of the name of a champion dog are two initials, Ch, that mean that she is a special Pug. A champion is a good representative of the breed and represents hours of competition and hard work. I explain this topic in more detail in Chapter 16.

After a Pug's name, you may find other initials that mean she has successfully passed obedience and agility exercises. The American Kennel Club (AKC) gives these titles after a dog has successfully passed the requirements set for them. For example, the initials CD, CDX, UD, or UDX mean that your Pug's ancestors have trained hard to earn obedience titles. The CD is the basic Companion Dog (CD) title, CDX (Companion Dog Excellent) is more advanced, while UD and UDX (Utility Dog and Utility Dog Excellent) are the most difficult. See Chapter 15 for more information about obedience titles.

As for agility titles, NA (Novice Agility) denotes a beginner's agility title. More advanced titles are: OA (Open Agility), AX (Agility Excellent), MX (Master Agility Excellent), and Master Agility Champion (MACH). Again, you can read more about agility in Chapter 15.

Getting Your Pug's Paperwork

Before you leave the breeder's kennel or home, you should receive lots of written information about your new puppy. Many shelters and breed rescue groups can also give you information about how to care for your Pug and whatever papers, if any, were given to them from the Pug's previous owners.

Here's a quick look at what you should get from a conscientious, reputable breeder:

- ✔ AKC registration
- ✔ Bill of sale
- ✔ Copy of the puppy's pedigree (see "Reading a pedigree" earlier in the chapter for details)
- ✔ Health guarantee
- ✔ Record of the puppy's medical information
- ✔ Information about care and training

Registering your Pug with the AKC

If both Pug parents are registered with the American Kennel Club, their offspring are also eligible for registration. When you take Puggy home for the first time, the breeder should give you her application for registration, which is supplied by the American Kennel Club for this specific litter. After you and your breeder sign this application, mail it to the AKC with the fee, which ranges from $15 to $25 and — voila! — Puggy becomes a registered Pug.

Many people make a mistake and think that the dog automatically gets registered when the breeder gives them papers from the AKC. Although the breeder gives you an application, it's only part one of the process. You have to fill out the actual registration for your puppy and send it in to AKC with a check.

After she's registered, your Pug receives an official record of ownership in your name, and a 60-day pet healthcare insurance trial policy. Her registration also makes your Pug eligible to compete in AKC events, such as showing in conformation, obedience, and agility.

Getting a health guarantee

Be sure to ask the breeder whether the puppy comes with a *health guarantee*. The health guarantee gives new owners 24 to 48 hours to take the puppy to their own veterinarian for a check-up. (Some breeders allow a few more days for the vet visit.) If, for any reason — health-related or non-health-related — an owner doesn't want the puppy and decides to return her with her AKC registration, the breeder should return the total purchase price.

After that time, and usually up to the age of 24 months, many breeders happily replace a puppy at no additional cost if the first one develops a genetic, life-threatening illness. The new puppy should be of comparable value and come with her own registration.

The health guarantee should be in writing and written in a language you can easily understand and agree to follow.

Finding out about health information

Your breeder should let you know what health care your puppy has had and what follow-up visits to the veterinarian for vaccines are necessary. I provide more information about vaccines and why they're so important to your puppy's health in Chapter 13.

If you've never had a Pug before, your breeder should also show you how to care for her and give you instructions on trimming her nails, cleaning her ears and wrinkles, and brushing her teeth. You can find more information about grooming in Chapter 9.

When you take Puggy to the veterinarian for her first examination and immunizations, take along the medical records your breeder gives you.

Soliciting training advice

Your breeder has spent many years raising Pugs and can provide a wealth of information about them. If you've never trained a Pug before, housetraining her and teaching her how to walk on a leash can be a challenge. I talk about training more in Chapter 11.

Ask your breeder as many questions about training and care as you can think of. Her job is to send you and your puppy out into the world with as many training tools as possible so that you can enjoy each other's company for many years to come.

Part II
Living with Puggy

The 5th Wave   By Rich Tennant

"I think the Pug's been up on the counter
again. There are several distinct paw
prints in the butter tub."

In this part . . .

Settling into life with your Pug is a snap with the info I share in this part. I start off by telling you what supplies to stock up on to prepare for your Pug's arrival. Then I explain how to make sure that your Pug's happy and safe in his new home. In addition, I give you the lowdown on a Pug's eating and exercise regimens. Finally, I provide some pointers about keeping your Pug well groomed.

Chapter 5

Preparing for Your Pug's Arrival

In This Chapter

▶ Getting some supplies your Pug will need

▶ Keeping Puggy safe in your home and your yard

*O*ne thing's for certain: Your new Pug requires some pet supplies to make him happy and comfy when he comes home. Okay, make that a lot of pet supplies. It's amazing how one cute little Pug can need so much stuff. Then there are all those fun extras that just scream, "Take me to your Puggy!" But don't panic. This chapter tells you what you need and what you don't. The luxuries are up to you.

Shopping for the Basics

Shopping for things your Pug needs is the fun part of getting a dog. I have a feeling that when you go out shopping for the essentials, you also find some nonessentials that you think Puggy (or you) just can't live without. That's okay. He's worth spoiling.

A word of caution, though: The cost of pet supplies can add up quickly. If you're a shopper and like to compare prices, you can save a little money here and there. I'm sure you'll find lots of places to find Pug paraphernalia, but here are some places to start looking:

- Pet supply stores
- Discount stores with pet departments
- Farm stores
- Your veterinarian's office
- Grocery stores
- Mail-order pet catalogs
- Web sites

Getting a crate and some bedding

To your Pug, a wire pet carrier with a soft mattress to snuggle up in is a cozy retreat. It's also the first thing you need to put on your shopping list because you'll begin using it as soon as you bring Puggy home. The carrier helps you housetrain your Pug, and it's a safe place for him to hang out if you can't keep an eye on him. For more information about how to use the carrier to house-train your Pug, see Chapter 10.

When shopping for the carrier, buy the size that an adult Pug uses but don't go much bigger than that. He doesn't need a confined space the size of a bedroom because if the carrier is too big, he thinks it's okay to relieve himself in there.

Consider purchasing two carriers — one for the house and one for the car. If you have the room in your car, let Puggy ride inside the carrier on car trips because the carrier gives your Pug some protection from injury in case you're in an accident. See Chapter 12 for more on traveling safely with your Pug.

As for what to put inside the carrier, you have several choices. If you have an extra lightweight blanket or quilt, consider putting that inside the carrier. Old bed sheets work well, too, as long as you can easily put whatever bedding you use into the washing machine and dryer and you're not going to be upset if Puggy destroys it.

Don't put any expensive bedding inside the carrier. Your Pug may chew it up and possibly swallow the padding, which can be dangerous. And keep an eye on him while he's in his carrier to make sure that he doesn't start tearing up and eating the material. When you know that Puggy isn't going to destroy his bedding, then you can give him a real doggy mattress, if you want.

When you and your Pug are just hanging out in the TV room, you can get a separate doggy bed for him to catch some zzz's on. Sure, you can take the mattress out of the crate and use that every night, but you may find that doing so is too much trouble. If you can swing it with the checkbook, an over-sized floor pillow works great. You don't have to get it right away, but it's something to think about adding down the line. Just don't leave him alone with it. Otherwise, you may come back into the room and find that your little darling sweet Pug has transformed the cushion into confetti.

Tinkering with toys

Ah, Puggy toys. You can find rubber squeaky things in a variety of colors, shapes, and noises; braided rope pulls; stuffed animals; fleece toys; and bones, bones, and more bones. Sure, all those toys look like fun dangling from pet supply store shelves, but what should you choose for your Pug?

Well, the fact is that he'll probably love just about everything, but that doesn't mean you should buy out the whole shop. Too many playthings may only confuse him, so for now, stick to the essentials. For example, fleecy toys in all shapes and sizes are good, as are hard nylon and solid, hard rubber toys.

Dog toys are the right size if they're big enough that Puggy can't swallow them, yet small enough to fit comfortably in his mouth. They should also be hard enough that your Pug can't break them apart and eat the pieces, yet soft enough for Puggy to chew.

Pugs of any age love to have things to gnaw on, but chew toys are especially good for a young puppy who's still teething. All Nylabone trademark products are safe because they won't splinter and cause damage. Also, any very hard rubber toys are great for chewing. Some rope toys are specifically labeled as dental floss chew toys, and dogs love these. Chewing helps his gums and teeth to stay somewhat clean and healthy. See Chapter 9 for more information about keeping your Pug's teeth clean.

Avoid giving your Pug your old socks, shoes, and clothing as toys to play with. It only encourages him to chew up your good things when you're not looking. Children's toys aren't a good idea, either. Small plastic parts on dolls or stuffed animals can come off and choke your Pug if he swallows them.

Braided rope toys are okay unless they begin unraveling. Keep an eye on these toys because if your Pug swallows the strings, they can cause blockages in his intestinal tract. Lightweight rubber or plastic squeaky toys are okay, but again, watch your Pug when he's playing with these. The squeakers inside can be dangerous if he swallows them. Throw away any toys when Puggy begins taking them apart.

Some breeders give their Pugs rawhide chews, but those can be dangerous if you don't watch your Pug the whole time he's playing with them. When the rawhide begins wearing down, it gets gummy and can get caught in your dog's throat, leading to accidental choking.

You can find many digestible bones, toys, and teeth-cleaning products that Puggy can safely chew and have fun with at the same time. However, if you're watching your Pug's weight, you want to limit the number of these items that you give him each day. The reason? These items have calories.

Rotate toys frequently so your Pug doesn't get bored with the same things all the time. Keep one or two in his carrier at all times and one or two in each room where Puggy spends time.

Outfitting your Pug with a collar and leash

You also need to get Puggy his first collar and leash, but wait until you bring him home to do that. It's much easier to carry him into the pet supply store so that you can try different sizes on him to make sure you get the best fit.

Always buy the collar size that fits that day. Don't get one that's too large now, thinking Puggy can grow into it. He may or may not, and in the meantime, if he's wearing one that's too big, it's useless if it falls right off his neck the minute he puts his head down.

Keep checking how Puggy's collar fits as he grows. Puppies grow fast, so you have to replace the collar if it gets too tight. You may have to make two or three trips to the store to buy bigger collars as your Pug grows up. In Chapter 11, I talk more about buying collars and leashes and explain how to use them when training your Pug.

Prepping for mealtimes

You also need some mealtime supplies. I recommend getting these supplies before bringing Puggy home so you're not running around trying to get everything after your dog has arrived.

Food and water bowls

So many different kinds and sizes of feeding dishes are available in the stores — ceramic, metal, plastic, acrylic, stoneware, porcelain, and stainless steel. I prefer the stainless steel designs for both food and water and think they're a must-have. A stainless steel bowl doesn't stain, splinter, or rip; in fact, it can last a lifetime. It's also very easy to clean, doesn't tip over, and doesn't slide around on the floor.

For traveling with your Pug, several different food and water containers are available. Check out the collapsible models, which are handy if packing space is tight. Otherwise, I always use small stainless steel dishes, even for traveling.

If Puggy spends a lot of time in the backyard, you may want to get a second water dish that stays out there all the time. Stainless steel is again the best choice, even for an outdoor dish, and well worth the expense.

Dog food

If you purchase your Pug from a breeder, ask the breeder what kind or brand of food she's been feeding him. That way, you can purchase it ahead of time, and it'll be waiting when your Pug makes his grand entrance into your home.

For at least the first few weeks after you bring your Pug home, continue feeding him what he was eating at the breeder's. He's bound to feel a little nervous in a new environment, and if you change foods right away, his stomach could easily get upset. See Chapter 7 for more information about feeding your Pug.

Likewise, if you acquire an older Pug or a puppy from a rescue organization, ask what kind of food the previous owners have been feeding your Pug. You want to stay on the same food at least for two or three weeks so his system doesn't get upset. You can begin mixing in another food after that.

If you want to buy another food, look for a premium-quality dog food. There are so many available that it's easy to feel overwhelmed. In Chapter 7, I explain the differences between foods.

Garnering the right grooming tools

Grooming your Pug isn't hard, as long as you have the right tools for the job.

Brushes and combs

Your Pug doesn't need a lot of grooming tools, but he does need these basics to keep his coat and teeth in good condition:

- Rubber brush with rubber teeth
- Steel comb with a really fine-tooth side
- Toothbrush and toothpaste
- Shampoo

See Chapter 9 for more information about using these items on a regular basis.

Consider getting two brushes and two combs. For some reason, these grooming aids have a way of disappearing around the house. You can always keep one in the bathroom to use after you bathe Puggy and another in the room where you and your Pug spend most of your time together.

Nail clipping equipment

You need to purchase some nail clippers or a battery-powered cordless nail sander so that you can trim Puggy's nails once a week. When he's a puppy, you can use the smallest guillotine-type clippers. (You may want to pick up some styptic powder in case you get a little close to the quick when trimming; the powder stops a nail from bleeding.) But as he grows, you may find that the battery-powered nail sander is faster and far more efficient.

Although you may feel overwhelmed with the nail sander at first, it's worth getting used to it. After two or three times, you'll love using it. With the cordless sander, you don't have to worry that you may clip off too much of Puggy's nails and hurt him. The sander gradually and safely takes off tiny bits of nail.

Look for the sander in a home improvement or hardware store. The box may or may not say that you can use it for pet grooming, so consult the store clerk. See Chapter 9 for more details on how to give your Pug a perfect pedicure.

Grabbing scoopers and bags: It's a dirty job, but . . .

Cleaning up Puggy's messes in the yard isn't anyone's favorite job, but if you have a two-piece pooper-scooper, the pickup detail is much easier. The scooper consists of two long-handled tools — one for scooping the stuff up and the other for holding the stuff until you can dispose of it properly in a waste container.

You can find pooper-scoopers in a variety of sizes in most pet supply stores. Use your scooper to clean your yard every day — your lawn stays healthier that way, and so do you and your family.

When you're away from home, small plastic bags, like the ones you get at the grocery store, are just the thing for cleaning up after your dog. Although these bags easily fit into your pants pockets, pet supply stores stock several types of clever and convenient little containers already filled with tightly folded-up plastic bags that attach to your leash.

Creating a Safe Environment for Your Pug

If your environment is safe for Puggy to roam around in and you don't have to worry about him getting hurt inside your home or out in the yard, you can relax. If not, you have some work to do. But don't fret because the work isn't too hard. In fact, with a little bit of creativity and some products you can purchase from pet supply or hardware stores, your Pug can be in the safest home in the neighborhood.

Pug-proofing the yard

For your peace of mind, you may want to go through your yard to make sure it is totally contained and there's nothing dangerous that your puppy can hurt himself on, such as sharp sticks or corners.

Landscaping issues

Although Pugs aren't known for being super-destructive, puppies can still make their mark on your landscaping — and it isn't pretty. They do like to dig every now and then, and Pugs sometimes find that plants make good, yummy chew toys.

In turn, plants can have their revenge on your Pug. Rose bushes or any other plants with sharp thorns can scratch Puggy's eyes, so cut them back or put fencing around them so that your Pug doesn't accidentally bump into them.

Likewise, some plants and flowers are poisonous if dogs eat them, so either get rid of them or block your Pug's access to them. Although these may look pretty in your yard, the following outdoor plants can be deadly to Puggy:

- ✔ Azalea
- ✔ Castor bean
- ✔ English holly berries
- ✔ Foxglove
- ✔ Jimson weed
- ✔ Mistletoe
- ✔ Oleander
- ✔ Poinsettia leaves
- ✔ Sago palm
- ✔ Water hemlock

Another good idea before you bring your Pug home is to ask your local nursery for a list of common plants in your area that are poisonous to Pugs.

Putting up fencing

A fully fenced-in yard is the most important thing you can provide for your Pug. It offers him room to run around (off his leash) without you having to worry about him running into the street and possibly getting hit by a car or taking off down the block and getting lost.

Depending on where you live and your budget, you can choose from many different kinds of fence. Brick, stone, or cinder block are the most permanent materials and require almost no maintenance, but they're also the most expensive. Fences of wood, plastic, and wrought iron are less expensive but require regular maintenance for painting and repair. Chain link is another option, but it needs to be continually checked to make sure nothing has come loose, producing sharp corners that could damage Puggy's eyes.

If your Pug is a digger, he can easily dig underneath chain link, so be on the lookout for digging with this fence.

Another option is the invisible fence designed especially for dog owners. But despite what manufacturers may claim, this is not a foolproof method of fencing because some dogs just ignore the warning beep and following shock they receive when they cross the fence line and leave the yard, anyway.

When shopping for fencing, be sure to tell the salesperson that you're putting it up because of your dog. He or she may suggest dog-friendly materials you hadn't considered.

Because Pugs aren't inclined to be jumpers, you don't have to worry about building an 8-foot fence. You just need your fence to be tall enough so that Puggy doesn't think of scaling it. Although a 4-foot fence is probably sufficient for a Pug, because you're going to the expense of putting up fencing anyway, you may want to think of putting up a 5-footer in case you ever decide to add a larger dog to your household later on. The foundation also has to be deep enough that he can't think of digging out, either, although Pugs aren't usually known for being escape artists.

You can also use fencing to section off part of your yard. Think of it as a safe area for your Pug to use for short periods. You can keep his favorite toys and a clean water dish in this mini Pug yard and create a potty area with low spreading sturdy plants, grass, cement, or gravel. This Pug-size playground is a great idea if you don't want him using the whole backyard as a bathroom or if you're afraid he might scratch himself and possibly injure his eyes on your rose bushes or cacti in another part of the yard.

Don't leave your Pug in this enclosure all the time. He'll be much happier if he's with you in the house as much as possible.

Make sure that you have secure gates. The safest gates are padlocked and made from solid wood or metal so that no one can look into your yard and see what a cute Pug you have and possibly steal him. Secure gates also keep Puggy from leaving the yard.

Keeping your Pug out of the pool

If you have a pool or hot tub in your yard, you may want to put a barrier up around it while your Pug is a puppy or if he's a senior. Pug puppies or seniors aren't very sure-footed, and they can easily miss a step turning a corner around the pool, accidentally slip and fall into the water, and drown.

Although some adult Pugs do swim, most don't and naturally avoid going anywhere near the edge of the pool. Even if your Pug does swim, you don't want him taking a dive unless you're around to supervise. He can easily forget where the pool exit is and drown.

Wrought iron with a locked gate works well as a pool fence because you can still see the pool in the yard and keep unwanted swimmers out, at the same time. You can also rent a chain-link commercial fence for the pool area. It's not as expensive as you think, and installation doesn't involve any permanent drilling into the concrete.

Pug-proofing the house

While he's inside, your Pug also needs some safe areas where you don't have to worry that he may get hurt or destroy your possessions.

Using baby gates

You probably have rooms or furniture in your home that you'd rather not let Puggy have access to while he's young. If so, baby- or child-safety gates can be a big help to you. These gates come in all different sizes and materials, such as wood, plastic, and mesh, and they can become permanent or temporary, depending on what you need. They easily attach to doorframes or walls and can be removed and stored away when company comes or Puggy becomes a good citizen around the house.

 Look for gates that are easy to use and lightweight enough to move from room to room. Many have mesh or wide slats, which are great if you want to keep Puggy inside a room. He can still look through and not feel so isolated and most Pugs won't think of chewing through the plastic models. If your Pug does have a bad habit of chewing, however, you may want to find metal gates.

 Baby gates can also be handy for confining your Pug to just one or two rooms until he's completely housetrained. Oh, and if you need housetraining tips right now (because you just finished cleaning up *another* mess), head over to Chapter 10.

You can find baby- or child-safety gates at discount stores, pet supply places, baby stores, and mail-order pet supply catalogs.

Installing doggy doors

So, what's a doggy door anyway? It's a hard rubber or metal insert that's cut into the wall or door that leads to your yard. The big door can be closed, yet Puggy can still hop in and out of the house whenever he wishes through this minidoor.

Dog doors come in all different designs and materials and fit into any type of door, including a sliding patio door, and even the wall of the house. You can purchase dog doors at pet supply or hardware stores, or through pet catalogs.

The best thing about a dog door is that your Pug can use it to go to the bathroom outside after he's fully housetrained. If you're worried that other animals might use the door from the outside, you can always close it off with the insert it comes with at night. Most animals don't want to venture into your home during the daytime when Puggy is out and about. Or if you're worried that burglars may use it by crawling through, remember that the person would have to be awfully small to be able to fit through a Pug-size door.

Hiding the trash

Pugs love trashcans, especially the kitchen containers with yummy leftovers or the bathroom receptacles filled with tissues and other paper products that smell interesting (to Pugs, at least).

However, some items in the trash can be fatal if your Pug eats them, such as small meat or poultry bones, spoiled food, razors, or cosmetic products containing alcohol.

Fortunately, it's easy to keep trash out of your Pug's sight and mouth. All you need are some babyproof cabinet locks. (And, don't worry, they're pretty easy to install.) When they're locked into place, only an adult or an older child can open the cabinet holding the trash can; there's no way Puggy can use his flat face to nudge it open. Look for these locks at baby, hardware, or pet supply stores in your area.

You can also simply close the doors to rooms where you keep trashcans.

Making cords disappear

To a Pug puppy, a dangling electrical cord is really one very long rope toy! After grabbing one end of the cord in his mouth, a Pug loves to see how far he can run. Meanwhile, the appliance it's attached to goes flying into the air before crashing on the ground or on top of Puggy, possibly hurting him. Electrical outlets are another household doggy danger because Pugs like to chew on the outlet, not knowing that a slight electrical current courses through it.

These problems are easily fixable. You can cover the outlets you don't use with baby safety covers. These are available in hardware, baby, or pet supply stores, and they just lock right into the outlet. Tack dangling cords firmly to the baseboard or consider unplugging an appliance when you're not using it.

Chapter 6

Bringing Your Pug Home

Eureka! You've found the perfect Pug, and it's almost time to take her home. You want to do everything just right, and you're eager to get started. Now, if only all those questions about what to do with Puggy once you get her home would stop flying through your brain. Never fear. This chapter walks you and your Pug through her first few days at home, one paw at a time.

Getting Your Pug From Here to There

The days, hours, and minutes are ticking down now to the time that Miss or Mr. Puggy touches down and make a splash in your home. Hopefully, you've purchased all your doggy supplies, such as the crate, food, grooming tools, and toys. If you need more information about supplies, see Chapter 5.

Despite the fun of a pet, bringing a new puppy or dog into your humble abode can be an overwhelming task. Everything you do affects your dog, and her health, safety, and well-being are in your hands. To get started on the right paw, you need to take a few important steps before Puggy enters the house.

Choosing the right day and time

With a little advance planning, your first day with Pugsly can be successful. To have a smooth transition when you pick her up, choose a weekday (or a Saturday, if possible) when you can stay home to devote most of your attention to your new dog. If it's feasible, you may also want to plan on staying home with your new Pug the day or two after you bring her home, as well, just to help her get further accustomed to her new surroundings.

 And the earlier in the day you can pick her up, the better. Plan on arriving at least an hour or two after your puppy has had breakfast. In addition, request that your Pug receive only about half the amount of the normal morning meal. Some puppies get carsick, so the smaller the amount of food in her tummy, the better. Don't worry. She won't starve. When she gets home and settles in a bit, she has plenty of time to make up for that lost grub.

Ensuring a safe journey

Hopefully, the breeder, Pug rescue group, shelter coordinator, or pet store clerk has given you some tips on how to take your Pug home safely. For more information on purchasing a Pug from a breeder or pet store or adopting from a rescue or shelter organization, see Chapter 4.

After you and Puggy leave her former home, you're in charge of transporting a very special, but possibly soggy or drooly, Pug package. Bring along some extra towels in case your puppy has an accident — either of the bathroom or the upset-tummy variety — in the car. This may be your Pug's first car ride, so she may get carsick.

Protecting your Pug in the car

Cuddling your Pug in the car for the ride home may sound irresistible, but it's not the safest way to go. Here's why:

- A new dog can be a big distraction while you're driving and possibly cause an accident.

- If you're involved in an auto accident, that little love bundle resting on your lap can go flying headfirst into danger.

- Wiggling around, a Pug can easily fall off your lap during a sharp turn and become injured.

 The best way to protect your dog is to use one of the many dog seat belts or doggy harnesses available in many pet stores (they're not very expensive), or to place her in a wire pet carrier lined with newspapers. The newspapers can absorb any mess she may make. For more information on training your Pug how to use a wire pet carrier, see Chapter 10.

But just because this is the right thing to do for your Pug, she may not agree. Be prepared to hear some whimpering from your Pug if you restrain her either in a harness or inside a wire carrier. Okay, it may be more than a whimper —

a lot more. Puggy may suddenly find her own voice, and it's a pretty loud one. This may be the first time she's confined in a carrier without her brothers and sisters, and she thinks the whole thing is a bad idea.

Don't give in by taking her out. A comfy new blanket inside the crate can help. If the breeder sends your Pug home with a soft toy she was raised with, this also gives your Pug a familiar, safe feeling in the crate. To reassure your dog that she's not alone, ask a passenger in the car to talk to her. Eventually, Puggy may even settle down and fall asleep for most of the ride home.

Whenever you give your Pug a stuffed animal or any toy in her crate, be sure to remove any decorations, such as button eyes or a hard plastic nose, that your dog could chew up and possibly swallow.

Preparing for lengthy car trips

If you have more than a three-hour drive home, take along some bottled water and a new stainless steel water bowl in case your puppy gets thirsty.

Don't rely on a water fountain or faucet on the way home. Believe it or not, all waters don't taste the same, as every community has a different type of water containing different chemicals. Your Pug may already be feeling a little nervous, so her stomach may be doing the jitters just from leaving home. Strange water could upset her tummy even more and lead to vomiting or diarrhea.

Along the way, you may want to make a pit stop, but think twice before taking your puppy to the bathroom in a strange place. Unless you have more than a six-hour drive home, your puppy may not want to go potty in a place with strange smells. Instead, she'd rather wait until she reaches her final destination and settles in. She may not want to go to the bathroom at home right away, either, because everything is so new. But at least she'll be staying there and has time to become accustomed to her new digs.

If you have more than a six-hour car ride home, take along a large plastic tarp and newspapers. Lay the tarp covered with newspapers on clean asphalt or concrete — an empty corner of a shopping mall or parking lot without traffic works well. Your puppy can safely use this for a bathroom spot. If your puppy was raised to eliminate on newspapers, these give her a familiar reminder of what she's supposed to do here. You can easily dispose of them in a trash container when they're soiled, and the tarp stays clean.

Avoid grassy areas or highway rest stops with designated pet areas. These spots are ripe for transmitting diseases from other pets that may be ill or may not have been vaccinated. Your puppy doesn't have enough immunity yet to ward off infectious diseases. And keep her on a leash so that she can't scamper away from you.

Introducing Your Pug to Home Sweet Home

The day you take your Pug home is the first day of the rest of her life with you. A hearty welcome lets your puppy know that her new digs are a fun place to be. So feel free to fuss over her and enjoy every minute of her homecoming. Just don't overdo it. She's just left behind all she has ever known — her comfy puppy area, perhaps a few rambunctious brothers and sisters, plus familiar sights and smells. Take things slowly and put yourself in her paws.

Introduce your Pug to her new world in slow, loving stages. Don't expect her to feel totally at ease with everything and everyone right away. Some puppies are just born more secure or have been handled more by their breeders or exposed to more things at an earlier age, so they can just waddle into a new place and be totally comfortable immediately. Other Puggies aren't as sure and need more time to feel secure around new people and objects. These Pugs need more attention and reassurance from you that their strange new world is a good Pug world. It can take a few days, weeks, or even months for these Pugs to adjust to everything.

Making your pooch comfortable

Hopefully, you've already Pug-proofed your home so that your Pug can be safe and sound behind your four walls. For more information on Pug-proofing, see Chapter 5.

Resist the urge to do everything you've always wanted to do with your Pug all at once. Likewise, hold off on showing her all the things you've purchased or prepared for her arrival. You don't want to give her the whole enchilada the first time because she doesn't know what to do or look at first.

Instead, I suggest the following steps when you enter the house with your dog for the first time:

1. **Take her to the room where she will be spending most of her time.**

   The family room or den works great if that's where you like to hang out, too.

2. **Sit down on the floor with her.**

   After a few minutes, she feels comfortable and wants to venture away from your lap.

3. **From there, you can gradually begin to take her on a tour of the rest of your home.**

Plan to use the whole day and hopefully the next one, too, to let Puggy realize what a wonderful new household she's moved into. To your plump little Pug, everything looks twice the size it is, and the house and yard have tons of new aromas to check out.

Taking your Pug on the grand tour

First impressions do count, even for Pugs, so you want to walk her slowly through all the rooms just so she can get a good sniff of every part of her new digs. Talk to her in an upbeat, happy voice and tell her the names of the rooms and special objects as you're giving her the home tour. The tone of your voice reassures her that everything is A-OK.

Sometime within the first two hours at home, she needs to visit the potty area. Walk her outside to the area where you want her to eliminate all the time. Although it would be great if she actually did use the same space every time she needed it, she may not be ready to use the same spot. That's okay. (Chapter 10 offers specifics about how to housetrain your Pug.)

The next stop is your dog's favorite location: the place where she can always find her food. Show her the dining area and the location where she can always find a clean, cool bowl of water. Ideally, your in-house café has flooring that's easy to mop up because Pugs can be dribbly eaters and water drinkers.

After about an hour, your Pug may be ready for her first dining experience at her new address. Or maybe she isn't. It's not unusual for a new puppy to want to skip a meal or two. Not to worry. After her opening day jitters settle down, she'll be more enthusiastic about devouring every last crumb of food you put into her bowl. You can find what you need to know about feeding your Pug in Chapter 7.

Your new Pug wants to know that you didn't forget about toys, so along the way, show her one or two of her new playthings.

Pug puppies are so funny. Things like a tall vase on the floor may worry or frighten your Pug at first. She may back up from it, run around it, or bark at it. And maybe she does all three. If so, let her sniff or approach it on her own terms without insisting that she make friends with the strange new object immediately. After she realizes the vase can't hurt her, she leaves it alone but may always be wary of it.

Napping is normal

You also want to show your Pug the comfy new wire pet carrier you've bought for her, but don't feel bad if she doesn't use it right away.

After a few hours of exploring this new world, your Pug may suddenly poop out wherever she is. This is perfectly normal. Pugs take a few naps a day — trying to do everything is tiring when you're little — so don't be surprised if your puppy suddenly flops down and nods off in the middle of the room.

Rest assured that you don't need to relocate her to her permanent sleeping quarters right away. Let her relax where she is but keep an eye on her when she wakes up. Maybe before the next siesta session, you can encourage her to sleep inside her new digs.

Putting your normal routine on hold

Introducing your Pug to her new world takes time. If possible, try to clear out your calendar for the first few days and reschedule as many household chores and errands on your to-do list as possible. If you also cut down on the amount of time you spend chatting on the phone or going online, you have the luxury of really getting to know your Pug without too many interruptions.

These days are the only time she's ever a new dog in your house, so now's the time to get her started on the right paw. Besides, after a Pug comes into your life, things around the house will never be the same again.

Acquainting Your Dog with Family and Friends

When your Pug has a feel for the place where she can hang her leash, it's time to meet the family and friends. Ask relatives and friends to introduce themselves one at a time. A crowd of new faces and new voices can be intimidating to a puppy, or even to a grown dog, just coming into an unfamiliar location.

Get comfy on the floor with Puggy and have children and grown-ups greet her on the ground level. If people aren't standing over her, they don't look so big and scary. When your dog is moving around the house on her own, she begins to feel confident and ready to take on the world of humans. In no time at all, she can accept the fact that, yes, people are lots taller than a Pug, and that's okay.

Introducing Puggy to children

Pugs and kids make a great match, but children need to be taught that Pugs are living creatures who shouldn't be disturbed when they're eating or sleeping and shouldn't be lugged around like a stuffed toy. Sometimes youngsters don't realize that they can be too rough or that puppies can get hurt. For example, playing chase with Puggy may seem like fun, but children need to know that this is a no-no.

A puppy can easily get underfoot and accidentally stepped on. Young tykes also have to know that your puppy gets tired and needs to rest quietly. You also need to pay attention to those little kid hands, which are great for cuddling a small dog but shouldn't be used to poke at your Pug's bulging eyes. Pug eyes are fragile and can be easily injured. Children shouldn't pull at your Pug's curly tail or ears either — that hurts!

With the proper instruction, however, children can easily become great Pug playmates (see Figure 6-1 and the color insert). If this is a child's first introduction to a dog, what you teach her now hopefully stays with her for the rest of her life, or at least until you have to remind her again, which you may have to do.

Older children also need some guidance around a new puppy. They may think that teasing or playing tug with Pug is appropriate play behavior, but it's not. Teasing makes Puggy distrustful, and playing tug encourages aggressive behavior. Bigger kids may also want to take the puppy with them on a bicycle or a skateboard, which isn't safe.

Figure 6-1:
Pugs are good playmates with kids and balls as long as the action doesn't get too rough.

©Judi Crowe

For your Pug's safety, now's the time to teach children what they can and can't do with your Pug. Here are a few tips to remember when introducing your new Pug to young kids:

- ✔ Supervise, supervise, supervise! Don't leave Puggy unattended when she's meeting children for the first time. For the first few weeks and even months, parents need to watch their children at all times around a new Pug. It's the best way to make sure that the kids don't accidentally hurt the dog.

- ✔ Don't expect a child — even a mature one — to completely take care of the dog. Feeding, housetraining, and grooming are big jobs that need a grown-up. Children make wonderful helpers, however, so be sure to include them.

- ✔ When supervising your Pug around children, have the camera ready because these first experiences captured on film make wonderful mementos years later. Take this perfect opportunity to enjoy seeing your children relate to the new family pet.

- ✔ Insist that small children sit on the floor before they can hold Puggy (see Figure 6-2). When children are this low to the ground, the dog can't slip out of little arms and fall.

- ✔ Show youngsters how to pick up a Pug — use one arm to carefully lift the dog from underneath her rib cage behind the front legs and the other arm beneath the rear. The dog should be pointing away from the child.

- ✔ Suggest to children that they be gentle and not squeeze the dog. Children don't always know their own strength and may hold the dog too tightly and hurt her.

- ✔ Watch to make sure that the Pug doesn't fall off a lap and onto the floor.

Figure 6-2:
Small children should sit down on the floor before greeting a Pug.

©Judi Crowe

Meeting and greeting the relatives

When the word gets out that a new Pug is living at your place, everyone you know wants to come and check her out. Pugs are such celebrities! Although it's natural for you to want to show your Pug off, setting some visitation rules first is a good idea. Meeting too many new faces all at once can confuse a little gal.

For the first day, try to limit introductions to the immediate family. Doing so gives your dog a chance to figure out who the people in her everyday life will be. Ask the other relatives, neighbors, and friends to delay their visits for a few more days, until your Pug has had a chance to get the hang of things.

When the time is right to meet your Pug, introduce the other family members one at a time. Here are a few pointers:

- ✔ Let people, including kids, say hello to Puggy at a normal pace in a normal tone of voice. She's not so fragile that you have to whisper, but dogs can always sense if people aren't acting or speaking normally. They may become frightened if they suspect that something isn't right.

- ✔ Don't allow people to rush in and hover over her. A dog can feel threatened if someone is leaning over her.

- ✔ Request that your family members try not to shriek about what a cute dog your Pug is. Because dogs hear things much louder than people do, a shriek sounds louder than a fire truck siren to a young Pug. You don't want to scare the poor dog out of her wits!

- ✔ Don't let people offer a toy or a treat when they first meet your dog. Give Puggy a chance to bond with the people and not be distracted by the goodie. The treats and toys can come later.

- ✔ Let your Pug sniff the new person as much as she wants. Dogs use their sense of smell to check someone out — their noses are so sensitive that they can detect smells that still remain on someone's clothing from other animals or other places they've been. It's their way of asking, "So what have you been up to?" When Puggy feels satisfied that she knows the answer to all of her sniffs and snorts, she can relax around a stranger.

The best way to greet a Pug is to feel friendly and confident. When someone is afraid or unsure of himself, dogs pick up on that feeling and may become fearful, too. An outstretched hand with the palm facing up held near your Pug's nose gives her a chance to sniff out whom she feels safe around and whom she's not so sure about. After your dog has finished her sniffing routine and attempts to make eye contact with someone, the person can begin that slow and gentle petting.

Although some puppies roll right into a household and take lots of commotion in stride, some need a little more time to feel at ease. You can tell when your Pug feels okay around someone because she bobs her curly tail from side to side and wants to climb all over that person.

Saying hello to other family pets

If you have other pets at home, imagine how they feel when your new Pug suddenly waddles into the house and steals all the attention! They were there first, and now this stranger is camping out in their quarters without their permission (yet, anyway). It's only normal if they seem miffed and aren't so eager to greet the newest member of the family so warmly.

From your Pug's point of view, sharing space with another creature is usually no big deal. As puppies, Pugs are curious and investigate other dogs, cats, birds, and small house pets like hamsters and rabbits. Older Pugs generally get along well with other pets in the home.

But to be on the safe side, don't throw them all together in the same room at the same time! And before your Pug meets your kitty, make sure that the cat's claws are clipped. Although your cat may have good intentions when he meows "howdy," he can accidentally scratch Puggy's precious eyes and injure them.

Keep the dogs on a leash or put your Pug in her carrier when kitty or other creatures enter the room (see Figure 6-3). Doing so gives everyone a chance to sniff each other out from a safety zone. After an hour or two, when you see wagging tails and no one is snarling, you can gradually begin to take the leashes off or let your Pug out of her carrier.

Figure 6-3:
It's safe to introduce Puggy to new dogs, but be sure to use a leash. You never know if the other dog is friendly.

©Judi Crowe

Don't leave small critters, such as rabbits, hamsters, pet mice, and gerbils, loose with a young Pug. The Pug wants to play with them and doesn't realize that she could accidentally hurt them.

Bedding Down the First Night: Ensuring You and Puggy Get Some Zzzzzz's

Puggy's first day at home has been a barrel of laughs, but by nighttime, you're ready to crash. In the meantime, your dog is still going strong, and you can't hit the sack until she does.

Synchronizing the snooze schedule

Accept that your Pug may not be ready for bedtime when you are. Lucky Pug has probably had a few naps throughout the daytime, which you didn't. Right after your own dinner, Puggy may drift into dreamland, but don't be fooled into thinking she'll stay asleep all night. She won't.

Try waking your Pug about two hours before you're ready to go to bed. This gives her a chance for a final play session and a trip to the potty location before it's time for the real lights out. A half-hour before you're ready to go to bed and when she seems ready to crash, take her to her wire pet carrier and let her sniff it out to her heart's content. Give her a good-night kiss and place her inside the wire pet carrier, along with a few toys and a blanket. Be sure to give her a tiny food treat, too. Then get into bed and turn out the light.

Sharing the bedroom

The best place to put the wire pet carrier is in your bedroom next to your bed. This way, your Pug knows that you're nearby, and she can hear your voice when you reassure her that all is well. Your Pug's first night in your home can be a quiet and restful one if she doesn't think you've left her all alone in a strange and dark room

Expecting the whine and the whimper

Yes, your Pug will probably make a little noise when it's time for lights out. Although a little whimpering may be acceptable, a loud commotion isn't. Sure, your precious little Puggy sounds so pitiful and lonely inside the carrier, but it's not a good reason to take her out. If you do, she knows that if she makes a fuss, she gets out of jail free. Resist the temptation and try to tough it out during the first nights at home.

Sometime in the night, you may hear a persistent whimper, and that may mean that she really needs a bathroom break. Little puppies have little bladders that fill up quickly and may not wait until morning.

If you take her out of the carrier to go to the bathroom, take her to the potty area right away and resist the temptation to play with her or cuddle her. You want your Pug to learn that potty time is not playtime. After she has done her business, give her a tiny treat, put her back inside the carrier, and flip the light switch. After a few minutes of fussing, she'll probably quiet down.

Getting enough rest yourself

Although having a new Pug in the house is exciting and fun, it can also be tiring. To avoid having an energy meltdown, try the following:

- ✔ Try napping when she does during the daytime so that you can get some zzzz's yourself.
- ✔ Realize that this schedule doesn't last forever. Eventually both of your time clocks will be in sync.

Chapter 7

Providing a Proper Pug Diet

*W*hat a Pug wouldn't do for a cool, clean bowl of fresh water to chase down his breakfast, lunch, and dinner! Pugs love to slurp, not to mention chow down. If they had their way, they'd insist upon having every different kind of dog food sold in the pet food store. Luckily, it's your job to do the food shopping, but knowing what to buy can be difficult. Of course, you want to make your Pug happy at mealtimes, but you want him to be strong and healthy, too.

Getting started with good eating habits is very important because it helps prevent Puggy from becoming obese, which can lead to other health problems. In this chapter, I give you all the do's and don'ts of catering your Pug's meals.

Filling the Water Bowl

As basic as it sounds, water is the most important thing your Pug needs to stay healthy. That's because a dog's body composition is 60 percent water. He can't afford to lose 10 percent or more of his body's water supply without becoming ill. Losing 15 percent may be fatal. Therefore, always keep a stainless steel water bowl (see Figure 7-1) filled with fresh water for your Pug. (If you need more information about why stainless steel bowls are better than the plastic or ceramic models, see Chapter 5.)

Figure 7-1:
It's healthier
if your Pug
drinks and
eats from a
stainless
steel dog
bowl.

©Judi Crowe

Be sure to wash out the water bowl every day before refilling it. If Puggy has been investigating holes in the garden and drops dirt clumps into his bowl, you may need to change it more often. A floating bug doing the backstroke in the H_2O? You wouldn't drink a glass of water with a naughty gnat in it, so don't let your dog do it, either. Fresh, clean water (right out of the tap) promotes good Pug health.

Your Pug gets used to the taste and quality of your tap water. So if you're leaving home with Puggy, take along some water for him from your own kitchen. Although every town you visit does have tap water, it also has a different chemical composition in its water. Sometimes you can taste the difference, and sometimes you can't, but often it's different enough to upset your Pug's tummy and give him diarrhea.

Keeping him on the same water source he's accustomed to from home or even on filtered water prevents digestive tract difficulties while you're traveling. If it's inconvenient or you forget to take water from your own tap, you can always stop at a supermarket and buy a supply of bottled water. Bottled water has been filtered and is far gentler on Puggy's tummy.

Establishing a Good Food Routine

Other than lots of hugs and kisses, you should give your Pug a quality, well-balanced dog food that provides good nutrition. Of course, the many advertisements about dog food can be overwhelming at first. But you can't go wrong if you feed Puggy a premium dry food, called *kibble,* mixed in with a little premium canned food and some water. See the section "Knowing Your Pug's Nutritional Requirements," later in the chapter, for further information.

Preparing the first few meals

Before you bring your Pug home for the first time, find out what kind of food he was eating at his old home. If you've purchased your Pug from a reputable breeder, ask what he fed his Pugs. Then arrange to feed him the same diet for at least the first few days. Here are a couple other things to remember about your Pug's first few meals.

- ✔ Just as different water sources can disrupt Puggy's digestion, so can a new food. Avoid surprising his system with a different diet and a different address both at the same time.

- ✔ Give your Pug at least an hour in his new home before you offer him his first meal.

- ✔ Plan on staying with him when you feed him the first few meals. It's even a great time for you to take ten and have a snack or cup of coffee yourself! The household is new to Puggy, and he may be concerned that he'll be left alone in an unfamiliar place.

Check out Chapter 6 for more information about acclimating your Pug to his new home.

Pugs live to eat, so expect them to normally attack their food bowl as if they have never seen food before. If Puggy passes up the first meal at home, it probably means that he's still settling in. After the first day or so, you can look forward to your Pug licking the bowl clean, trying to get every last crumb.

If he rejects two consecutive feedings, however, something must be wrong. Your Pug must not be feeling well, so be prepared to call the veterinarian. A healthy Pug doesn't even think of skipping meals.

Picking an eating area

You may wonder where to leave your dog's water and food dishes. It doesn't really matter if you have the refreshment center in your kitchen, dining room, living room, or bedroom. But you should keep the water and food dishes in the same place all the time. Puggy always needs to know where to go to get a long drink of water and his next meal.

Another option is to leave the water dish in the same place in the house all the time but to feed Puggy inside his wire carrier. As Figure 7-2 shows, the advantage of feeding him in his carrier is that if you take him on a trip, his normal meal routine stays the same, no matter where you put his carrier.

Figure 7-2:
Feeding
your Pug in
his carrier
makes him
feel at home
if he travels.

©Judi Crowe

Setting a schedule

Pugs love routine, but forget giving your Pug a PDA to help him keep track of
what time things are happening. Pugs have their own inner alarm clocks that
tell them when they should eat, sleep, and play, and they don't hesitate to
remind you if you're late rustling up the grub.

Be sure to feed Puggy at the same times every day. You may even want to
choose times that coincide with your meal schedule so that they're easier for
you to remember.

Measure the amount of food you give Puggy each time so you know exactly
how much food he's getting. I leave a measuring cup inside the container of
dog food so it's handy when I'm feeding.

Pug puppies should have three meals a day. They would happily stay on this
schedule forever, but by the time they're 12 to 14 weeks of age, they should
be reduced to two feedings a day. They should stay on the two-meal-a-day
plan for the rest of their life, unless they need to add some weight.

Knowing Your Pug's Nutritional Requirements

A good food for your Pug contains the right mixture of protein, carbohydrates,
fats, and fiber. Don't forget that he also needs the all-important vitamins and
minerals, which he's already getting if you're feeding him a dry food that's
labeled "nutritionally complete."

At each stage of his life — from puppyhood to senior citizen status — Puggy needs these basics, but the percentages change according to what his system requires. To help you select the right food for the right age, dog food companies have different recipes for puppies, mature dogs, and seniors. Some companies even make food for dogs on a special diet, such as "lite" formulas for overweight dogs. Your veterinarian may also suggest when it's time to switch to a senior food.

Choosing commercial dry dog food (kibble)

Although it may look dull and boring to you, dry commercial dog food, otherwise known as *kibble,* is your Pug's main nutrition squeeze. Kibble is a complete meal package with all the nutrition he needs. Feeding dry food has many advantages:

- It gives Puggy's mouth a workout by helping to scrape tartar from his teeth.
- It's less expensive in the long run because you feed less than canned food. Based on a price per pound, large bags cost less than small bags.
- It's easy to store — no refrigeration required.
- It stays fresh for three to six months.
- It doesn't have a strong odor.
- It's easy to take with you if you're traveling.

When buying kibble, check the package label to determine whether the pieces are the right size and texture. The dog food companies make small dog food chunks that Puggy can easily fit into his mouth. There's no sense in buying large, extra-hard pieces that take your Pug forever to eat.

If possible, store the contents of the kibble bag in a closed, airtight container, preferably inside the house. For animals on the loose in your neighborhood, an open bag of dog food left outside is a sure invitation to dinner. Keeping the food in a closed container also helps to keep it fresh longer. If you can't keep a large bag sealed, then buy the smallest bag available. The food should always have a fresh smell and never be stale or moldy.

Reading the ingredients label

Although commercial kibble bags list the ingredients in their recipes, trying to figure out what's inside a bag of dog food by reading the label is like trying to read a foreign language. The food contains some strange-sounding ingredients, and they're mostly written in very tiny print!

What you can decipher may sound good, but to be sure, look for a label that says "meets AAFCO nutrient profiles for all stages of a dog's life." This means that you can feed this food to your Pug throughout his lifetime.

AAFCO stands for the Association of American Feed Control Officials, which sets the standard for animal nutrition requirements and pet food ingredients. When AAFCO approves a food, it must be

- A recipe that meets the nutritional levels that it establishes

- A food that dogs have actually eaten during a testing process

- A recipe that is very similar to another brand of food that has successfully passed a feeding testing trial

Look for a food with a label that says it has passed AAFCO feeding trials and not simply "according to AAFCO guidelines," which is not the same thing. A food is much more reliable if it has been fed to dogs over a long period of time and the dogs haven't had any problems after eating it.

Buying quality dog food

When buying food, remember the following things to ensure that you're getting good, quality food for your Pug.

- Avoid foods that contain animal by-products. *By-products,* in dog food speak, mean anything from the animal, such as hair, feet, and feathers, to who knows what else.

- Look for whole ingredients rather than ingredients that aren't specific, such as chicken instead of chicken meal. *Chicken meal* is just a generic term for some part of a chicken. This could be the chicken neck or wing ground up so finely that it becomes meal, not a breast or a thigh.

  Sure, you may be reading that proteins, fats, or carbohydrates are inside, but unless the label specifies what kind of protein, such as chicken, beef, or egg, the food could contain any type or amount of protein, which you may not want your dog to eat. All the ingredients should be foods that you recognize, such as apples, brown rice, or oatmeal.

- While regular brands include wheat, corn, or soybeans as a primary ingredient, quality foods list their protein (such as chicken, egg, meat, lamb, turkey, or duck) first. The first few ingredients listed make up the largest percentages of the total ingredients contained in the food. Ingredients listed last represent the smallest amounts of the total.

Because a quality food has ingredients that are easy to digest, it's more concentrated, and you don't have to feed as much. This type of food is easier on a dog's system and less expensive in the long run. You'll also have fewer stools to clean up.

You're more likely to find a better selection of quality dog food in pet food stores rather than discount outlets or grocery stores. These stores simply don't have the room to display the wide variety of dog foods available, so generally go with one or two high-volume foods.

Adding vitamins and supplements

If you feed Puggy a quality premium kibble, you don't need to add extra vitamins and supplements to his diet. Everything he needs is inside the kibble. Premium kibble contains all the necessary vitamins and minerals.

If you add extra vitamins or minerals to Puggy's diet, you could upset the balanced diet he's already getting in his kibble. Giving extra vitamins and minerals to a young Pug may actually cause more harm than good. You don't want Puggy to grow too much too fast because that could cause rear-end lameness, otherwise known as *hip dysplasia*. For more information on this inherited disease, see Chapter 14.

Dining on canned food

Just as with dry food, it's a good idea to read the labels on canned food. Practically all canned food contains mostly water — nearly 75 percent — although it also contains some meat and vegetable ingredients. Some canned recipes are complete meals, but other recipes need to be mixed with kibble.

Although you could feed your Pug a canned brand that has total nutrition, it isn't a good idea to give him only that. For one thing, it still has a high moisture content and has no crunch factor, which is very satisfying to Puggy teeth. The best way to use canned food, even the complete meals, is to mix some in with the dry food. But it's worth pointing out that canned food is far more expensive than dry food. It may also have an odor that you may dislike, even though Puggy thinks it's pretty terrific.

Don't forget to refrigerate any leftover, opened canned food to keep it fresh. After a few days in the refrigerator, it may begin spoiling and may not be safe for your Pug. If you're traveling and plan to take some cans of dog food, don't forget the can opener or a cooler with ice to keep it fresh.

Opting for semi-moist food?

Here's the lowdown on semi-moist (also called soaking or soft) food: It's not worth opening the freezer door for. Semi-moist food is usually found in the freezer section of pet food stores, but is seldom available in supermarkets or discount stores. It has less moisture than canned food, which makes it more chewy.

Sometimes it comes packaged in individual servings, but unfortunately, the serving sizes are often too much for a Pug to eat in a single meal. If the food comes in a loaf, you have to cut a frozen slice and then defrost it. You need to thoroughly thaw it before serving, so you have to plan ahead. No one, least of all Puggy, enjoys an ice-cold meal.

Have you ever eaten frozen food that has stayed in the freezer too long? It's yucky. If you choose frozen, semi-moist food for your dog, check the expiration date on the package before purchasing or serving it. Your Pug won't appreciate food with freezer burns, either.

The cost of the semi-moist food is another factor to consider. Semi-moist food is more expensive than dry food but less expensive than canned-food complete meals. Consider, too, that semi-moist food contains all sorts of ingredients that aren't terrific. It has more sugar, salt, preservatives, and artificial coloring agents than you really want your Pug to eat. Sure, Puggy may gobble it down, but stop and think about what he's getting.

Handing out the treats

Giving out treats is probably one of the best things about having a dog. Pugs, especially, are thrilled to get more food. And there's no shortage of treats on the market.

Leave it to commercial food manufacturers to make so many different kinds of tasty morsels, although a few independent bakeries have sprung up in several U.S. cities that specialize in making treats just for dogs. There are biscuits and lots of little nibbly things in all different sizes, shapes, and flavors. Or you can try making your own petite Pug yummies. Check out a pet food cookbook for some great ideas.

Cut-up fresh fruits and veggies also make wonderful treats for Puggy. Nothing is better for your Pug on a hot summer's day than a few small pieces of watermelon or sliced strawberries, but be sure to cut them into very small pieces. Carrots, especially, need to be diced because Pugs tend to inhale without taking the time to chew them first. There are a few foods you should avoid feeding your Pug. See the section "Avoiding Dangerous Foods," later in the chapter, for information.

Don't give out more than 5 to 10 percent of Puggy's daily food allotment in treats. Most goodies contain sugar, which leads to obesity and tooth decay. Besides, your Pug will want them all the time if you give them out too much. Just like the standards you set for regular dog food, treats should also be healthy and kept to a minimum.

Too many treats may make Puggy pick at his food, hoping that something better will come along. As soon as you see that he's not eating his kibble, the temptation is great to give in to his wishes.

Keep all treats in a closed container or up on a high shelf. Pugs have been known to empty out open containers left lying around.

Edible chewy toys can also stand in for treats. Found in pet food stores, these edible toys, usually in the shape of bones, have flavors such as carrot, liver, and chicken. Gnawing on these toys helps keep your dog's teeth clean. Although these things don't hurt your Pug if he devours them, bear in mind that they do contain artificial ingredients, which you probably want to give sparingly. They're not meant to substitute for a meal. Stick to natural food sources as much as possible. To find out more about nonedible chew toys, see Chapter 5.

Passing up table scraps

There's a fine line between people food treats and table scraps. Although most low-fat foods that you eat are okay to give Puggy, hold these to a minimum. His main diet should consist of his kibble, with only an occasional treat.

Above all, don't give your Pug food scraps directly from the table or else he'll forever be hanging around the dining room. If you do have healthy leftovers, such as chicken, rice, cottage cheese, veggies, or eggs, save them for your Pug's next mealtime and mix them in with his regular food. Be sure to dice or shred these morsels and combine them with kibble, or else Puggy eats the table food and ignores his kibble.

When you do give your Pug some of your leftovers in his kibble, be sure it isn't the fancy food, such as chicken with spices or vegetables and sauce. Your Pug can't digest these delicacies and could get diarrhea or severe stomach upset. Try washing the chicken or vegetables off with some warm water. If you can't get rid of the gourmet touches, then don't give the food to Puggy.

Making Changes as Your Pug Grows

The amount and type of food that your Pug eats as a young puppy changes as he matures. He has different nutritional needs at different times in his life.

Continually evaluate how your puppy looks as he grows into adulthood and even after that. If he suddenly looks too skinny, it means he is growing and needs a bit more food. Or if Puggy looks pudgy, it's time to cut back on the amount of food you give him. Like people, dogs' weights change in response to how sedentary or active they are.

Preparing your puppy's diet

Everything your puppy needs to eat for steady growth and good nutrition is available in a premium kibble food mixed with a small amount of quality canned food. Many dog food manufacturers make a puppy recipe with small chunks that are easy for a young puppy to chew.

At 10 weeks of age, a puppy should be fed three times a day. By the time a puppy is 12 to 14 weeks old, he's ready for two meals a day. Many veterinarians recommend transferring from puppy food to the adult recipe by the time a Pug is 12 to 14 weeks of age. Research shows that dogs are more likely to develop hip dysplasia if they're fed too much protein, which is contained in puppy food at a young age. For more information about hip dysplasia, see Chapter 14.

When increasing the amount of food you give your Pug puppy in his daily diet, do it in small increments. First, just add barely ⅛ cup of kibble at each meal. After a few days, see how Puggy looks with this new amount. You can always add slightly more or even cut back the extra food at one of the meals.

One way to tell whether you're feeding your puppy the correct amount of food is by looking at his ribs. If you can see them sticking out, he's not getting enough. If you can't even feel them, he's too fat. If you can feel his ribs but you can't see them, he's probably just right.

Graduating to the adult recipe

Between the ages of 12 to 14 weeks, you should begin transferring from the puppy recipe to the adult one. Exactly when during that time depends on how your Pug looks and acts. If he's becoming less active, then begin the switch at 12 weeks. Puppy food has more calories than the adult recipe does, and Puggy may not need as many calories if he isn't as active.

Don't make a sudden switch from puppy to the adult recipe overnight. Do it gradually. At first, feed him a combination of one-fourth adult food and three-fourths puppy food. Keep him on this diet for three or four days. Next, give him a mixture of half adult food and half puppy food and keep him on that for three or four days. Follow that with three or four days of three-fourths adult food and one-fourth puppy food, until finally Puggy can eat entirely the big-boy adult recipe.

Adult dogs usually eat the same amount of food they did as puppies. They just don't have that extra meal that you cut out at 12 to 14 weeks of age.

Why Puggy, what big eyes you have!

Suppose that you've already given Puggy his dinner and just made a sandwich for yourself. It's TV time, so you've left the sandwich on a plate on your TV chair while you get up to get a cool beverage. When you come back, the sandwich is gone, and Puggy is smacking his lips! Yup, your little angel must've been extra-hungry to chow down on both your meal and his own.

But how can you tell whether your Pug is really hungry or if he just looks that way? That's hard to answer because Pugs always *look* hungry.

His big googly eyes have that "poor me" look. So the sooner you can read his expression and body language, the sooner he won't be able to fool you!

If you do decide to give your Pug more food because he's hungry, avoid adding more kibble because kibble has calories. You don't want him to get too fat. But here's where the fresh fruits and vegetables come in mighty handy. They fill Puggy up without adding the extra calories.

When feeding a quality premium kibble, most adult Pugs eat between ½ cup to ¾ cup of adult recipe kibble soaked with a little water, plus 1 to 2 tablespoons of some quality canned food.

Avoiding Dangerous Foods

I'm sure you don't want to give your Pug anything that can make him sick. The following food items can be downright dangerous and maybe fatal, so be sure to avoid giving them to your Pug:

- **Chocolate:** Too much chocolate can cause dehydration and diarrhea.

- **Onions:** Raw or cooked onions can cause an upset stomach.

- **Grapes and raisins:** Grapes and raisins both have toxins that are deadly to dogs.

- **Table scraps other than the healthy fruits and veggies already listed in this chapter:** Commercial food that is formulated especially for your dog is far healthier for him than your food.

- **Bones, such as chicken, turkey, pork, or beef:** They can splinter and, if swallowed, can pierce your dog's intestines.

- **Beverages other than water:** Be aware that alcohol is deadly for Pugs.

- **Any strange food objects he may pick up off the ground when you're out walking:** They can be so badly decomposed that you have no way of knowing what they were, originally. Things like gum, cigarettes, or parts of dead animals can also be killers.

Discovering a Food Allergy

One minute, your Pug is resting comfortably next to you. The next minute, he's violently rubbing his body along the carpet and thrashing back and forth, trying to scratch himself. He may have a food allergy. Although any food may make your dog allergic, most of the time the type of protein or grain used in the kibble or canned food is the culprit.

Making your own dog food: Labor of love or a lotta hassle?

Many people today make their own dog food because they think it's healthier than commercial dog food, which has preservatives and some artificial flavors. As a result, some owners report that their dogs have more energy and that their dogs' skin and coats look better.

Although preparing a homemade diet has become very popular, many veterinarians aren't so enthusiastic about it. It means using raw meat — which carries the risk of E. coli and salmonella poisoning — and a long list of other fresh ingredients, including pureed veggies, cooked rice, and vitamins, all mixed together. Homemade dog food also calls for fresh raw bones to be given with the ground-up mixture or in between meals. Why raw bones? Oddly enough, when they're not cooked, the bones don't splinter. Raw bones, such as turkey necks, are soft enough to break down when a dog starts chewing them, but they don't break into sharp pieces.

Obtaining fresh raw meat, including the bones, can be a challenge in some cities, but local butchers can be a great source. Although freezing the raw meat makes it less fresh than it would be unfrozen, it may be a more convenient way to prepare it. Fresh fruit, veggies, and rice are much easier to get than the raw meat and not that much trouble to grind up.

Some dog lovers have formed cooperative homemade food groups. They buy the raw meat in bulk, and each person takes a turn making all the food for all the dogs in the group. However, transporting the food gets tricky sometimes because it needs to be kept refrigerated.

Another alternative is to feed your Pug a combination of the commercial and the homemade food. This feeding system gives you more personal freedom because you're not tied down to having to prepare fresh dog food every day and may offer your Pug the best of both worlds. You can give your dog commercial food one week and raw food the next week. Some people feed their dogs a commercial diet all the time but supplement with just the raw bones and give fresh fruits and veggies here and there.

Not every dog does well on the same diet. Check with your veterinarian before starting your Pug on a natural diet to make sure that all the ingredients are safe to give your dog.

Besides itchy skin, other allergic symptoms include

- ✔ Ear infection
- ✔ Diarrhea
- ✔ Digestive problems
- ✔ Hives
- ✔ Rash
- ✔ Vomiting

If Puggy develops any of these symptoms, take him to the veterinarian. After treating the allergy, your veterinarian can evaluate what you're feeding your Pug and tell you what sorts of changes to make.

If your Pug has a bad reaction to any food, stop feeding him that food. Sometimes you don't know what food caused a reaction until you've given it to your dog twice. If you're feeding a combination of two or more foods, try removing one of them at a time to see how it affects your dog. Wait a week before reintroducing the food that didn't bother him back into his diet.

If your Pug has any serious symptoms that make it difficult for him to breathe, rush him to the veterinarian immediately.

Chapter 8

Building Up a Pug Sweat: Exercise Advice

*T*he Pug may be an official member of the Toy family, but when it comes to working out, your Pug is pretty sturdy. She's more than ready to get up and out of the house in search of the perfect stretch session. All you have to do is clip the leash onto her collar, and she's set to be your best walking or hiking buddy.

Exercise is exactly what a Pug needs to maintain her good health. Don't forget that playing games with your dog also counts when helping to flex her muscles — as long as Puggy stays out of the heat. Have any doubts? Not to worry. In this chapter, I tell you everything you want to know about making an exercise plan for your Pug.

Understanding the Importance of Exercise

No doubt about it: Exercise makes the heart and mind grow stronger.

Getting regular exercise helps your Pug's respiratory and cardiovascular systems adapt and expand to enable them to send more blood pumping to the muscles and other organs. Take away exercise, and everything slows down to slug speed. It also prevents Pugs, who have a tendency to get a little chubby, from getting even heavier, which is a health no-no. Obesity can be a serious problem because it leads to heart disease, respiratory problems, and arthritis. Unlike other breeds, however, Pugs don't require a lot of intense exercise; even a little amount goes a long way.

Putting Puggy on a regular exercise program helps her stay healthy throughout her life. Of course, Pugs at different ages require different amounts of exercise. I talk more about that subject in the section "Getting Physical: Taking Your Pug's Age and Home into Account," later in the chapter.

How does exercise work for both dogs and people? Without getting too technical, a good exercise program sends a signal to the body's *endorphins,* the special biochemical messengers in the brain, to get going and make you feel happy. Their job is to give you a feeling of euphoria and overall well-being. In Puggy's case, being in a good mood helps prevent her from having those bad doggy habits, such as licking or chewing at the skin on her legs, taking apart the furniture, or digging up the new tulips in the yard. Exercise-induced happiness also talks Puggy out of barking without a stop, and feeling restless.

Choosing the right activity

What kind of outdoor exercise can both of you do safely? Walking, walking, and walking.

Unlike running, walking is easy on your joints (and your Pug's joints) and gently raises your heart rates. Jogging is too hard on Puggy's feet, and she can quickly overheat. Besides, she can't go as fast as you probably need to go to get the benefits. Pugs aren't great swimmers, either, because they have heavy bodies and short, thin legs. Outdoor hikes may be okay if you don't go too far too fast. You can also play games with your Pug for some exercise (see the section "Playing with Your Pug," later in this chapter). But, pound for pound, walking is still your best bet when it comes to exercising with your Pug.

The only equipment needed for walking are some good walking shoes for you and a well-fitting collar and leash for your Pug (see Figure 8-1). I talk more about kinds of leashes in Chapter 12.

To jump-start your exercise program, don't try to make up for lost time by doing a rigorous routine right away. That only tires both of you out and discourages you from sticking with your new fitness plan.

If you and your Pug haven't gone walking for a long time, you need to build up to even just a few minutes a day. Hopefully, Puggy can be all the inspiration you need to get moving. Her love for the great outdoors can really be contagious. Pugs like being outside, and if they have a safe and secure fenced yard, they love nothing more than racing around it.

Although your Pug would probably also enjoy running outside the yard without a leash, that's not safe for her. Too many dangerous things can happen to her while she's off her leash, especially if you live near a busy street and she runs out into traffic.

Figure 8-1:
To be on the safe side, keep Puggy on a leash outdoors.

©Judi Crowe

Realizing that an active Pug is a happy Pug

The more places your Pug gets to go to, the better. Pugs are curious, intelligent dogs, and they thrive on having things to do. When Puggy doesn't have a job or isn't busy with tasks to accomplish or problems to work out, she can get bored.

Exercise is a great way to combat Pug boredom. Sure, she's a lap dog and does a lot of serious lounging around the house, but don't underestimate your Pug's sedentary lifestyle. Your dog is smart and likes to use her mind. She also loves to be around people, and when Pugs are left alone for too long, they can find things to get into that you may not approve of. It's nothing for a Pug to investigate that loose piece of carpeting sticking up in the great room. Next thing you know, shredded carpet tufts are decorating the house.

Giving your Pug a chance to get out and about gives her some new things to look at and think about, plus it burns off some energy (see Figure 8-2). Check out the color insert for more looks at good ways to exercise your Pug.

Two Pug heads may be better than one as far as being active goes. If you're away for most of the day, you may want to consider adding another Pug just to keep the first one company. One dog definitely amuses the other one, and they're both exercising one another.

Figure 8-2:
Puggy looks forward to getting her exercise.

©Judi Crowe

Of course, two Pugs can get into double the trouble, but at least they're happy. Just be sure to think carefully before making that choice and don't get another dog on a whim. You don't want to regret your decision later.

Getting Physical: Taking Your Pug's Age and Home into Account

Two main things determine when and where you can exercise your Pug: where you live and how old your dog is. You need to weigh both of these factors when designing an exercise routine for your pet.

Location, location, location

Whether you live in a tiny apartment or a sprawling ranch, it's still important to make sure that your Pug gets the appropriate amount of exercise. A bigger dwelling may make exercising your pet easier, but you can still find ways to keep Puggy active in a small space.

For the apartment Pug

If you live in an apartment with your Pug, you're already taking her outside a few times a day to go to the bathroom. As much as you'd like to think this is exercise, it really doesn't count. Sorry.

To give your housebound Pug some exercise, take her outdoors for a 15- to 20-minute walk at least once a day, in addition to her bathroom trips. You can also take her to a large outdoor area, such as a park or a safe, paved site where there isn't any traffic. Then give her some room to roam by attaching an 8-foot leash or a retractable leash to her collar. A *retractable leash* is very strong and uses a pulley to extend as far as 12 feet.

Another idea for helping your Pug keep in shape indoors is to walk her up and down the hallways for 15- to 20-minute sessions. As long as you're not making a lot of noise, this activity shouldn't disturb the neighbors. Although you don't have to go fast, do walk at a brisk pace. Or, if you have stairs in your building that are safe but not too steep, you can climb up and down some stairs with her, if you're physically able to do so. Stair climbing is a healthy way to exercise because it gets your heart rate up. A Pug likes the challenge of having something new to do and will be eager to reach the top (or bottom).

If you decide to climb stairs with your Pug, be careful and don't try to race. Discourage her from running ahead of you because doing so could be dangerous. Both of you could trip or fall down the stairs.

To reduce the threat of falling, wear comfortable, flat-heeled athletic shoes. Also try using a short 4-foot leash so that you can control how far and how fast she climbs the stairs.

To prepare for stair-climbing exercises, train your dog not to pull on the leash. For more information on training, take a look at Chapter 11.

During a heat spell, or even during very rainy or stormy weather, you may not be able to take your Pug outdoors for her workout. Because during these periods she gets less exercise than normal, cut down a little on the amount of food you regularly feed her. She isn't burning off the extra calories, and you don't want her to get fat.

For the Pug with a yard of her own

If you have a safe, fenced-in yard that Puggy can run around in, your dog is one lucky duck! She has the freedom to move around without feeling constrained by a leash.

Your outdoor area doesn't have to have lots of acres for Puggy to use and enjoy. An area big enough for her to take several long strides before having to turn around too soon works out well. For your Pug to even want to use an area, it should have a surface that is safe and easy on her feet. Make sure that no sharp rocks or objects that can damage her toes and feet are sticking up. For more information on having a safe yard, see Chapter 5. You can use the following surfaces for your Pug's workout:

- ✔ Grass
- ✔ Soft, smooth gravel
- ✔ Packed-down dirt or compressed soil
- ✔ A combination of concrete walkways and grass

Even a small concrete patio can be enough for your Pug to run back and forth on. Or you may want to opt for a *dog run,* which is a small, chain-link enclosure with either gravel, dirt, or cement on the floor. The size usually depends on how much room is available, but it could be as small as 4 feet wide by 8 feet long.

Your Pug shouldn't spend long days outdoors in such a tiny space. That's way too confining and can certainly make Pug bored, bored, bored. This area doesn't provide any source of exercise for your dog.

To give Puggy even more workout time, install a doggy door connecting the inside of your house to your Pug's fenced-in yard. If you don't have to worry about dog theft in your neighborhood, your yard is a safe place for your dog to get outside and back inside again whenever she wants.

If you like the idea of the doggy door but don't want your Pug going outside whenever she wants to, you can close it off. Most doggy door models come with a metal slat that you can slide over the opening to prevent your Pug from getting out. This works well for owners who are gone during the day and may not want Puggy out in the yard without being supervised. For more information about the different types of doggy doors that you can install, see Chapter 5.

Just because your Pug has her own space in the great outdoors, don't forget about getting her out for a stroll in the neighborhood, too. Although a yard is great to have, seeing the same thing day after day, year after year, can get boring. How many times can you expect your Pug to sniff and check out every flower and shrub in the yard without her thinking that a siesta is really a lot better way to spend her time? Here's where taking your Pug for a walk in the neighborhood at least a few times a week can help.

Exercising through the ages

The amount and type of exercise that you give your Pug naturally changes as she ages. Her body has different needs as she progresses from puppyhood to senior life.

For the puppy Pug

Puppies are just more naturally active than older dogs. Every day, they discover something new in the world that they hadn't noticed before, and for a youngster, that's pretty exciting. They also manage to keep themselves busy moving around from room to room or from place to place in the yard.

Because your puppy Pug is on the go so much, you don't have to give her as much exercise as a mature or senior Pug. Of course, I'm certainly not stopping you from having a good time with your Pug and getting outdoors just for the sheer joy of it, but it's not mandatory for a puppy because she exercises without any help from you.

You don't have to convince a Pug puppy that she wants to go out for a walk. The minute you go to pick up the leash, she lets you know she's ready and very willing to go off with you.

If you want to take your puppy walking on a leash, don't plan on going very far. She's still a little gal, and she's not done growing yet. Her legs are pint-size, so she isn't able to go as far as you can. For the first few times, saunter out for only about 5 to 10 minutes. If you're not careful, your Pug puppy can become injured just because she doesn't have the coordination that older Pugs do; sometimes she's all legs.

In fact, skip any long walks, hiking trips, or serious agility conditioning until Puggy is about 18 months old. It takes that long for the growth plates of her bones to close. For more information on agility competition, see Chapter 15.

For the middle-aged Pug

If your middle-aged Pug is healthy and doesn't have any orthopedic problems, she'll probably love getting out as much as she can. All workout systems are a-go for the Pug who's between 18 months and 10 years of age.

For the senior Pug

Getting enough exercise is still very important for the older Pug.

As she ages, she stiffens up more because she doesn't have as much flexibility in her joints. Unfortunately, Puggy Senior isn't so eager to get off the couch and investigate a strange noise or see who's coming in the front door. And if she does play indoor exercise games, you may find her shuffling instead of racing after a toy.

When she's settled into her favorite comfy spot, it's pretty hard to convince her to give it up to go chase a rope, but you have to try. Notice that I did say "try" and not "force." If your Pug needs some incentive to get up and do something, consider enticing her with the following:

- A treat
- The sound of her leash
- Your voice: "Come on, Puggy, ol' girl. Let's go see if we can go find some dragons today."
- A few loving pats in the hope that she leaves the couch and follows you to the front door
- A new toy

Good exercise for a senior Pug includes walking throughout the house a few times a day, playing a few short rounds of fetch, or going outdoors for a stroll several days a week.

Older Pugs have even less tolerance for hot weather than they did when they were younger. On hot days, limit the time she spends outdoors. If she likes running around in one particular room of the house, take extra care and, if you don't have air conditioning, put a fan in that room to keep it cool.

Avoiding the Last Supper Before Exercise

The last thing you want to do just before taking Puggy out to exercise is to feed her. Sure, it gives her energy, but not until she digests it and her body begins to process the food. Because this process could take a while, all that delicious kibble just sits there in her tummy.

Wait at least an hour after you feed Puggy before you take her out for a walk. If you're going on an exciting outdoor adventure, such as a hike, wait even longer — about two hours.

Feeding just a little

Say that the weather is pretty hot where you live, and the only time you have to take Puggy out for her 20-minute walk is early in the morning. And say that she's very conditioned to expect that you serve her breakfast to her first thing after she awakens. Well, okay, maybe she is spoiled a little!

Here's a situation where it probably doesn't hurt to give her just five or six pieces of kibble. No, it isn't her real breakfast, but she thinks it is, and when she's done eating, she's a little satisfied. This small amount doesn't upset her system when you go out for a walk, but it's just enough to take the edge off her hunger. Then after you come home, you can serve her the regular breakfast.

Feeding after exercise

If your Pug misses a meal (heaven forbid!) while you're out exercising with her, be sure to wait at least an hour before giving her regular entrée to her. This gives her system some time to settle down before it gets busy starting to metabolize the kibble.

If you feed Puggy too soon after she exercises, she may feel like vomiting it all up. And don't let her gulp down a whole bowl of water when she gets home, either. A few slurps are probably okay, but no more than that. Otherwise, she may vomit.

Getting Out of the House

Sometimes the hardest part of going for a walk is taking the first step out of your house, which typically has too many distractions — the phone, a nice warm bed, the TV, and the computer, for example. Actually, for people who resist going out to exercise, any excuse works as a reason that they can't do it.

If getting out of the house is a challenge for you, consider these suggestions:

✔ Choose a day and time when you can regularly commit to taking Puggy out for exercise.

✔ Choose your workout clothing the night before and lay it out with Puggy's leash.

✔ Choose an exercise, such as walking, hiking, or ball chasing, that you like to do with your Pug.

Making sure Puggy's up to the challenge

If you haven't gone walking with your Pug yet but want to begin, start off slowly. Your Pug is probably in good enough shape to go walking, but before beginning a serious fitness program to prepare for competing in agility (see Chapter 15), ask your veterinarian to give your Pug a thorough examination.

The exam is just a precautionary measure to make sure that Puggy doesn't have any health problems that may get worse with exercise, such as the following:

✔ Diabetes

✔ Heart murmur

✔ Hip dysplasia (see the following paragraph for more information)

✔ Musculoskeletal disorders

✔ Patellar luxation (see the following paragraph for more information)

Even as a young dog, Puggy should be checked by a veterinarian before doing any serious exercise, to make sure that her kneecaps haven't slipped out of place. This condition is known as *patella luxation,* which I discuss in Chapter 14. After the age of 2, Puggy's hips should also be x-rayed by a veterinarian and evaluated by a board-certified veterinary radiologist to verify that she doesn't have rear-end lameness, otherwise known as *hip dysplasia.* For more information on this inherited disease, also see Chapter 14.

When you're ready to get going on an exercise program with Puggy, you need to check out one more thing: the weather. See the section "Sitting Out the Hot Times," later in the chapter, for details about avoiding the outdoors with your Pug when the mercury is rising.

But if the weather is cool and comfortable, how much exercise do you and Puggy need to have to be fit? Walking outdoors for 15 or 20 minutes a day for a few days a week is all you and Puggy need to get started. If you feel that you can both handle longer walks, then slowly increase that time. Keep in mind that Puggy takes much shorter steps than you do and feels like she's walking farther than you are.

When going out the first day, follow this advice:

✔ Don't try to make up for lost time by doing too much.

✔ Don't push Puggy to go farther when she's panting a lot or seems out of breath.

✔ Don't go too fast.

✔ Don't wear uncomfortable shoes or clothing.

✔ Don't leave home if it's too hot for Puggy (see the section "Sitting Out the Hot Times," later in this chapter).

Advancing to twice-a-week outings

If walking the same route outside your home gets boring, or if you want a change of pace from your regular routine, put Puggy in the car and drive to a new location twice a week. Just going to a different place may likely invigorate both of you. For more information about safe ways to take your Pug for a car ride, see Chapter 12.

After you decide to become more active with your Pug, you'll be surprised how easy it is to find other places to go. Here are some interesting places to take Puggy:

- ✔ Outdoor shopping centers
- ✔ Small neighborhood parks
- ✔ Outside and around civic buildings
- ✔ The corner grocery store
- ✔ Swap meets or sidewalk art fairs
- ✔ Boat or car shows
- ✔ Errands with the kids
- ✔ Safe country trails or hiking areas
- ✔ Beach walkways

Be sure to check ahead of time to find out whether pets are allowed at these places or special events.

For the first few outings, don't overdo it. If you're accustomed to walking with Puggy for 20-minute sessions, don't suddenly jump to spending an hour. You'll both be pretty tired afterward, and your feet will certainly feel it. I know, going for a walk with your favorite dog alongside the ocean on a beautiful summer morning is tempting, but just be careful!

Securely fenced-in dog parks are another place to take Puggy for additional exercise. The dogs here aren't on their leashes and are looking for other dogs to play with. These parks usually have separate areas for big dogs and little dogs. In some cities, dog parks are free, but in others, you may have to pay a fee to enter. You probably want to find out ahead of time whether there's a charge. In addition, you should ask what hours they're open and whether they require some kind of ID, such as a proof of rabies vaccination. That way you haven't wasted a trip if they're closed or if you don't have your wallet or dog's ID.

Be sure to supervise your Pug at the dog park. Other dogs may not be as friendly as yours, so if you sense that your dog feels threatened, take her home before any fights break out. You're also responsible for cleaning up any mess she makes in the dog yard.

Sitting Out the Hot Times

All the best-laid plans about taking your Pug outdoors for a good time can fall apart if one thing happens: hot weather.

Limiting outside time

Hot or humid weather can be deadly to Puggy when she's outdoors. She can easily overheat and get heatstroke. I give more information about heatstroke in Chapter 13, but basically, the problem is that the Pug's flat face and short muzzle can't cool down her body temperature. Dogs with long muzzles have an easier time in the heat because their long muzzles give the hot air some time to cool as it travels past the nasal passages on its way to the lungs.

Your Pug's health and well-being should always be your first priority. Get used to checking the temperature before taking even one step outside with Puggy.

If it's 80 degrees or higher and the humidity is high, don't let your Pug stay outdoors for more than 10 or 15 minutes. Pugs who live in hot climates should venture out only in the early morning or late afternoon after the temperature cools down.

And be sure and take some cool water along if you do head outside. I talk more about this in the section "Taking a Pug pack: Bringing water along," later in the chapter.

Finding shade outdoors

In some areas of the country, the weather can change quickly. For people, this isn't usually a problem, but for Pugs, it can be a big one, especially if the weather suddenly turns hot and humid.

If you find yourself outdoors and it's too warm for your Pug, find some shade to stand beneath as soon as possible so she can cool off. Some good places to look for shade include the following:

- Buildings with wide eaves that you can stand beneath.
- Big trees with overhanging branches. If you have to walk from tree to tree in order to get back home or to your car, that can help, too.
- A phone booth where you can call a friend to pick you up!

Never leave your Pug unattended outdoors in the heat.

Taking a Pug pack: Bringing water along

If the weather is warm, don't even think of leaving home for more than 10 minutes without taking along a container or two of cool water for Puggy. You probably want to carry some along for you, too.

Gathering to talk Pug: Pug Hill, New York

There's a wonderful camaraderie among Pug owners. For example, if a Pug owner is driving along and sees someone walking a Pug, he or she may pull over to the side of the road to check out the Pug and chat with the person at the other end of the leash.

In some places throughout the country, people even get together just to meet other Pug owners and to see other Pugs. For example, some New Yorkers meet at Pug Hill in Central Park. Every Sunday morning, 10 to 30 Pug people gather on a grassy hilltop beside the Alice in Wonderland statue. The crowd really gets going around noon.

Blacks, fawns, show, and rescue Pugs — it doesn't matter what they are. If they have a flat face, big googly eyes, and a short compact body, that's the only thing their owners need to hang around Pug Hill. For the dogs, this is Pug heaven. They have the freedom to run around and sniff out other Puggy bodies. The owners get a chance to talk Pug. Although some people keep in touch throughout the week, most strike up conversations on the spot about their dogs' snoring, where to find a good vet, and anything else related to Pugsly.

Going for a walk outdoors? Carry a lightweight backpack that has room for water inside. Also available are packs you can wear around your waist that water bottles can fit into. You also can find padded shoulder straps that are specially designed to hold water containers and that are very convenient to tote. Be sure to take along Puggy's travel water dish, too. They make portable collapsible dog water bowls just for this purpose. For more information on supplies, see Chapter 5.

TIP

Check local outdoor camping stores to find all types of inexpensive, lightweight water carriers for both you and your dog.

REMEMBER

During warm weather, put some bottled water in the freezer. About a half-hour before taking your Pug out for a walk, get the bottled water out of the freezer. That way, it has some time to thaw but is still nice and cold when you're out in the heat.

Planning a long drive before getting out of the car and taking a walk with your Pug? Take the water out of the freezer right before you walk out your door. For extra insurance that your water will stay cool, take along an insulated ice chest filled with ice chips. Giving your Pug a few pieces of ice also helps keep her cool. Likewise, you can use the blue reusable ice freezer packs under her bedding to keep her crate cool while traveling or when stopped.

Playing with Your Pug

Who could resist having some fun with a loveable Pug? Playing with your dog is one of the best things about having her. Plus, she's always ready for a good game. Luckily, there's no shortage of good, sturdy dog toys that you can buy for Puggy.

Don't play tug of war over a toy with your Pug. Although her teeth are strong, they're little and could get yanked out of her mouth if you pull too hard.

Chasing a ball

As you can see in Figure 8-3, Pugs like balls, especially if they aren't too hard. If you're playing ball with her in the house, you certainly don't want to throw something that can knock a hole in your wall. Besides, she needs to be able to get a grip on the ball so that she can bring it back to you, if she does bring it back. After chasing the ball, a Pug loves to tease you and carry it around the house or spend some serious time gnawing and chewing it.

For the best roly-poly choices, consider these tips:

✔ Select balls for Puggy that are the right size for her mouth — not so large that she can't get her mouth around them and not so small that she can swallow them. If she swallows a ball or toy that's too small, she could choke.

✔ Select balls that aren't so soft that she can chew pieces off and possibly swallow them. These small parts can become lodged in her throat.

If your Pug does retrieve the ball, resist the temptation to keep throwing it without giving her a rest. Wait a few minutes before you throw it again to make sure she's breathing normally.

Tossing some toys

The best fun is tossing a toy a few feet away from you but low to the ground for Pug to chase and hopefully retrieve.

She feels so proud when she brings a toy back to you — if she does! Or she may prefer to strut around the house with the toy. Just watching her trot through the great room on through the kitchen and making a beeline for the bedroom is enough entertainment for both of you. What she's really thinking while carrying a toy around is, "Am I terrific, or what?"

©Judi Crowe

Figure 8-3:
Most Pugs
love chasing
a ball.

Some Pugs chase anything. That can be a ball, a rope toy, Nylabone chews, or even the red glow of a flashlight. Fleecy or furry animals are big favorites. So are Kongs (hard rubber toys), especially if they're filled with cheese or peanut butter — with those, it's probably a one-time chase, though!

New toys are always appearing in pet supply stores, so keep checking to see what your Pug may enjoy. Sometimes, the process of picking new toys is trial and error. What you think your Pug will like doesn't really do it for her, while another choice that you're not all that thrilled over may make your Pug jump for joy. See Chapter 5 for more on picking Pug toys.

One quick word of warning about tossing toys: Don't throw a toy up in the air for her to catch. She could injure her back on the way down, as can many breeds.

Chapter 9

Grooming Your Pug Pretty

- -

In The Chapter

▶ Preparing to spruce up your pet

▶ Giving your dog the brush-off (that's a good thing)

▶ Giving Puggy a bath

▶ Brushing Pug teeth

▶ Inspecting Pug eyes

▶ Checking and cleaning your dog's ears

▶ Maintaining wrinkles

▶ Trimming nails

- -

*L*ooking at your Pug's short-haired coat, you probably find it hard to imagine that he needs much primping and preening to keep him clean, but even Pugs need some grooming. And while you're at it, his pearly whites could use a good brusha-brusha, his ears need to be wiped out, and a pedicure would really be the frosting on the Pug. Oh, and one more thing: Those Pug wrinkles just scream, "I'm cute but grimy and need a good cleaning."

Puggy doesn't need the services of a professional groomer, however; you can handle the job yourself. In this chapter, I tell you how easy it is to keep your Pug looking like a Hollywood celebrity by spending only a short time on his beauty routine at home.

Preparing to Fluff and Puff Puggy

Grooming is first and foremost a bonding experience. Here's a chance for you to dedicate a few uninterrupted minutes of your time to your Pug pal. I'm not talking about having to spend hours fussing with your Pug. You can probably get the whole beauty treatment — brushing; bathing; cleaning teeth, ears, and wrinkles; and trimming nails — done in under an hour.

Using nutrition to look good

Having a Pug with a shiny coat that doesn't shed too much or shower flakes of dandruff all over your home and clothing begins from the inside out. In fact, the kind of food you feed him directly affects how his coat looks. A good premium kibble with whole, natural ingredients and the right type of vitamins and supplements gives your Pug everything he needs to have a soft,

luxurious, and healthy coat. For more information about feeding your Pug, see Chapter 7.

Keep in mind that you should groom your Pug before you feed him. Although some Pugs love to be fussed over, others get too nervous to keep their food down if they know they're getting their toenails clipped or having a bath.

The sooner you start grooming Puggy, the better — say a day or two after he settles into your household. He needs time to accept the idea that grooming is a way of life, and no fussing is allowed! Use an upbeat, happy voice, and he thinks this is a fun time.

Choosing a day to groom

Pick the same day every week and call it the Groom Puggy Day. Having a regular schedule makes it easy for you to remember to do whatever sprucing your Pug needs. If you don't pick a day, it's too easy to slack off. Before you know it, four months have gone by, and an odd odor is coming from your dog. Can you imagine what you would feel and look like if you went without bathing, washing your hair, brushing your teeth, or trimming your nails for four months?

Once a week, you should also clean out his wrinkles, wipe out his eyes, clip his nails, and brush his teeth and coat. Unless he's been outside rolling around in the dirt, you really don't have to bathe him once a week. Once every three weeks is probably sufficient.

Setting up a table

Putting your Pug up on a table makes it much easier for you to trim his nails, brush him, and clean out his ears. If he's up high, he's less tempted to fool around. Besides, with Pug at eye level, you can see his whole body up close.

Any sturdy table that you have at home works if it's waist-high for you. You don't want to have to bend over to see Puggy. Unless you have a table with a non-skid surface, I recommend putting a plastic tablecloth down on the table first so your Pug doesn't slip.

If you're so inclined, you can purchase a special dog-grooming table through animal supply catalogs or pet supply stores. These tables are wobble-proof with a nonslip rubber top. They're also portable so that you can move them anywhere, and they fold up easily for storage. The tables also have an extra attachment, called a *grooming arm,* that's pretty neat and worth the investment. It clips on to Puggy's collar so that you can work on him without having to hold him or worry that he may fall off the table.

Never turn your back or leave your Pug unattended on a table. He can easily slip and fall off.

If a table isn't available, sit down on the floor and place Puggy directly in front of you in a corner of the room. This way, he can't wiggle away.

Gathering your supplies

Put all the grooming tools for Puggy together and keep them in one place. Hunting for these things every time you groom your Pug is time consuming, so save time and energy, and organize!

If you have a wall near the bathing area, hang the equipment up on a pegboard. Or if you plan to bathe Puggy one time in the kitchen sink and another time outdoors, keep all the tools in a plastic container. Many types of plastic organizers are available that can fit under the sink or in a drawer.

Inspecting Puggy's body

Just before Puggy's spa session is a good time to give him a mini physical. To make it easy, put him up on a table. Here's your opportunity to do the following:

- ✔ Carefully inspect your Pug's body for any strange lumps that may be cancerous or any open sores that haven't healed. If you find anything suspicious, have your veterinarian check it out. Your inspection may catch something before it gets worse.

- ✔ Check to see if there's a *foxtail,* which is a sharp bristle end piece of dried grass hiding out in Puggy's chest, paw pad, or ears. You

can pick it off before it works its way down deep beyond the fur and into his skin and causes a painful infection.

- ✔ Check your dog's eyes and ears for any signs of redness or strange discharges, which may signal that an infection is brewing.

- ✔ Check your dog's coat for signs of any flea dirt (which looks like tiny pepper specks), skin rashes, or bald spots. If you find flea dirt, chances are that you find fleas, too. Begin treating fleas immediately, if they show up. Your veterinarian should examine any skin rashes or bald spots.

Here's a quick rundown of the supplies that you need:

- Brushing (before the bath):
  - Rubber brush with rubber teeth or pumice stone
  - Steel flea comb with a really fine-tooth side
  - Chamois cloth to wipe away dead hair
- Bathing:
  - Kitchen sink, bathtub, or shower
  - Two nonslip mats

    One for your dog so that he doesn't slip and one for you so that you have traction
  - Quality doggy shampoo and spray conditioner (see the section "Choosing the right shampoo," later in this chapter, for more information)
  - One or two large cotton towels or high-velocity dryer
  - Washcloth
  - Rubber suction cup and grooming noose

    The cup attaches to the side of the sink or bathtub, and the noose fits across the dog's chest and over one leg so he can't go anywhere.
  - Spray shower attachment for an indoor bath or a hose adapter for an outdoor bath
- After-bath grooming:
  - Cotton balls
  - Ear cleaner
  - Nail clippers or electric hobby grinder
  - Styptic powder (see the section "Training your Pug to like the experience," later in this chapter, for information)
  - Canine toothbrush and toothpaste

Beginning with a Good Brushing or Comb-Out

Wondering what you should do first — bathe Puggy and then brush? Or brush first and then bathe? The answer depends on whether you want a lot of dead hair neatly piled in your bathtub or spread out all over you and the rest of the house. Because very few people would opt for the latter (with the possible exception of Pigpen from the *Peanuts* cartoon), I suggest using a brush with rubber teeth or a steel comb with a really fine-tooth side to remove all the dead hair from Puggy's coat *before* you give him a bath.

On the weeks you don't give him a bath, brush or comb your Pug for a few minutes at least once a week. Doing so helps to remove the dead hair before it falls out on its own. It also stimulates the skin to produce natural oils, which help promote growth for the next crop of hair.

With his collar on, prop Puggy onto the table so that he faces away from you. If you aren't using a grooming arm (see the section "Setting up a table," earlier in the chapter, for an explanation of this term), hold on to your Pug's neck to support him. Then follow these steps to brush him:

1. **To loosen dead hair, brush him a few times in the opposite direction his hair grows.**

2. **Brush him along the top of his back from the top of his neck to the base of his tail.**

3. **Brush his sides, from front to back.**

    Don't press down too hard with the brush — doing so can hurt Puggy!

   Don't forget his neck and legs.

Shedding and more shedding

Lucky Puggy's short-haired coat never tangles or mats, but if he's a fawn-colored Pug, he makes up for it by having two coats — an undercoat and a top coat. Some black Pugs have only one coat layer, but both colors shed heavily and produce brushes full of dead hair. (See Chapter 3 for more on the different colors of Pugs.)

Although he sheds year-round, your Pug sheds even more in the summertime, when his undercoat falls out to cool him off. The plush fawn blanket of hair he wore in winter looks sparser and darker in the warm months because the undercoat is gone. When the temperature begins to cool off, your Pug sheds slightly less.

He needs his coat to keep him warmer in winter. Don't be fooled if you don't see a lot of hair floating around the house in cold weather. Puggy still sheds, and you can't get out of brushing him, even during the winter months.

Dog hair grows in cycles. When hairs first sprout up, they should be strong and healthy and look shiny. As soon as they stop growing, they look dry and begin to fall out. These dead hairs are the culprits that wind up everywhere — woven into your navy blue suit, stuck into the velour sofa, and floating on top of your soup! With a good diet, regular brushing, and bathing, Puggy's coat becomes healthier, and he doesn't shed as often.

4. **Reach underneath and gently brush his chest and belly and beneath his neck.**

5. **To brush his tail, hold it by the tip and gently unfurl it.**

   Carefully brush or comb it from the base of the tail to the tip.

6. **If you're not bathing him, finish the brushing session by rubbing him down with a wet but wrung-out chamois cloth.**

   Doing so picks up the loose hair.

7. **Spritz his coat lightly with conditioner for a smooth final finish.**

The color insert shows Pugs getting brushed.

Shampooing Your Starlet

Fortunately, your Pug is small enough to fit into your kitchen sink for a bath (see Figure 9-1). Other good spa spots are the big bathtub or shower in your bathroom, or even outdoors on a warm day.

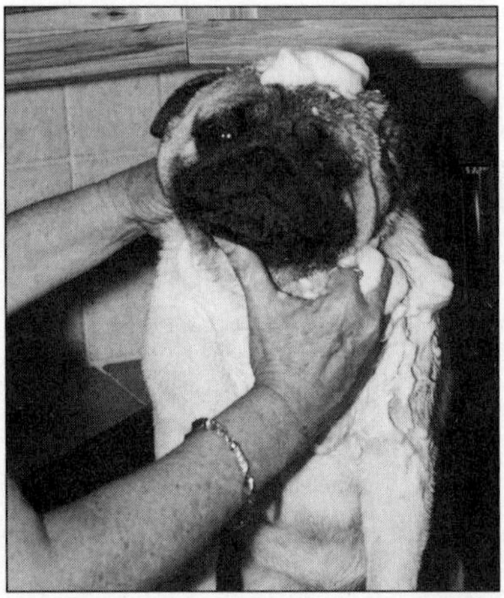

Figure 9-1:
Your Pug can easily be bathed in a sink.

©Judi Crowe

Don't bathe your Pug more than once a week. Too much bathing can dry out his coat. Getting a bath once a week or once every other week is ideal. During the winter, when he doesn't go outdoors much, you can stretch the bath to once every three weeks. How do you know how often you should bathe your Pug? If his coat already has an offensive odor, bingo! Give him a bath.

But before you plop your dog into the water, take him outside to go to the bathroom first. You don't want him to have to relieve himself right after he gets out of the tub. That's the fastest way to get dirty all over again. Besides, he may get a chill! Another precaution to take before the spa treatment: Block off any exits from the bathing area so he can't run the other way when he figures out he's going into the tub. Sure, some Pugs love their baths, but others wish the bathtub would be outlawed.

Make sure that you have good light wherever you give Puggy a bath. If the lighting is poor, add a quality fluorescent shop light to hang near the tub.

Rub a dub dub: Putting Puggy in the tub

Get all your bathing supplies ready before you head into the bathroom. (See the section "Gathering your supplies," earlier in the chapter, for more on what you need.) Nothing's worse than getting halfway through the bath only to realize that you've left the shampoo in the other room.

When you put your Pug into the tub, keep his nylon collar on so that you have something to hold on to if he gets a little restless. Don't grab Puggy by the top of his forehead if you need to control him. You can damage his eyes, which are very sensitive. Instead, hold on to his chest or put your hand under his chin.

If you're into music, turn some on. It doesn't matter if the music's country, classical, or just plain rock-and-roll. Music soothes the savage beast — as well as your not-so-savage Pug. Here are the steps to follow for your Pug's spa drill:

1. **Place one nonslip bath mat into the tub for your Pug and one on the floor for you to stand on.**

2. **Gently place a cotton ball inside each of Puggy's ears.**

   These help to keep the water out of his ears.

3. **Lift him into the tub.**

   Hopefully, this isn't a fight. If so, use the rubber grooming noose. (See the section "Gathering your supplies," earlier in the chapter, for more on this item.) The more times you bathe Puggy, the less he wants to give you a hard time. Some Pugs just have to become accustomed to the routine.

4. **Attach a rubber suction cup to the side of the tub and put the connecting rubber grooming noose over one of Puggy's legs.**

5. **Brush his teeth.**

   See the section "Look, Mom, No Cavities: Keeping Your Pug's Teeth Clean," later in this chapter, for details.

6. **Turn on the warm water.**

   Before wetting him, test the water temperature on the inside of your arm to make sure that the water is tepid and not too hot or too cold.

7. **Fill the sink or tub with barely enough water to cover your Pug's feet.**

8. **Gently spray and spread the water over his body — not his head and face.**

9. **Drizzle a small amount of shampoo onto your Pug's back.**

10. **Use a rubber brush to lather the shampoo into his coat upward from his tail toward his neck and down onto his legs, on his abdomen, and up over both sides of his neck.**

    Keep the soap out of his eyes.

11. **Use a wet washcloth to wipe off his face, eyes, and the outside of his ears.**

    You can also clean out his wrinkles now. I talk more about this in the section "Maintaining Worry-Free Wrinkles," later in this chapter.

12. **Begin rinsing the shampoo off down his body.**

    Here, the rubber brush really gets a workout. Hold the water sprayer in one hand and the brush in the other and brush out the shampoo as you rinse it off (see Figure 9-2).

Figure 9-2:
A water sprayer is a great way to rinse off Puggy, and he even likes it!

©Judi Crowe

13. **Get all the soap out of Puggy's coat!**

    If any residue is left on his feet, he'll be itching later on.

14. **Spray on some conditioner.**

    Brush it through his coat and then rinse very thoroughly.

15. **Check Puggy's ears for any sign of debris and clean them, if necessary.**

    I talk more about this in the section "All the Better to Hear You With: Caring For Puggy's Ears," later in this chapter.

Getting back to nature: Opting for an outdoor bath

If you're one of those outdoorsy kinds of Pug owners, you're probably thinking it may be fun to give Puggy a bath outside on a warm day. Doing that is okay, and the routine is the same as what I describe in the previous section; however, you do need to take some extra precautions when Puggy goes skinny-dipping on your front lawn:

✔ Use your garden hose hooked to a faucet inside the house so that you can control the water temperature to keep it lukewarm. Water in the outdoor spigot is too cold for your Pug, who can catch a chill even when it's warm. Use a hose adapter that's sold at a hardware or a waterbed supply store.

✔ Use a nylon leash to keep your Pug in place. A leather lead can shrink when it's wet.

✔ Use a towel on the grass for your Pug to stand on, or bathe him on concrete.

✔ Use your thumb on the water stream directly from the hose instead of using a nozzle. Doing so cuts the water pressure so that you don't hurt your dog.

Choosing the right shampoo

Ever see shampoo commercials on TV? The models are sudsing up their hair while dancing and having a ball. Too bad those commercials don't show glamorous Pugs shampooing their coats. Can you imagine? If they did, you would know how many different kinds of doggy shampoos you can find. Shampoo companies make products for every kind of canine coat and skin problem. Here are some shampoo choices:

- **Botanical extract:** Made from all-natural ingredients. It's milder and doesn't lather as much as other shampoos.

- **Color-enhancing:** Available for white, black, and red dogs.

- **Degreasing:** For dogs with too much oil in their coats. If Puggy's fur separates and feels greasy, it may be too oily.

- **De-skunking:** For dogs who've been skunked. See the nearby sidebar, "What if Puggy gets skunked?" for more information.

- **Flea and tick:** For dogs with a flea or tick problem, or you can just use it as a preventative.

- **Medicated:** For allergies caused by flea bites, grass, and pollen. Also for mites.

- **Oatmeal:** For itchy skin or allergies.

- **Puppy:** Similar to baby shampoo, it doesn't sting puppies' eyes.

What if Puggy gets skunked?

Although you hope it never happens, it can: a skunk encounter of the smelly kind. When Puggy meets a skunk outdoors, all he wants to do is to go over and say, "Howdy!" But the skunk isn't so palsy-walsy. In fact, the experience can actually stink. Skunks have no manners and think nothing of shooing other animals away with their pungent spray. Here's a very short-lived relationship where your Pug gets the worse end of the deal. The skunk odor is so strong (who can forget it once you've smelled it?) that, as soon as you bring Puggy indoors, your whole house reeks from the stink.

Getting sprayed by a skunk can be irritating to your Pug's coat, and he needs to be bathed. Don't try tomato juice or vinegar because those products don't work. And although you can try some shampoo products on the market, you can also make this recipe at home:

In a plastic bucket, mix the following ingredients well:

1. **Mix 1 quart of 3-percent hydrogen peroxide, ¼ cup baking soda, and 1 to 2 teaspoons liquid soap.**

2. **Wet Puggy down with water, apply the mixture deep into the fur, and work it through his coat.**

3. **Leave the solution on for about 5 minutes, or until the odor is gone; let your nose guide you. Some heavily oiled areas may require a "rinse and repeat" washing.**

4. **Rinse off with tepid water.**

Pour the leftover solution down the drain with running water. Never store mixed solution in a closed bottle or sprayer. Pressure can build until the container bursts.

Courtesy of Paul Krebaum © 1993

Use shampoo made for dogs, not for people. The ingredients in human shampoo are too harsh for a Pug and may irritate Puggy's coat. If you're bathing your Pug once a week, use a high-quality dog shampoo that contains natural ingredients rather than a cheaper one with artificial stuff. The high-quality shampoo doesn't leave a residue on your Pug's skin.

An oatmeal shampoo containing a conditioner with aloe vera is a good general shampoo to bathe Puggy in. Besides, it smells good!

Toweling off

After his bath, the next step is getting him dry. Towels made from 100 percent cotton are best for drying your Pug. They're absorbent and soft, and they don't scratch his coat. Here's a quick way to dry your dog:

1. **While he's still standing in the tub and before he shakes the water off himself, wrap a towel over him.**

2. **Apply gentle but firm circular motions to dry your Pug.**

3. **Using your fingertips, knead the towel to dry the coat at its base, from the roots up.**

4. **Blot the insides of his ears and the top of his head.**

5. **Wipe off his neck, throat, and each leg.**

6. **Carefully pat the groin area dry and lift Puggy's curly tail and blot the water beneath it.**

7. **Now you can take your Pug out of the tub and let him air-dry himself if it's warm enough.**

Or if you prefer to use a hair dryer, use a high-velocity, professional-quality dryer made for pets — not a human dryer model. Human hair dryers blow at very high temperatures, which can spot-burn Puggy's delicate top coat while his undercoat stays wet. Pet hair dryers have heating coils that prevent them from reaching a high temperature. These dryers can stand alone so that your hands are free to brush the coat while the dryer spreads the warm air around at the same time.

Although a pet hair dryer can cost between $50 and $200, the expense is well worth it when you consider how many times you'll be bathing Puggy throughout his lifetime.

Give your Pug a small food treat when you're finished bathing him. This tells him that he was a good dog to let you fuss all over him!

Look, Mom, No Cavities: Keeping Your Pug's Teeth Clean

Taking care of your dog's teeth by regularly brushing and checking them for any signs of infection or disease is a lifelong responsibility that helps your Pug stay healthy.

Poor dental hygiene can create bacteria, which spread to the heart, liver, and kidneys. This situation is very dangerous to your Pug's health.

Feeding your Pug a good-quality kibble can help keep his teeth clean, if it isn't soaked too long in water. (For more information on feeding Puggy, see Chapter 7.) Otherwise, the carbohydrates in the food can stick to his teeth and create plaque — a combination of bacteria, stray food particles, and saliva. Canned food doesn't help to remove plaque. One of its ingredients is sugar, which adds to the plaque buildup.

If plaque isn't brushed away, it builds up and becomes tartar. Tartar then moves in and imbeds itself between the teeth and gums and creates a small sinkhole where the bacteria multiply. The bacteria invade the gums and cause gingivitis — and the gums swell and bleed. Once a dog has gingivitis, his teeth fall out.

Give Puggy hard nylon bones or raw marrow bones to chew on. These items clean his teeth and don't splinter off and hurt him.

Checking for diseased gums or cracked teeth

Puggy's charming wide-tooth smile doesn't happen by accident. His jaw is slightly undershot, which means that his lower jaw is longer and sticks out past the upper jaw. Because the entire face is shortened, his teeth are often squeezed in sideways very close together. To handle the scrunch, some of the teeth crowd onto others, creating spaces for food particles to get caught in the gums and cause trouble.

It takes a second every day to lift up your Pug's lips one side at a time to look at his gums and teeth. Make sure that his gums aren't red or swollen and that none of his teeth are cracked. Swollen gums are a sign of gingivitis or that a tooth is impacted with debris. If a tooth is cracked at the base, bacteria move in and cause more decay.

As soon as you take your Pug home for the first time, begin getting him accustomed to letting you check his mouth. Start by holding his head with one hand and gently lift one lip and quickly put it down with the other hand. Tell him, "Good boy! Good boy!" Keep repeating the drill, progressing to lifting both lips, one a time, and holding each lip up just long enough for you to peek inside Puggy's mouth. After you have the lip action going, you can progress to adding a toothbrush and then toothpaste.

Getting your Pug to hold still long enough for you to see anything may be a challenge, but a little training can go a long way toward convincing him this is a good idea. For more information about training, see Chapter 11.

While you're checking out Puggy's mouth, be on the lookout for other signs of oral disease. If your Pug has any of these signs, take him to the veterinarian as soon as possible:

- ✔ Aversion to touch on his muzzle
- ✔ Bad breath
- ✔ Brown or yellow crust stuck to teeth enamel
- ✔ Excessive drooling
- ✔ Red line along the gums
- ✔ Skipping meals

Brushing your Pug's pearly whites

Although brushing your Pug's teeth may seem odd to you, this routine is one of the most important things you can do to safeguard your dog's health. You're helping your dog to rid his mouth of harmful bacteria. And once you both get the routine down pat, your tooth-brushing session can be a piece of cake, er, kibble.

Use a doggy toothbrush and a toothpaste formulated just for dogs. Human toothpaste foams up, and if Puggy swallows this, it can upset his stomach. Canine toothpaste safely dissolves inside your Pug's mouth, and, unlike the people product, doesn't require any water to rinse it off.

Start slowly to get Puggy comfortable with having a strange object in his mouth. At first, run your finger inside his mouth along the tooth and gum line. In no time at all, he'll like the sensation and will push his gum into your finger for the dental massage. Later, add a small slip of gauze and a little bit of the doggy paste. Ease the paste around the teeth gently but firmly. When he's comfortable with that, go ahead and move on to using a toothbrush. At first, just brush one side of his mouth once across, and then build up to a few times as he readily accepts the brush.

Brush your Pug's teeth once or twice a week and when you give him a bath. I'm not kidding about how often to do this. The more care you give his teeth, the fewer dental problems he'll have.

Getting a little help from the vet: Professional cleanings

Sure, you can brush away debris resting on your Pug's teeth yourself, but at least once a year, your Pug needs to go to the veterinarian for a professional dental scaling. Your veterinarian anesthetizes him before doing the job because he has sophisticated cleaning tools that dig down deeper to clean bacteria before it damages your Pug's teeth. Your veterinarian can discuss the pros and cons involved with putting your dog under before beginning any procedures.

Eyeballing Puggy's Eyes

Those big googly eyes that Pugs are famous for are very sensitive. Because they bulge out, too many bad things can happen to your Pug's eyesight. A thorn from a rosebush or a swipe from a cat's claw can scratch his cornea and damage his eyesight. Being so low to the ground, your Pug can run into all sorts of things that lurk and stick into his eyes and cause eye problems.

Check your Pug's eyes every day to make sure that everything looks normal. His eyes shouldn't be tearing excessively or be red or swollen. Then, once a week (maybe after bathing Puggy), wipe his eyes and eyelids clean with a cotton ball soaked in warm water. You can also use a warm washcloth to clean his eyes. If you spot an eye problem, take your Pug to the veterinarian as soon as possible.

All the Better to Hear You With: Caring For Puggy's Ears

Puggy's cute little foldover ears make a great hiding place for dirt, grime, and who knows what else. A shoe could even be underneath those ears! Well, maybe a small one, anyway. The one thing you don't want to have inside your

Pug's ears is an ear infection. Infections hurt and itch, and your Pug may be scratching and rubbing to alleviate the discomfort. If it's really bad, he scratches them so hard that they bleed! You certainly don't want your Pug to suffer when you can easily take care of the problem with regular cleaning.

Besides good old-fashioned dirt and a buildup of regular ear wax, allergies and other conditions (such as hypothyroidism, overactive adrenal glands, diabetes, or ear mites) can also be the culprits responsible for your Pug's ear infections. For more information about keeping your Pug safe and healthy, see Chapter 13.

Checking ears to help prevent infection

It takes only a minute to flip over the top of one of Puggy's ear flaps to check inside to see whether anything funny is going on in there. You want to see healthy ears, which are slightly pink and not red. Red means trouble and an infection.

With Pug ears, you can sometimes smell a problem before you see it. Your nose picks it up right away. A brown or black waxy buildup down inside the ear canal accumulates and sends off a very earthy, but somewhat nasty, odor. It's your cue to enter your Pug's ear, stage left (or right), and clean up the act.

Check your Pug's ears every day (see Figure 9-3 and the color insert). Doing so helps you catch any problems before they get any worse. You want to make sure that the insides of his ears feel warm to the touch, but aren't bright red. A few cleanings can clear up most ear infections within a few days, but you may want to take Puggy to the veterinarian if a problem doesn't clear up.

Figure 9-3:
Cleaning Puggy's ears on a regular basis helps prevent bad ear infections.

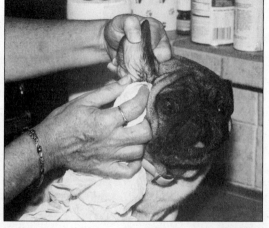

©Judi Crowe

If your Pug's ears aren't clearing up, he may have ear mites. These tiny pests live in the ear canal and wreak havoc with their constant irritation. Your veterinarian can prescribe a stronger cleaner for these unlucky creatures. No, ear infections and ear mites aren't contagious to other dogs or people.

Looking into Puggy's ears isn't a one-shot deal. It's a regular doggy job you have to keep repeating if your dog has problem ears. If you let a few days go by without checking his ears, don't be surprised if he's rubbing his ears on the carpet or scratching wildly at them.

Doing regular cleanings

Ask your veterinarian to give you a safe ear-cleaning solution to do the job right. Although a few types of ear cleaners are available in a pet food store or through a dog supply catalog, these products usually contain alcohol, which can dry out and irritate your Pug's sweet little ears and make them itch even more.

Here are the steps to follow for cleaning your dog's ears:

1. **Using one hand, lift up one of your Pug's ears and, using your other hand, squirt some ear cleaner into the same ear.**

2. **Place your thumb and forefinger on each side of the base of the ear and press your fingers together a few times, compressing the ear slightly each time.**

   You should hear a squishing sound. The cleaner is breaking up the waxy debris stuck to the inside of Puggy's ear.

3. **Insert a long rectangular piece of rolled cotton — about 6 inches works well — into the ear as far as it can go.**

   Don't worry about hurting the eardrum. It's located far down his neck, and you can never reach it!

4. **With your finger in the middle of the cotton, rotate the cotton around a few times in his ear and draw it out of the ear.**

   If Puggy's ears are really dirty, the cotton may be a yucky shade of dark brown.

5. **Repeat, inserting the cleaner and a new piece or side of the cotton one or two more times, until the cotton comes out clean.**

6. **Repeat the process with the other ear.**

Give Puggy a small food treat to reward him for putting up with this ear invasion!

Don't use cotton swabs, baby wipes, cotton balls, or tissues to clean your dog's ears. These items aren't big enough to absorb all the liquid from the cleaner or get all the debris. In addition, don't go digging inside Puggy's ears with anything other than cotton strips. Anything sharp can hurt his sensitive ears.

If your Pug's ears aren't dirty, then don't clean them! Cleaning without a reason can cause yeast infections.

Maintaining Worry-Free Wrinkles

Part of the Pug's appeal is his wonderful wrinkle factor. Who can resist the V pattern of wrinkles on his forehead? Then there's the irresistible *nose roll* — the deep fold of skin that lies above his nose. It even wiggles whenever he sniffs. Despite the Pug's physical appeal, keep in mind that taking care of your Pug's wrinkles and nose roll is serious business.

When filled with debris, the wrinkles can make Puggy feel very uncomfortable. Your Pug can be so bothered by the dirty wrinkles that he tries to clean the folds himself by rubbing his head sideways against a door frame. Yuck! Puggy rubbing his face on the carpet? Better check his nose roll.

Clean the nose roll and other wrinkles every day — bath or no bath — to prevent odor.

Some Pugs have larger nose rolls than others, but even the smaller ones need to be cleaned.

The best thing to use for cleaning Puggy's nose roll is a damp washcloth (see Figure 9-4). To rid the roll of rank stuff, take these steps:

1. **Take Puggy's cheek in your left hand.**
2. **Lift the folds and look for redness, moist sores, rashes, or musty smells, which may mean infection.**
3. **Run the damp washcloth through the roll from one side to the other.**

   Repeat on the other side.
4. **To help keep the wrinkles cleaner longer, spread a small amount of earwash onto a gauze square and use it to wipe the wrinkles and folds on your Pug's face and nose clean.**
5. **Clean the smaller wrinkles under the eyes the same way.**

A bald spot or a rash in your Pug's wrinkles means there's a fungus among us or a staph infection. Chin acne also pops out if the face isn't cleaned. Take Puggy to a veterinarian to know for sure.

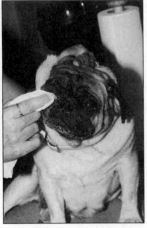

©Judi Crowe

Figure 9-4:
Keeping your Pug's wrinkles clean is easy with a damp washcloth.

Dogs Need Pedicures, Too: Clipping Your Pug's Nails

Hear that click, click, click on your floors? That's the sound that your Pug's nails make when he stands or walks in the house. It means his nails are too long, which isn't good. Just that little bit of extra length is enough to throw your Pug slightly backward off balance. Not only can this make Puggy look like he's had one too many because he can't walk in a straight line, toenails that are too long hurt his toes by forcing them to spread outward.

Nails that are too long are a menace to other Pugs and people. They can scratch and hurt you, another Pug's eyes during playtime, or even a Pug's own eyes accidentally when he's rubbing his face. Long nails get snagged in the carpet or your clothing and can rip and bleed.

Worse yet are those too-long toenails that curl over the edge of the toes and then downward into the foot, puncturing the pad. If your Pug didn't have his *dewclaws* (thumbnails) removed when he was a baby, they, too, can hurt Puggy if they're not trimmed regularly. They curl over and dig directly into his skin.

Knowing when and where to clip

Just like people's nails, dogs' nails come in a variety of shapes and sizes and grow out differently. Some dogs are just born with short nails that hardly ever need trimming, no matter what surface they walk on. Other dogs have longer nails to begin with and continually grow out longer nail tips.

Fawn Pugs are always ready to ride.

This black Pug loves to give kisses.

Judi Crowe

Elaine Gewirtz

Judi Crowe

The Pug standard describes the breed as even-tempered, playful, with a round head and square body.

Judi Crowe

This puppy's head is already perfectly round, but his ears still need more time to grow out and reach the outside corner of the eye.

Tony Nunes

This charmer helps his
owner celebrate Halloween.

Meg Callea

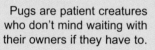

Pugs are patient creatures
who don't mind waiting with
their owners if they have to.

Elaine Gewirtz

Pugs are good travelers. As long
as they have a warm lap and a
toy, they can go anywhere.

Judi Crowe

Pugs enjoy the brushing experience.

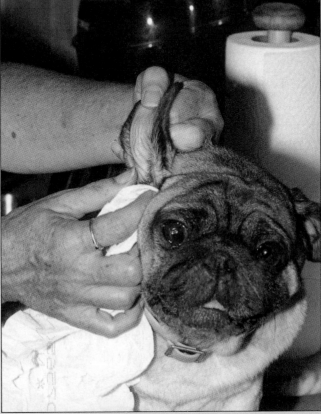

Judi Crowe

Keeping ears clean is easy, and Pugs don't mind having it done.

Judi Crowe

Although they can't be the dog's sole caregiver, children can certainly play a role in caring for your Pug. Having a child feed the dog a treat is a good start.

With supervision, Pugs are gentle with children and make good playmates.

Judi Crowe

Judi Crowe

These puppies are the result of generations of conscientious breeding.

Judi Crowe

Pugs like having other Pug companions. Besides, it's hard to have just one.

Playing with a ball in the pool is great exercise, but going for a walk works just as well.

Trust curious Pugs to investigate everything in the house.

Every Pug should know how to sit and stay and obey other basic commands like down and come.

Even wearing a bandana won't hide this Pug's clearly defined black and fawn facial markings.

Because of their color, black Pugs seem smaller and finer boned,
but these features should be the same on fawn Pugs as well.

Feeding a good-quality diet containing plenty of protein and calcium speeds up the nail growth even more. A few days after you've trimmed the nails, they're ready to be done again. If you don't think you have to cut your dog's nails because Puggy can exercise them off by walking or running on concrete, guess again.

So how do you know when nails need to be cut and how much should be taken off? If nails are clicking on the floor or curling over the edges of the toe, they're too long.

Although Pugs have black nails, some fawn Pugs have clear or white nails, which make cutting easier. Each of these nails has a clear white area above the *quick* — the pinkish part of the nail containing a nerve and blood vein — that grows out at the tip. All of the white tips are sanded or ground off. With the black nails, just grind off a small amount of the pointed end. If you've taken off too much, the nail bleeds slightly, and you know how far you can go. Use that nail to measure where the quick is on the next nail.

Pick one day of the week when you know you're available and make this your regular nail-trimming appointment. At the very least, trim your dog's nails once every two weeks right after his bath. The nails are clean, and you can see the quick easier. They're also soft and easier to cut. Do the job in good light — outdoors works best.

If you prefer to stay inside, a table comes in handy for the job. Putting your dog up there makes it so much easier, especially if you use a grooming arm and noose, leaving both your hands free. (See the section "Gathering your supplies," earlier in the chapter, for details about a grooming arm and noose.) Or you can work on his nails while he's lying beside you on the couch or in your lap.

Training your Pug to like the experience

Because you're going to be trimming your Pug's nails every week or every other week, you want him to like it. This happy outlook isn't impossible to achieve if you train yourself to do it right and if you relax! The more jittery you are, the more nervous your Pug becomes.

Start slowly by touching Puggy's feet. Hopefully, his breeder began getting your dog used to this process, but if not, spend a few minutes several times every day handling his feet and giving him a food treat when he doesn't pull them away.

Many types of doggy toenail clippers are available, but I like to use the smallest guillotine-type tool or a cordless electric nail sander. Let Puggy sniff these out several times before you use them.

Before beginning the pedicure, open a small container of styptic powder and pour a small amount of it into the cap. Hopefully, you don't need to use it, but if you do accidentally nick one of Puggy's nails and it bleeds a little, the powder is handy to stop the bleeding. You can also use a styptic pencil made for people. You can find styptic powder at most pet supply stores.

Sure, a nick may hurt your Pug, and he may raise a ruckus. You didn't do it on purpose, however, so don't feel so guilty that you stop trimming completely! Even the most experienced nail groomers occasionally nick a nail. With practice, you get faster, and your aim gets better.

When you're ready to cut, follow these steps:

1. **Pick up and hold one paw in one hand, but use your thumb to gently press upward on the pad of the toe you're going to cut first.**

   Doing so extends the nail automatically.

2. **With your other hand, clip or sand off the white tip or a little bit off the edge of a black nail.**

3. **Immediately give your dog a small food treat and tell him what a good boy he is!**

4. **If your dog fusses too much, just do one foot or even one nail during a single session.**

   Eventually he gets over it.

Never get angry with your dog. He'll hate the nail trimming even more. And if you really get frustrated, you can always call a professional groomer to do the job.

Part III
Training Your Pug

The 5th Wave   By Rich Tennant

"You know you're never going to get Pugsley to do his business in your remote control dump truck."

In this part . . .

I help you conquer the dreaded task of housetraining your Pug (it's really not that bad, I promise). In addition, I give you some advice about making your Pug mind his p's and q's through obedience training. One of the most important aspects of training is how you talk to your dog, so this part also clues you in on the do's and don'ts of effective communication, such as using positive phrases and being consistent. Finally, if you ever want to hit the road or the friendly skies with your dog, I give you some tips about how to travel safely with a Pug.

Chapter 10

Private Pug, Reporting for Duty: Basic Training and Housetraining

You already know that your Pug is the coolest canine on the planet, but does she do what you want her to do around the house? It's one thing for her to be the cat's pajamas and another for her to be wetting them or tearing them up. However, the good news is that with a little training, your Pug can become a model dog.

In this chapter, I tell you how to convince your Pug that she really loves her wire pet carrier. Believe me, those little babies have many advantages, if used properly. One big one is that they make bedtime easier. Speaking of which, I also give you the lowdown on starting your dog on a sleep schedule so you don't have to get up with her in the wee hours of the morning. I also go over the basic rules of housetraining so that you can minimize the messes and teach your dog the proper place to go to the bathroom. Finally, I give you some pointers about how to make sure your Pug doesn't pick up bad habits, such as jumping, nipping, barking, or chewing you out of house and home.

Using a Wire Pet Carrier and Liking It

At first glance, a wire pet carrier may look like a mini-jail to you and me, but to your Pug, it's a personal multipurpose room. Wire carriers, also called crates, are very personal spaces that your Pug will come to love because, just like your bed, Puggy's carrier has a special feel and smell.

If you're leaving the house for a few hours and want to prevent Puggy from chewing the furniture, put her in her carrier. Likewise, if you're having some repair work done in your home and want to make sure your Pug is out of harm's way, her carrier makes a great safety zone. It can also help you house-train your Pug because dogs don't like to make a mess where they sleep. See the section "Running through the Housetraining How-To's," later in this chapter, for more on how to use the crate when housetraining your Pug.

Why use a wire pet carrier instead of one of the many hard-sided models you see in the stores? The wire carrier allows more air to flow through, and it isn't as hot inside. Because she easily overheats, your Pug needs to stay cool inside her crate, especially during warm weather. (For more information about Pugs and the dangers of overheating and heatstroke, see Chapter 13.)

Even if you have two Pugs (and twice the fun), each dog needs to have her own carrier.

Finding the right size and type of carrier

Wire pet carriers come in all different sizes and shapes, but you don't want one that's too big or too small. Your Pug should be able to comfortably stand up inside it without her head hitting the top, and it should be wide enough that she can comfortably turn around in it without her body crunching into the sides (see Figure 10-1).

Don't buy a carrier that's bigger than the one pictured in Figure 10-1. If it's too big, you don't want to move it around with you when you need it, and Puggy may think it's still okay to use the far corner as her lavatory.

Figure 10-1:
This wire
pet carrier
is just the
right size for
a Pug.

©Judi Crowe

When you go to the pet supply store to buy a carrier, take your Pug with you. Let your Pug test different sizes out by putting her inside. If you can afford to purchase more than one carrier, consider buying one for the car and one for the house. This way, you don't have to move them every time you want to take your Pug somewhere.

Putting it near the action

When's the best time to introduce your Pug to her carrier? Start right away when you bring her home. To find out more about putting Puggy in her carrier for the first time, see Chapter 6. She may not take to it right away, but with patience and the right training, your Pug may learn to prefer her carrier over your couch. Well, maybe not *every time*.

When you first bring your Pug home, put the carrier in your bedroom at night so that she doesn't feel abandoned while you're sleeping. In a strange, new place, she feels more comfortable if she knows you're nearby. During the daytime, move the carrier to a spot where you and Puggy plan to spend the most time because she wants to be where you are. The great room, den, and kitchen are usually good choices.

Keep Puggy's carrier out of the direct sunlight and away from any drafts or warm air vents that may be blowing toward the carrier. Your Pug needs to be cool and comfortable in her crate because it takes longer for cooler air to pass through her flat nostrils.

If you have small children in your home, teach them to respect your Pug's privacy and not go wandering into her crate uninvited. Puggy may not be too keen on sharing because a carrier is a dog's domain.

Getting Puggy in and keeping her there

Training Puggy to go happily into her carrier and enjoy staying there is easy if you believe that it's the best place for her to be if you can't watch her. In short, if you think that your Pug's carrier is great, so will she. However, if you don't like putting Puggy into her carrier, she can pick up on your emotions, and she won't like going in there, either. When you realize what a good training aid a carrier can be, your Pug will think the same thing and look forward to settling down inside her special location.

Take off Puggy's collar before you put her inside the carrier. If you leave it on, it may catch on something inside, and your Pug can accidentally choke.

Dispensing treats and meals in a carrier

When you begin training your Pug to use her carrier, don't expect her to wander in there and stay in there on her own. She needs some convincing, and she may need a few training sessions before Puggy realizes that you're serious about her using this new pad.

Every time you want your Pug to go inside her carrier, show her a small food treat — a small biscuit works great. Keep a metal container filled with biscuits near the carrier so the treats are always handy. Be sure to say, "Puggy, carrier." When she comes close, show her the treat and toss it inside the carrier. She runs in to get it, and after a few times, she begins to associate the word *carrier* with the place where she gets a treat. Don't be surprised if she runs inside her carrier first and waits for the treat before you're actually ready to give it to her! I talk more about training your Pug to come when called in Chapter 11.

If your Pug doesn't trot right inside after the treat, gently place the treat and Puggy inside the carrier, quickly shut the door, and leave. There's no reason to check to make sure that your dog likes it inside. If your Pug sees you hanging around, she probably thinks that you'll eventually take her out, so just walk away.

Another way to get Puggy to like going inside her carrier is to feed her meals there. After a few times, she runs inside her carrier and waits for food to be delivered the minute she hears the first piece of kibble drop into her bowl. In fact, if you have other dogs or small children, it's not a bad idea to continue feeding her inside her carrier. There she won't have to worry that her canine companions or the tiny tots may take her food. Also, if you go traveling with her, it gives her a familiar place to dine because some Pugs won't eat in strange places.

Stocking it with toys

To entice your Pug to hop into her carrier, you can also toss a new or well-loved toy inside in place of treats. If it's a toy that Puggy can chew on for a while, that's even better. The toy not only lures her inside on her own but also helps keep her there because she has something to do.

Try leaving a safe chew toy inside your dog's carrier. That way, if she gets bored with the new one, she always has the old one to keep her amused. For more information about different kinds of safe treats, see Chapter 7.

Periodically vary the toys you leave inside your Pug's carrier. After a while, the same old things get boring.

Placing an item inside that has your scent

Besides a comfy pillow, put one of your T-shirts or sweatshirts inside the carrier. Because the item has your scent, your Pug feels like you're close by, and she loves to snuggle down inside it. But, don't give her anything you plan on wearing again. There's a chance she may decide to chew it up!

Be sure to remove any buttons, zippers, or artificial decorations, such as sequins, from the clothing. Puggy may start chewing on these and can easily swallow the small pieces, which can cause an obstruction in her body. Or she can scratch her eyes if she lays on them.

There's no crying in wire pet carriers

After Puggy goes into her carrier, there's no guarantee she won't make a fuss the first few times. Ignore it. If you feel sorry for her and take her out whenever she cries, she figures out that she can get out by crying. Leave the house if you have to, but don't take her out of the carrier until she quiets down for at least a minute. If you choose to stay around, give her a strong verbal command — such as "No bark!" — when she carries on. Then, when she's quiet, tell her she's a good dog.

When you first begin carrier training your Pug, repeat the exercise a few times a day for short 15-minute sessions. As she gets the hang of it, lengthen her stays by ten minutes until she can quietly stay in her carrier for about a half-hour. Some Pugs can remain quiet in their carriers if they see you close by. Try putting her into her carrier for short periods while you're sitting in the same room, where she can see you.

Don't leave your Pug in the carrier for longer than four hours at a time. She needs to relieve herself after that long. Never use the carrier to punish your Pug. She won't understand what she did wrong and why you've suddenly put her inside. Besides, this is the place you want her to *like*, not dislike.

The carrier is also a great place for your Pug puppy to have a "time-out." This isn't punishing her. You're actually giving her a rest. Maybe she's gotten out of hand and is grabbing things she shouldn't around the house or is barking or biting too much and corrections aren't working as efficiently as they normally do. In that case, it's okay to put her inside the crate to chill out. Maybe she's just overtired and needed a nap. Or maybe you're tired and don't want to deal with her shenanigans. It's okay. You're not punishing her. Leave her in there until she's calmed down and you're ready to watch her. That could be up to two hours.

Setting the Snooze Schedule

Training your new Pug to sleep regular hours may sound silly, but doing so comes in handy when you like to get your zzz's and want to be on a regular schedule yourself.

Turning in at a decent hour

To help Puggy get on a regular schedule, set regular bedtime hours. Put her in her carrier about the same time every evening, and soon she'll be on your schedule. Right before you're ready to go to bed at night, take your Pug outdoors to her potty area. When she's finished, put her into her carrier. When you turn the lights out, she should go to sleep and stay asleep for most of the night. If you hear her whimpering during the night, however, it means she has to go outside to the potty area. In fact, for the first few months of puppyhood, your Pug may not be able to wait longer than six hours to relieve herself.

Don't ignore the bathroom call because your Pug may use her carrier for a potty if she can't get out. Dogs don't like to relieve themselves inside their carriers, but they will if they have no other choice.

As your Pug grows, she adapts to your schedule and is ready for bed when you are. When she's several months old or a full-grown adult, she can last the whole night without having to disturb you.

Rising with the sun isn't fun

Believe it or not, you're in charge of setting your schedule every day, not your dog. When the sun comes up, your Pug may think it's time to get up, too, and she may whine and cry. But unless you're a natural early bird, this may not be the time you set your alarm to go off. If you think your Pug has to relieve herself, then, by all means, take her out of her carrier. When she's done, resist the urge to play and fuss with her; instead, bring her right back to the carrier and close the door. Hopefully, she plays quietly with her toys or goes back to sleep until it's time for you to get up.

Never let Puggy bark and howl in her carrier when she wants to get out in the morning. That's a big no-no! In a firm voice, tell her, "Puggy, no bark!" Then when she quiets down, you can take her out.

Running through the Housetraining How-To's

Housetraining. Just the word itself makes people nervous.

Getting the message across to your Pug that she can't use the dining room drapes for her own personal bathroom (see Figure 10-2) can be a challenge. No one likes the thought of cleaning up a mess — even a small one — from a

Why Toys aren't harder to train

Many people with Toy dogs say that house-training is the main problem they have with them. The truth is that small dogs are no more difficult to train than medium- or large-sized dogs. Just because a little Pug's plumbing system is smaller than a bigger dog's but still relative to her size doesn't mean that a Pug can't control herself. Most of the time, it's the owners who miss the opportunities to teach Puggy the potty rules.

Here are some reasons that many Pug owners have a hard time with training:

✔ Toy puppies need to go to the bathroom more often than larger puppies do.

✔ Many Toy dogs live in apartments, so it's not always convenient to get outside quickly. People and their pets have to use stairs or an elevator.

✔ Pugs don't like to go outside when it's cold or rainy.

✔ Pug puppies are so low to the ground that it's hard to tell whether they have squatted down to relieve themselves or not.

✔ The messes are so tiny that they often go undetected, especially on a rug.

✔ The accidents are so small they can easily be wiped up and disposed of.

✔ Owners think Puggy is so small that she couldn't possibly understand the potty plan.

✔ Owners aren't diligent about taking their Pugs outside when they need to go. It's easier to just clean up the mess.

To effectively train your Pug, you need to establish the potty rules and stick to them right from the time you bring her home. To keep this goal fresh in your mind, remember the following:

✔ Spending a concentrated amount of time right in the beginning to housetrain your Pug is easier than cleaning up messes for months or even a year.

✔ Your Pug is smart and can understand exactly what you tell her as long as you give clear instructions.

✔ A little dog still needs to do big-dog things, such as go to the bathroom outside even when the weather is cold or rainy.

✔ A Toy dog may think she's being a good dog just by leaving her own clean area and going to the bathroom in a far corner of the house.

little dog, but it happens. The training process takes time and patience, but eventually your Pug catches on. She's a naturally clean animal and doesn't mean to make you unhappy — it's just that she doesn't know where the correct potty area is.

If you can schedule your vacation time around Puggy's arrival, or stay home with her the first few days you have her, you can get a jump-start on housetraining. You can monitor her bathroom calls and introduce her to what you expect. On the other hand, if she's left alone all day, she has to use the same area where she's confined to go to the bathroom. As a result, it may take longer to convince her this isn't the spot you intended for her bathroom responsibilities.

Figure 10-2:
This Pug
tried to aim
for the
paper but
missed.

©Judi Crowe

Showing your Pug where the bathroom is

Your Pug has to know where you want her to relieve herself outdoors before
she can go there. So showing her where "x marks the potty spot" is the first
step in housetraining.

 If you want your Pug to use the same area outside every time she goes to the
bathroom, begin training her by putting on her leash and collar and taking
her there. Plan on staying outdoors with her for about 20 minutes. Bring a
cup of coffee or a book if you need additional entertainment, but don't just
fling your back door open and expect your Pug to know where to go and what
to do on her own.

Even if you have a fenced-in yard and it's safe for your Pug to run around,
keeping her on the leash confines her to the location you want her to use
each time. Stand or use your patio chair to sit comfortably in the same place
and keep her on the leash.

Let your Pug sniff around in the same area as much as she wants to. Ground
sniffing is something Pugs love to do. After she exhausts all the smells in the
same place, she relieves herself right there. Return to that location every
time she needs to go potty, and soon she chooses this spot, even when she's
off the leash, as her favorite.

I know it's tempting, but resist the urge to start strolling around the yard with Puggy. Otherwise, she goes sniffing from place to place, postpones going potty, and the result is that you're out there all day with nothing to show for your efforts. Then the minute you take her back into the house, guess what?

Following the potty rules

The rules of housetraining are really pretty simple after you get the hang of them. The good thing is that when you figure out how to keep your Pug from messing in the house, you know how to train your next Pug or any other dog you may have.

The key is preventing Puggy from making a mistake in the first place. Here are the basic daily potty rules:

1. **First thing in the morning, take your Pug out of her carrier, put on her leash and collar, and take her outside to the place in your yard where you want her to eliminate.**

    If the carrier isn't clean when you take her out, there's usually a reason — either the carrier is too big or she's been left in it too long. (See the section "Finding the right size and type of carrier," earlier in the chapter, for more information.) If your Pug's carrier is too big for her and she has to go to the bathroom, she simply walks over to the far side and goes potty there, figuring it's far enough away from her sleeping spot.

2. **Tell her to go potty and stay with her in the same area until she does.**

3. **When she goes to the bathroom where you want her to, always praise her by saying, "Good girl, Puggy!"**

    For more information about praise, see the section "Using encouraging words," later in this chapter.

    Avoid giving her a treat as praise because she'll be going outside and waiting for the cookie instead of doing her business.

4. **Feed her breakfast and then take her outside again and repeat Steps 1 through 3.**

    She needs to go out after every meal.

5. **Take her inside for playtime but keep an eye on her.**

    Every 20 to 30 minutes, your Pug has to relieve herself again, so be ready to take her back outside. If you can't supervise her, put her back into her carrier.

    If you see her sniffing the floor and walking in circles during playtime, it's time to go outside again. Also, if she goes to the door and waits or paws at it, she probably has to go out.

6. **Immediately after she wakes up from a nap, take her outside so she can relieve herself.**

7. **Right before bedtime, take your Pug outside and then put her into her carrier for the night.**

Dedicating yourself to potty breaks

For the first few weeks that you have your Pug, your life revolves around Puggy's plumbing. Is spending all that time running outside with your Pug worth it? You bet. Putting in the time now quickly teaches her the house rules so you won't be housetraining her forever. Before you know it, she's going to the door herself and waiting for you to let her out on her own.

To train your Pug to relieve herself on a regular schedule, take your Pug out at the following times:

- ✔ As soon as she gets up in the morning
- ✔ After every meal
- ✔ After a 20-minute play session
- ✔ Each time you take her out of her carrier
- ✔ After the last playtime at night, right before bed
- ✔ After Puggy has been in her carrier for five to seven hours at night if she keeps whining to go out

Don't limit your trips to only these times. Leave it to a smart Pug to surprise you by feeling the urge to go outdoors when it's not on the schedule. Sometimes, she may rush out of the room to go to a corner where you can't see her. Be sure to follow her, pick her up quickly, and take her out the door.

When you take your Pug outdoors to eliminate, don't rush her. You can't hurry a Pug, and trying to encourage her to go faster only frustrates you, which then frustrates her.

To help maintain a positive attitude when housetraining your Pug, remember that you're really getting to know your Pug and her habits better, and you're also spending real quality time with her. Observing her closely pays off double later on when you want to teach her some basic obedience. By watching her every move, you may get an inkling of what she's thinking.

If others in your household share the responsibility of caring for Puggy — including getting her housetrained — everyone has to be on the same team and play by the same rules. Call a family meeting and discuss what it will take and what everyone will have to do to get Puggy housetrained. Explain the rules and see whether all family members agree on the concept and whether

Jingle bell Pug

To teach your Pug how to let you know when she has to go outside, try letting her ring her chimes — er, make that jingle the bells! Teach her this cute little trick, and you'll both love what Puggy can do when she wants to go outside. Here are the steps to follow:

1. **Hang two or three bells (each one measuring 1 to 2 inches wide) from the doorknob or handle of the door leading to the yard where you're teaching your Pug to relieve herself.**

   Make sure they hang near your Pug's nose.

2. **Rub a small piece of hot dog on the bells.**

3. **Show your Pug what you've done and allow her to sniff the bells.**

4. **When the bell rings, praise your dog by telling her she's a good girl!**

5. **Promptly take her outside and give her a tiny piece of hot dog.**

6. **Repeat this three or four times a day for a few days.**

7. **When she rings the bells without your prompting, make a big fuss and praise her before taking her outside.**

they think they can keep an eye on your Pug at all times when they're on duty. Although everyone means well, some people would rather clean up a mess on the floor than get up and go outside. If this happens once or twice, your Pug soon figures out that this behavior is acceptable. Here's a bad habit in the making! You may not want to rely on these family members for house-training, but definitely keep them in mind when Puggy needs extra kisses.

Using encouraging words

What are the magic words to help housetrain your Pug? You don't need anything too fancy, just some simple positive phrases such as "Puggy, good girl!" or "Good job, Puggy!" when she's gone outside to relieve herself. Keep your tone upbeat and positive when she does well and don't say a word when she disappoints you.

Don't give her a lot of different words to try to understand while she's trying to urinate at the same time. She only gets confused. I talk about this in more detail in Chapter 11.

How much praise should you use and how often? Every time your Pug goes in the correct spot, praise her like she just won the lottery! But more important than the words themselves is the tone of your voice. A high, happy tone lets Puggy know that you're pleased, while a low tone makes her think you're unhappy.

When you praise your Pug for good behavior and ignore the bad, she feels better about herself and soon learns that the good, and not the bad, behavior gets a reaction that she loves. Pugs and all creatures thrive and do their best on positive reinforcement.

Mopping Up Your Pug's Messes

Having a dog means that, yes, you'll have messes to clean up every now and then. It's just part of having a dog.

Plan on keeping an odor neutralizer in the house for emergency clean-ups. For extra protection, add a stain remover without ammonia. You can find many good spray-on products in both pet supply and grocery stores that you can use on the boo-boo area. Get rid of any stains and odors as quickly as possible because Puggy may return to the same area if it smells familiar. Dogs prefer to urinate and defecate where they've been before. Besides, you don't want your home to smell like a public potty area!

If your Pug has an accident in the house, never, ever hit her, rub her nose in the mess, use a rolled up newspaper to swat her, or do anything else that's negative. She can't make the connection between what she did and your reaction to it. These actions only frighten poor Puggy and ruin her self-esteem for future training.

Instead, be patient and realize that your Pug may still be very young and she can't always control herself, especially if she didn't have access to outside for a long time.

Confining Puggy to a small area

To prevent accidents when you first bring your Pug home, don't give her free run of the whole house right away. That's too much area for you to monitor. Instead, choose one room that's small, can easily be closed off, and has a floor that's easy to mop up. Don't worry about giving your Pug only one or two rooms to roam around in. As she learns the routine and starts going to the door when she wants to relieve herself, you can give her free run of the place.

If you can't watch your Pug, put her in her carrier. Besides having a bathroom mishap, she can get into all kinds of other trouble around the house, including chewing on your brand-new, custom-made sofa, if she's not supervised. She's safe in her carrier, and you don't have to worry about any accidents.

Going back to basic training

Even after your Pug is housetrained, she may goof up and mess in the house. If she does, don't panic! Instead, double up on your efforts to supervise her when she's outside her carrier. Perhaps you weren't as diligent this time as you were in the beginning about getting your Pug outdoors immediately after a meal. Or maybe she got distracted by a fun toy and had an accident on her way to the door.

One or two mishaps in the house don't mean that your Pug has forgotten everything and suddenly become unhousetrained. No, it just means that she doesn't quite have the act down 100 percent yet. She'll bounce back as soon as you begin to focus on her training again.

In fact, to get your Pug back on the housetrained track, return to the basics, as follows:

- ✔ Use only positive words to tell your Pug when she's done a good job. Don't punish her in any way for a mishap.

- ✔ Use your watch or wall clock to remind you when it's time to take Puggy outdoors during playtime. Hint, hint: It's every 20 minutes or when she's making obvious signs that she needs to go out.

- ✔ Use discretion when allowing Puggy access to other rooms of the house. Supervise her at all times.

- ✔ Put her inside her carrier when you can't watch her.

Reacting properly to accidents

If your Pug has an accident in the house, the best way to handle it is to say nothing or very little. If you yell loudly or scold her in any way, she just sneaks off and finds a place where you can't see her and goes to the bathroom there. Surely you don't want your Pug doing that, so simply avoid any negative response.

Your Pug had to go to the bathroom — it's a natural act — so urinating and defecating aren't wrong. It's just the place that's wrong. You don't want her to think that you're angry at her because she had to relieve herself. And being stern with her after she's done the deed only confuses her.

If you catch your Pug in the act of relieving herself inside the house instead of going to the door and waiting for you to take her out, say, "Puggy, no!" and promptly take her outside to the potty area. If you find a puddle on the floor and your Pug's not even close to it, don't correct her. It's too late, so just ignore the situation, clean it up, and forget about it.

Building a Better Pug: Teaching Her Which Behaviors to Avoid

Although it would be very nice to have a Pug around the house who behaves perfectly and doesn't do anything you don't like, that's not going to happen. After all, dogs don't know what things you like or dislike until they start doing them! If your Pug does something you'd prefer she didn't do, it's your job to let her know — but in a positive way.

Putting the kibosh on jumping

Your Pug really can't help jumping up to greet you. She loves your attention and gets excited when you or guests are around. Pugs also jump up because they want to get a better look at what's happening far above them. When you're a Toy dog, you have a limited perspective because you're so close to the ground.

If you don't want your Pug leaping on you, and she's at least 4 months old, now's the time to convince her that she can still enjoy life if she keeps all four feet on the ground (see Figure 10-3). This means, though, that you have to make it worth her while to stay low by rewarding her with a food treat or some good petting when she doesn't jump.

To convince Puggy that you don't want her to jump up, think about all the ways you've encouraged her to act like a leaping lizard. After you realize what you do, you can change your reaction when Puggy's around. For example, have you done any of the following?

- Looked at her and smiled the first time she jumped at you
- Talked lovingly to her when she put her paws up against you
- Picked her up the moment she came to you
- Tapped your leg, indicating it was okay to jump the moment she approached you
- Given her a food treat when she leaped up

No doubt you've done one or more of these things, but it's never too late to correct this behavior. To retrain Puggy and stop her from jumping on you, follow these tips:

- Completely ignore your Pug when she jumps on you. I know how hard this is, but if you ignore her, she realizes she's not getting the reaction from you that she wants.
- Do nothing when she tries to jump higher and faster at you.

✔ When she stops jumping, and she will, then and only then get down to her level and look at her. She was hoping to see you all along.

✔ When she has all four feet on the ground, tell her what a good dog she is and give her a treat.

✔ Teach her to sit as soon as she starts to jump up. For more information about teaching Puggy to sit, see Chapter 11.

Figure 10-3:
Pugs need to be trained not to jump up.

©Judi Crowe

She may jump again now that she has your undivided attention. If so, ignore her again and wait until she stops hopping up to get to you. Reward her lavishly again when she stops jumping. You may have to repeat this exercise several times until Puggy gets the message.

What to do when friends come over and your Pug still wants to jump on them? Tell visitors in advance to just ignore her. When she stays on the ground, then they can greet her and give her a treat that you've supplied for them on the spot.

What if your guests ignore your Pug, but she still jumps? When the doorbell rings, attach Puggy's leash to her collar. That way you can correct the behavior the minute she goes to jump by pulling back on the leash. Say, "Puggy, no jump!" or "Puggy, off!" When she gets the message, be sure to praise her with a treat or the words, "Good girl, Puggy!" every time she keeps four on the floor when visitors arrive and she doesn't jump.

Making the furniture off-limits

It's amazing that a roly-poly Pug has the athletic ability to hop up on the furniture, but she does. After Puggy thinks that settling in on the nice comfy couch, bed, or chair is okay, she doesn't hesitate to pick out the best spot and claim it for her own. If you don't care that she's on the furniture, then enjoy your happy companion. If, on the other hand, you don't want her up on the furniture, you have some work to do to discourage this behavior.

To discourage Puggy from roosting in the best seats in the house once she's already set up camp, don't say anything to your Pug but gently lift her off and place her on the floor (see Figure 10-4). Tell her she's a good girl or give her a treat when she's *not* on the furniture.

Figure 10-4:
You may have to show your Pug where the floor is if she's on the couch.

©Elaine Gewirtz

Pugs love to be comfortable (who doesn't?), so make sure that she has a comfy dog bed on the floor to lie on instead of the couch. For more information about bedding, see Chapter 5. To encourage your Pug to choose her bed over yours, put an old article of your clothing and some of her favorite toys there. She's more attracted to that area if it feels and smells familiar.

Nipping the nipping

When Pug puppies are about 3 weeks old, their baby teeth start coming in. A few months later, these teeth fall out, only to be replaced by permanent adult teeth. Throughout this time, your Pug needs to ease some of the discomfort of her teeth coming and going by chewing. This is the reason that Puggy loves to chew on just about anything she can get into her mouth.

Your fingers, toes, and arms have a soothing effect in your Pug's mouth that may help her feel better, but her nipping can sure hurt you! All puppies try to bite the hands that feed them, but it's not because they want to be mean to you. They just don't understand the difference between you and a chew toy!

To teach Puggy to be gentle and not to bite, wait until she begins to gnaw roughly on your fingers. Then make a high-pitched squealing sound to let her know she's hurting you. This sound startles her and stops her from nipping. You can also tell her, "Puggy, no bite!" If she continues nipping, then she needs a timeout session in her carrier. Maybe she's overtired and just needs a nap. Give her a small treat and put her inside. Chances are likely that, after 10 or 15 minutes, she falls fast asleep. If not, it's okay to keep her there until you feel like you can deal with her again in, say, a half-hour?

Until she learns not to nip, be cautious with young children around Puggy. Her teeth can seriously hurt them and leave scars.

By the time your Pug is finished teething at around 6 months of age, she should lose interest in nipping.

Bucking the barking trend

It's one thing for your Pug to pretend that she's a big watchdog and bark to let you know someone's at the door. You probably appreciate that behavior. It's another thing if she barks at every cat strolling past the front window or every car driving by. Frequent barking can be irritating to you as well as to your neighbors.

If your Pug is barking at an unfamiliar person or object, don't pet her and reassure her by saying that it's okay. Barking isn't okay. Your dog thinks that you're really saying, "Puggy, it's okay that you're barking!"

Yelling at your dog when she barks doesn't convince her not to do it, either. To a dog, your yelling is the same thing as barking, and she thinks you're joining in the fun. So, to stop overzealous barking, try this advice:

- ✔ Try to figure out why your Pug is barking. Does she need attention or want to play? Is it feeding time, or does she need to go out?

- ✔ Tell your Pug to stop barking by saying in a firm voice, "Puggy, no bark!"

- ✔ Try to keep your Pug's mind occupied with additional exercise or training classes. Maybe she's just bored at home.

- ✔ Try putting your Pug's leash and collar on so you have some control over what she does, and tell her to "Sit" and "Stay." When she has some other activities to occupy her time, such as sitting and staying, she stops barking. Chapter 11 has more information about teaching these commands to your dog.

- ✔ Try teaching Puggy to bark only when you tell her to. That may sound strange, so allow me to elaborate. While your Pug is already barking, say, "Puggy, bark!" When she looks at you, give her a small food treat or lavish praise. Repeat this routine several times. Then, when she's quiet and isn't barking, give her the same command to bark. If she doesn't bark right away, be patient. With practice, your Pug thinks of this as a game, and because Pugs love a good game, she soon knows the difference between barking and not barking.

✔ Try putting Puggy in her crate when she barks and none of the other corrections are working. These are times when you just don't want her barking — someone comes to the door, or you have workers outside your home.

Halting the great escape

No doubt Puggy has everything her heart desires. She's always on a leash when going out for exercise, and her yard is fenced in and safe. Therefore, she has no reason to run away, right? Wrong. Your Pug may still go for the great escape and try to scoot out the front door the minute you answer the doorbell.

To prevent your Pug from escaping even a first time, remember the following points:

✔ Teach her to Stay before opening the front door. For more training information, see Chapter 11.

✔ If you have taught her how to Sit and Stay, ask her to do exactly that before you open the door. She must Sit and Stay before she can meet the guests. Reward her with praise or a food treat when she follows your command.

✔ Make sure Puggy is behind your legs as far back as possible so that you can catch her before she slips through and out the door.

✔ If possible, put up a baby gate to separate your Pug from the open door.

✔ If she insists upon seeing who's at the door every time you open it, put her collar and leash on her the minute the doorbell rings. Doing so gives you some control over your Pug's desire to get up close and personal with visitors.

✔ Carry her across the threshold each time. This may mean making two trips if your hands are already full with packages, but by not letting her walk out — even on a leash — she doesn't get the idea that she can do that on her own.

If your Pug does manage to get out the door despite your best efforts, and you've taught her to respond to the Come command, be sure and use it when you need to get her back into the house. If she doesn't respond to the come command, then kneel down and call her name to try and catch her. Hold a piece of food to entice her closer. Don't chase after your runaway Pug. Doing so only makes her run farther away.

Chewing the Fat Leather Shoe and Other Goodies

For a little dog, your Pug has a powerful jaw. While her teeth are coming in, she may want to gnaw on household objects to relieve some of the pressure on her gums. As a result, some of your possessions may become teething objects (see Figure 10-5).

Figure 10-5:
This is what happens if you leave your shoes lying around.

©Judi Crowe

Don't worry too much though; your Pug grows out of this unpleasant stage by the time she's 6 months old. In the meantime, I want to give you some ways to minimize the chances that your Pug makes mincemeat out of your favorite possessions.

Although some Pugs are into heavy-duty destructive chewing, others don't even bother with it. Lucky you, if your Pug falls into the latter category.

Keeping things out of sight, out of mouth

The best way to protect your precious items and your Pug's safety is to put Puggy in her carrier if you can't watch her. It's the only way to prevent her from chewing the table leg or your good couch (see Figure 10-6).

Figure 10-6:
Because this leather sofa feels good to a teething Pug, you need to supervise her at all times so she doesn't chew on it.

©Elaine Gewirtz

The next best thing to do to prevent your Pug from her destructive chewing habit is to go through your home and Pug-proof it, as follows:

- ✔ Pick up any loose things lying around, such as shoes, clothing, or other small objects.

- ✔ Tack any loose or dangling electrical cords directly to the wall.

- ✔ Limit the amount of free rein you give Puggy in the house so she can't find too many things.

- ✔ Close the doors to rooms you don't want Puggy going into.

- ✔ Remove anything valuable from Puggy's environment, such as furniture or area rugs that you couldn't stand to see chewed up. Puggy won't be a chewy puppy forever, so it may be worth the effort to move the Colonial-era side table or the brand-new Oriental rug into a closed room. When she's safely out of the chewing stage, you can try bringing it back in.

- ✔ Place a baby gate across any room containing furniture you don't want to worry about and you may not want to move.

- ✔ Secure closet and cupboard doors with baby locks to prevent Puggy from opening them and chewing both the doors and the contents inside.

Persuading your Pug to choose her own chew toys

As unbelievable as it sounds, you can teach your Pug to chew only her own toys. This is a great way to channel your dog's chomping ambitions.

Start by stocking up on a variety of safe but interesting chewy toys (see Figure 10-7). You can even take Puggy to the store to help pick out her own treasures. Look for sturdy chew toys, such as the strong, nylon products available in pet supply stores. If the toys are hard enough, yet soft enough for Puggy to chew, they usually can't break apart and damage her throat. Rope chew toys are especially good because they can also clean your dog's teeth at the same time.

Figure 10-7: Tackling this toy keeps Puggy from chewing your stuff.

©Judi Crowe

Never give Puggy any leftover cooked bones from the dinner table. Pieces can break off, and she can swallow them. All it takes is one little piece to rip a hole in your dog's intestine and cause major damage. Also, stay away from soft rubber or plastic toys because they can break apart and Puggy can swallow pieces, which may block her airway and cause death.

Never give your Pug rawhide chews! Although she probably loves them and gnaws on them for hours on end, they eventually shrink down and get gummy. Your Pug can easily swallow the small, slimy pieces, and if they lodge in her throat, they can obstruct her breathing.

Chapter 11

Doing-It-Yourself Training and Obedience Training

. . . .

In This Chapter

▶ Setting training goals

▶ Getting the proper equipment

▶ Working with your Pug on some basic commands

▶ Determining the best person to train your dog

. . . .

The thought of having a perfectly trained Pug who pays attention to every word you say and does exactly what he's supposed to do all the time is sure appealing. It can be life-saving, too. If your Pug accidentally slips out the front door and runs into the street, all you have to do is to call out, "Puggy, come!" and he turns right around and comes back to you. But the reality is that someone has to teach him a thing or two or three — or fifty — to get him to be that way.

Pugs are easy to train unless you've never worked with a dog before. Then the task can be somewhat overwhelming. But never fear. This chapter can help make the job seem less daunting.

In this chapter, I get you started on how to train your Pug to be a wonderful companion when you leave home. I explain how to get the right equipment and start with the most basic lessons. From there, it's an easy search to find good training classes or call in a professional, if you decide to go that route. The best part is putting it all together so you and Puggy can go out into the world and have a ball!

The leader of the pack

Like their ancestors the wolves, dogs first lived in packs in the wild. The members of each pack established an order, with every dog having a place and a job to do. The leader of the pack was the top dog and made all the decisions. All the other pack members came second to whatever the leader needed or wanted.

In the case of you and your Pug, you're the leader of the pack, and your Pug needs to know it. Maintaining leadership isn't that difficult with a Pug. Your Pug is probably easygoing to begin with, but if you don't assume the role of leader, this 18-pound wonder gladly steps up to the plate and rules the roost. So grab the reins and take charge because when he knows you're in control, he pays better attention to you when you start training him.

Deciding What You Want Your Pug to Know Upfront

Before you rush into trying to teach Puggy everything all at once, pick out some basic behaviors you think a well-behaved Pug should know. For example, here are a few things that your Pug can easily learn to do with some training:

✔ Walk nicely on a leash

✔ Sit down when you stop walking

✔ Lie down and stay if you're out walking and need to stop

✔ Sit and wait for permission before going through doorways

✔ Come back to you when you call him

✔ Wait for permission to greet strangers and other dogs

✔ Wait patiently at the veterinarian's office

✔ Stand still while the veterinarian examines him

Don't worry. These skills are easier to teach than you think. See the section "Teaching Basic Commands," later in this chapter, for more information.

With steady practice, a Pug can master these behaviors much faster when he's a puppy, but it's never too late to train a grown-up Pug. All the same principles apply, and the rewards are just as great.

Having the Right Equipment

To do any job right, you need the right tools. When it comes to training, Puggy's basic tools are his collar and leash. Think of Puggy's collar and leash like the steering wheel of your car. They help you lovingly guide him in the right direction and keep both of you connected.

When should he wear his collar? All the time, because the collar carries his identification tag, which helps reunite him with you in case he gets lost or stolen. Even if he's also microchipped or tattooed (for more information about these forms of identification, see Chapter 13), it doesn't hurt your Pug to have a second form of ID.

Cornering the market on collars

What kind of collar should Puggy have? Collars come in every color, pattern, and type imaginable, including your basic black and stainless steel, tie-dye, camouflage, hearts, and flowers. Beyond the flashy colors, you can expect to find these types of collars:

- Nylon with prong buckles, which can be either round or flat
- Nylon slip (a slip has a metal ring at both ends)
- Nylon with adjustable snap and quick release
- Cloth with adjustable snap and quick release
- Leather with round or flat buckles
- Leather slip
- Body harness
- Slip chain

Besides the price, what's the difference between the leather, nylon, mesh, or cloth models? Leather collars last the longest and don't stretch, but they're pricier. Mesh, cloth, and some brands of nylon stretch, so you should check the collar regularly to make sure that it still fits properly.

Picking the right type

How do you know which kind of collar to pick? It depends on what you want your Pug to be doing while he's wearing it.

If you're training your Pug to walk obediently beside you on a leash, get a collar that gives some resistance if he's straining at the leash and pulling you. A slip collar works best to prevent Puggy from pulling you. He doesn't like the resistance from the collar. Another option for outings is the harness, which really isn't a collar at all but an arrangement of adjustable straps that wraps around his body. A harness has a ring at the back where you can clip on a leash.

Take off the harness when Puggy gets safely inside the house. It's not designed to be worn indoors because those straps can get caught on all sorts of household objects, and your Pug can hurt a limb.

On the other hand, if your dog is already trained to walk politely alongside without pulling you, he can wear either a buckle or snap type of collar, whichever you prefer. In fact, if your Pug is mostly a homebody and doesn't venture out much, the buckle or snap collars are probably your best bet.

Ensuring the proper fit

After you narrow down the color and style of collar, you need to get one that fits properly. The collar should fit snugly around Puggy's neck without choking him, but you don't want it to be so loose that it falls off his neck when he drops his head! If a collar fits properly, you should be able to put two of your fingers comfortably between your Pug's neck and the collar.

To get the correct size collar, take your Pug along for the shopping trip. All pet supply stores welcome dog browsing. They know that Pugs usually end up picking out more than just one collar!

If you can't take your dog with you to buy a collar, measure his neck at home with a tape measure and add two inches. The two inches is the leeway you need for the leash.

Don't buy a collar that's too big or too small. Buy something that fits properly the day you get it. And don't buy a bigger size than what Puggy needs that day, thinking that he can grow into it. You don't want it falling off his neck. By the time Puggy is full grown, you've probably bought two or three collars to accommodate the changes in his neck size.

Looking for leashes

If you thought collars were colorful, wait until you start shopping for leashes. You can find everything, from expensive leather to economical nylon, cloth, chain, and retractable leashes. And to complicate your shopping, leashes come in all different lengths and widths, too.

Leather is the best material for leashes because it lasts the longest and is the strongest. In the beginning, it's a bit stiff, but the more you handle it, the more it softens up and gets easier to hold in your hand. The biggest problem you'll ever have with a leather leash is when you leave it lying around and your Pug chews it up!

As for the other types, nylon is less expensive than leather, but it slices through your hand if your Pug decides to bolt after another dog on the street, so it may not be a good choice. Skip the chain leash altogether because it's too bulky and uncomfortable to hold. Finally, although the idea of a retractable leash is clever, never use it when you go out walking with your Pug. On the street, you have no control if a bigger, menacing dog gets too close to your Pug. However, a retractable leash may come in handy if you take Puggy for a long car ride and he needs to get out and stretch his legs because the longer ones can extend up to 12 feet.

In terms of length, a six-foot leather leash is the most versatile, and it's great for everyday use. It's long enough to give Puggy some room to stretch out on an outing, yet you can easily gather it up if you need your Pug to move in closer to you at a moment's notice.

Teaching Basic Commands

When you're training your dog, you're communicating with him. But dogs need to figure out what human words mean before they can perform the tasks you want them to. So how do they do that? Puggy learns your vocabulary in three ways:

✔ **By getting a reward:** If your Pug gets a goodie every time he does a certain thing, he makes the connection. After a few times, he performs the behavior automatically because he knows you approve.

A reward can be anything that your Pug really loves. Although some Pugs love food, others may prefer a fun toy. If both of those bomb out, try lavishing words of praise or lots of petting. The trick is to find the reward that your dog loves the most and then use it when you want to teach him a new behavior.

To keep the training interesting for your Pug and to keep him on his toes, vary the reward. For example, if it's food, you can use small pieces of hot dogs one time and maybe chicken the next, which are both healthy. There are also many different kinds of package treats just for dogs that you can buy in pet supply stores or supermarkets.

✔ **By realizing that *no* means *no*:** Imagine your Pug always responding when you say no. That's because he knows when you say no, you mean it. Sure, it can be challenging not to cave in and give Puggy what he wants when he looks up at you with those sweet googly eyes, but stay strong. He has to know that you mean business.

✔ **By recognizing the tone of your voice:** Use a firm, no-nonsense tone of voice when you want Puggy to follow your instructions and use a higher-pitched tone to let him know he did the right thing. By firm voice, I'm not taking about being louder, because that doesn't get you anywhere.

Getting Puggy's attention

Before you can begin training your Pug to do anything, you have to have his attention. Basically, you need for him to look your way.

To get your Pug's attention, follow these steps:

1. **Look him directly in the eye.**

   Put his collar and leash on to help direct his head.

2. **Say his name.**

3. **When he looks at you, give him a treat.**

   If he doesn't look at you or looks at you briefly and turns his head away quickly, give the leash a gentle tug to move his head your way.

4. **Repeat his name and say, "Watch!"**

   The minute he looks at you, give him a treat.

5. **Repeat Steps 1 through 4 several times.**

Sitting is nice

To teach Puggy how to sit (see Figure 11-1), you need a few small food treats.After you have the treats ready, follow these steps:

1. **Position yourself so that you're directly in front of your Pug.**

2. **Hold a treat slightly above his nose and say, "Puggy, sit!"**

3. **Raise your hand slightly over his head.**

   As his eyes follow your hand, he lifts his head up and rocks backward into a sitting position. When he's sitting, give him the food.

4. **Praise him by telling him that he's a good dog!**

5. **Repeat this exercise a few times a day.**

©Judi Crowe

Figure 11-1:
You can
train your
Pug to sit
nicely.

Staying in one place

On many occasions, you need Puggy to stand and stay (see Figure 11-2) — at the veterinarian's office, while he's being bathed and groomed, or when you're out and he needs to wait.

©Judi Crowe

Figure 11-2:
Teaching
Puggy to
stand still
on a leash
outdoors
comes in
handy.

Understanding your Pug's body language

Dogs don't use words to communicate. Instead, they rely on their overall body position, facial expressions, and ear and tail movements to let other dogs and people around them know how they're feeling.

To find out more about your Pug, watch his body language. Does he have his rear end up and his front down, and is his little curly tail wagging back and forth? If so, he's play bowing, which means that he wants you or other dogs to come play with him. When a Pug is scared, he tries to shrink himself and look smaller by unfolding his curly tail and letting it drop slightly, pulls his ears back, and avoids looking at you. Rolling over and exposing his belly means he's surrendering. Or maybe he just likes to have his stomach rubbed! The more you observe your Pug's body language, the more you get to know what he likes and dislikes.

Be sure your Pug has his collar and leash on when you teach him this command.

Follow these steps when you want your Pug to stand and sit:

1. **Stand in front of Puggy and tell him to sit.**

2. **Hold his leash in your right hand and keep it at stomach level.**

3. **Raise your left hand with your palm facing Puggy.**

4. **Look at him and say, "Puggy, stay!"**

5. **Slowly walk backward from your dog.**

   Make sure to keep looking directly at him.

6. **When you get to the end of the leash, drop it on the ground and put your foot on it. That way he can't go anywhere.**

7. **Tell him he's a good Puggy.**

8. **Keep him there for about five seconds, then say "Okay," and give him a treat.**

Lying down

If you're ever out with Puggy and you need him to wait for an extended time, the Down command can help relax him.

To teach Puggy the Down command, he first has to know the Sit command (see the section "Sitting is nice," earlier in the chapter, for details) and then follow these steps:

1. **Tell Puggy to sit and give him a treat.**

2. **When he's looking at you, take another piece of food and lower it to the floor away from his nose.**

   Don't let Puggy get up. If he does, go back to the sit position.

3. **As Puggy begins to lie down, say, "Puggy, down!"**

   When he's down, give him the treat.

4. **Verbally praise him or give him a food treat.**

Coming when called

Practice this routine with his leash on and follow these steps to teach the Come command:

1. **Say, "Puggy, stand!" Then say, "Puggy, stay!"**

2. **With the leash in your right hand, face your dog and slowly walk backward, saying, "Puggy, come!"**

   When he follows you, keep walking backward.

3. **After a few steps, stop and say, "Puggy, come!"**

4. **When he's coming toward you, bend over and touch his collar.**

   Praise him by saying in a happy voice, "Good boy, Puggy!" You can also give him a treat if you want.

5. **Repeat Steps 1 through 4.**

Walking beside you without pulling on the leash

Teaching your Pug to walk beside you without pulling on the leash is easy with his collar and leash on. Just follow these steps, but keep in mind that learning this skill takes practice for your dog, so be prepared to spend several sessions working on it:

1. **Keep Puggy on your left side and hold the leash in your right hand.**

2. **As you start walking, say, "Puggy, heel!"**

   If he doesn't pay attention and lunges forward, turn around quickly and go the other way. Repeat this step several times.

3. **When he's walking without pulling you, be sure to praise him with compliments or treats!**

Deciding Whether to Train Your Pug Yourself or Seek Help from a Pro

Do you have the time and patience to train your dog, or do you think the job can be better handled by a pro? To help you decide, this section takes a look at both options and tells you what's involved in each.

Going it alone

Everyone in the family may want to be the head Pug trainer, but the truth is that only one person should fill that role. In fact, the designated trainer should be someone who

- Is available to train on a routine basis. (Pugs thrive on consistency and like to know what to expect.)
- Can work with Puggy in the same location until he grasps the concept and then take him to a new spot to test his retention.
- Has an upbeat attitude and likes working with animals.
- Uses praise and an occasional treat to reward Puggy when he does well.
- Isn't distracted by interruptions during training.

Above all, a healthy dose of patience when training helps your Pug learn at his own rate. Put yourself in his position: Would you want to follow instructions from someone who kept getting exasperated with you for not paying attention? Didn't think so.

If you ever feel yourself getting frustrated that your Pug isn't catching on to what you want him to do, quit for a while. Never work your dog if you feel angry or frustrated because he just stops doing anything.

When deciding which family member ought to train your Pug, pick the person who has enough time to do the task right. The truth is that although you have good intentions to work with your dog, sometimes life's responsibilities get in the way. You may work full-time and have a family and an active hobby and therefore are not able to spend the time regularly training your dog. If that's the case, perhaps another family member should do the job, or you should hire a professional trainer (see the next section for info about trainers).

Opting for professional help

Training your Pug by yourself is great, but if that's not possible, don't worry, because you do have other options.

Hiring a professional trainer

If you don't feel confident about trying to teach your Pug yourself, or if for some other reason you can't train your dog personally, a professional trainer is always a phone call away. To find one, ask friends, your veterinarian, or your breeder or look on the Internet. A good place to start is www.apdt.com, the Web site for the Association of Pet Dog Trainers.

Professional trainers work one-on-one with clients. They can come to your home, or you can meet outdoors. A pro can troubleshoot any problems you're having with your Pug and can give you ways to solve them. Pros offer a variety of services, ranging from a single visit to regular weekly appointments. But get your wallet ready because their fees are usually pricey, ranging from $75 to $2,000.

You should always feel comfortable with your trainer and like the things she's teaching you and Puggy to do after she leaves. If you don't click with the first trainer you call, call someone else, but above all, get your Pug trained!

Finding classes and instructors

Enrolling your Pug in a class may mean you have faster success at training him. Being around other dogs tests your Pug's concentration and introduces him to other dogs in a safe environment.

When should you start classes with Puggy? Three months old isn't too early. At that age, your Pug hasn't had too much of a chance to form bad habits. In fact, puppy kindergarten classes are great for young Pug puppies because they introduce the basic commands but are still geared to a pup's short attention span. They're also a great way for you to meet other puppy owners and share concerns about your dogs.

Although some classes are geared to first-time owners and provide more basics, other classes are more advanced and help people find out how to compete in the show ring with their Pug. See Chapter 16 for more information on dog shows.

You want to find a class that isn't so large that you and your Pug feel lost. When looking for instructors, ask if you can observe a class before you join. Doing so gives you some idea of whether you like the instructor and think the class is a good fit with your dog. When you observe the class, hopefully the instructor is giving clear instructions so you can easily understand what you're supposed to be doing.

To locate a good class and an instructor, ask the following people for recommendations:

- ✔ Friends with dogs.
- ✔ Your veterinarian.

- ✔ Your breeder.

- ✔ Members of the Association of Pet Dog Trainers (APDT). For more information about the APDT, check out the group's Web site at `www.apdt.com`.

- ✔ The local kennel club.

Chapter 12

Traveling the Great Outdoors with Your Pug

*O*ne of the best things about having a Pug is getting her out into the great big wide world and showing her off to everyone. Introducing your Pug around starts when she's a puppy. Meeting new friends is good for your Pug's development — the more the better, in fact. With plenty of good socialization as a foundation, she can be ready to provide love and companionship to friends and strangers, alike.

However, leaving home and venturing out into the community, either on foot or by car or plane, takes some planning. When you and Puggy venture out, you have to think about more than just yourself. You need to consider your dog's behavior and needs while you're away from home. In this chapter, I tell you how to take Puggy everywhere safely and, best of all, how to have fun while you're on the go.

Meeting and Greeting the Public

Part of having a wonderful Pug with a great personality is making sure she has been properly introduced to people and things around her early in life.

A good breeder often begins handling the puppies the day they're born and introduces them to different areas of her home, new sounds (such as a vacuum cleaner and the doorbell), and as many children and adults as possible. Then, when she's between 8 and 12 weeks of age and you take her home, your job is to continue the socialization that your breeder began.

Early lessons last a lifetime

The first 16 weeks of any dog's life is a vital part of her development. Whatever happens to your Pug during this time stays with her for the rest of her life. This short period is another reminder that dogs are descended from wolves. When young pups went exploring away from their mother, they had to be able to tell right away who was friendly and who was a threat. If they couldn't, they wouldn't survive in the wild for very long. Although Pugs no longer have to compete with wild creatures for their food and shelter, they're still programmed to protect themselves when they first venture out.

Although getting your Pug puppy out to meet the world when she's 3 months old may be a great idea for her mental and emotional development, most veterinarians don't recommend taking any puppy into the world until she's had her last vaccination, usually around 5 months of age. Before this time, puppies are still building up their own immune systems and may be susceptible to a few communicable diseases. See Chapters 13 and 14 for more information about vaccines and diseases.

To reduce the risk of contracting diseases at a young age, keep your Pug off public grass areas, parks, or high-traffic areas where loose dogs are apt to congregate and urinate or defecate. When Puggy sniffs these areas or steps onto grass that has been urinated on, she can pick up trouble. In fact, this is how some diseases are transmitted.

If you get your Pug after she's 4 months old, you can still arrange for her to meet the public, but she may need more time to feel comfortable around strangers than a younger dog. Between 4 and 6 months of age, Pug puppies are fully developed mentally, but their physical and emotional growth hasn't caught up yet. Your Pug may have already had some experiences or contact with people and other dogs that weren't so positive, so now she may be cautious and not very eager to have new encounters.

Introducing your Pug to the world

Besides people, a young Pug also needs to encounter different sights, sounds, and smells to know that the world around her is really an okay place. She needs to see, hear, and do everything! In fact, the more situations she comes across, the better. Out on the street, she should hear a fire engine's sirens blaring, car alarms going off, and children yelling. Likewise, a fire hydrant by the side of the road, a manhole cover, or a parked motorcycle should be no big deal to Puggy. She needs to know that people with oversize floppy hats and sunglasses, children on skateboards, and parents walking or jogging while pushing big baby strollers won't jump out and hurt her.

A Pug who has never left the house or yard may be fearful because she doesn't know that both everyday and unusual sights, sounds, and strangers won't hurt her. She may grow up afraid of children or senior citizens and could become aggressive out of fear.

So, how much socialization does a Pug puppy need, exactly?

Every Pug is different, and the amount of socialization she needs to feel secure varies depending on her genetics and how well her breeder socialized her as a young puppy. If her mother or father was a fearful dog, she may be that way, too. If one or both of her parents were secure, confident dogs, she's probably just like them. The tendency to be shy or outgoing is inherited, but early training or socialization can modify it. Basically, the more socialization that any Pug has at a young age, the more secure she becomes as she grows up.

At the very least, plan to socialize your dog by doing the following:

- Taking your Pug out several times a week. I'm not talking about staying out for hours at a time. Frequent, short jaunts of 10 to 15 minutes can do the trick, as long as each place you go is somewhat different.

- Taking your Pug out at different times of the day so that you can have a variety of experiences.

- Taking your Pug out, even for a few minutes, during different weather conditions. A loud thunderstorm teaches Puggy that being out in noisy weather won't necessarily hurt her (although she may not like coming home with wet fur).

Every new happening adds to Puggy's mental development. Plus, the time you spend with your dog helps to strengthen the bond that you two are developing with each other.

Where to go

When you get out, I'm sure you find your own favorite haunts that are ideal for socializing Puggy. But getting your dog socialized doesn't have to be a time-consuming activity. You can simply take your Pug with you as you run your own errands.

Many businesses and stores don't mind having a puppy visit for a few minutes. Have to drop off a pair of pants at the cleaners? Your Pug may love going inside the cleaners and meeting the clerk. My dry cleaner keeps biscuits behind the counter, or you can take some with you and ask the clerk to give Puggy a treat.

I always take a puppy with me when I go to the bank. Customers waiting in line often find a puppy a wonderful distraction, so most people never object and actually like my dog's presence. A bank official often gets up from behind her desk to come over and greet us.

When I take a dog to a public place that doesn't allow dogs indoors, I usually just hang around outside or walk my dog back and forth a little as if I'm waiting to meet someone. I find that people are glad to see a cute Pug and always have plenty of kind words to say to my dog. In a few minutes, my Pug can come in contact with more than two dozen people, some noisy cars, a few children, and maybe another dog out to get her own dose of socialization.

Here are a few of my favorite places to take a dog for socialization:

- ✔ Outdoor shopping mall
- ✔ Carwash
- ✔ Bank
- ✔ Plant nursery
- ✔ Post office (outside)
- ✔ Office buildings without security (hang around outside during lunchtime)
- ✔ School (Call ahead and ask if you can give children a short demonstration on dog care and answer their questions. If that's not possible, try taking your puppy for a walk near the school just as it lets out in the afternoon.)
- ✔ Construction site in a safe area
- ✔ Beach, river, or lake
- ✔ Auto dealership
- ✔ Sidewalk coffee bar
- ✔ Dog training classes or shows
- ✔ Nature area
- ✔ Video stores
- ✔ Newsstand
- ✔ Bus stop

- Home improvement stores
- Outside an ice cream store

What to do when you get there

What should you do with Puggy when you go out? The following list points out a few things to always keep in mind when you and your dog venture out into the world:

- Take your Pug on a leash.

- Take your time and don't rush. If you're cramped for time but still want to get your Pug out, go on a 5- to 10-minute outing at a more leisurely pace.

- Leisurely stroll around the areas that I suggest visiting (see the preceding section) — well, maybe not the bank!

- Warmly greet anyone who comes up to admire Puggy. Your Pug picks up on your confidence and feels braver.

- Let people who appear confident pet Puggy if they ask to do so. Avoid strangers who seem fearful of your dog. Their insecurity may rub off and doesn't make Puggy any braver.

- Bring along some dog biscuits. Put them in your pocket so they're easy to hand out at a moment's notice.

- Ask strangers who approach you and want to pet Puggy if they want to give your dog a treat. Your Pug begins to associate strangers with something she likes, namely, food.

- Give your dog a treat if she approaches an object or a situation and she's frightened. Again, she begins to associate a scary object with a positive thing (food).

- Tell your Pug she's a great dog when she investigates a new experience or person and doesn't shy away from it.

- Bring along a plastic bag to clean up any mess your Pug may make along the way.

Boosting your shy Pug's confidence

If you find that Puggy shies away from people by hiding behind your legs, shrinking down to the ground, or trembling or shaking from the noise and hubbub at an outing, your Pug's personality isn't very stable. So, you need to show Puggy that all these things are all part of life and nothing to feel afraid of. With time and patience, you can accomplish this.

Here are some specific things you can do to help your Pug build her confidence.

- **Enroll Puggy in a puppy kindergarten class if she's 4 months or younger or in a beginning obedience class if she's older than 6 months.** She gets exposed to new experiences that help her feel better about her surroundings. Check out Chapter 11 for more on puppy kindergarten and Chapter 15 for more about obedience classes.

- **Keep taking your Pug to as many different places as you can, as often as you can.**

- **Continue letting people give your Pug a treat and pet her if she allows it.**

- **If there's an object, such as a bicycle or a fire hydrant, that your Pug isn't too sure about, handle it or lovingly pat it like it's a precious gem.** When she sees that you like it, she likes it, too.

- **If she's fearful, don't coddle or pet Puggy by telling her it's okay.** It isn't. Otherwise, she thinks that you're praising her for feeling afraid.

- **Say nothing if Puggy is shy, or try laughing.** When Puggy hears that you're having a good time, she relaxes and feels more like joining in the fun.

- **When she's acting confident, praise your Pug by giving her a treat and telling her, "Good girl, Puggy!"**

Toning down the exuberant Pug

Maybe your Pug doesn't know the meaning of the word shy. She may exhibit the complete opposite type of behavior when you take her out: Your Pug is a little too happy to see everyone! You know what happens: When she sees other people, she drags you over to greet them and starts jumping all over them, even scratching their legs or snagging their clothing. That's what you may call too much of a good thing because not everyone likes a Pug who's so upfront and personal.

If you find yourself in that situation, here's what to do to calm your Pug down:

1. **When you see someone up ahead, anticipate that your Pug will want to jump by gathering up the leash, if it's loose.**

2. **Using the leash, make quick turns so that Puggy knows that you are in charge of the direction she's going.**

   Don't allow your Pug to pull you over to greet someone. Train her to walk nicely without pulling. For more information on leash training, see Chapter 11.

3. **Tell Puggy to sit down when someone approaches.**

   For more information on giving the Sit command, see Chapter 11.

4. **Make Puggy sit down before allowing someone to pet her.**

5. **If your Pug doesn't jump up and behaves politely when greeting a stranger, quickly reward her with a treat and tell her, "Good girl, Puggy!"**

6. **If Puggy does jump up on someone, you can quickly give the leash a quick tug downward and say, "Puggy, off!"**

   Be sure to give her a treat when she has all four feet on the floor.

Riding in Cars with Pugs

Taking your Pug in the car with you is another good way to let her see the world and get socialized. You can drive Puggy to experience new sights and sounds and to encounter people who don't live within walking distance. However, keep in mind that you need to take some precautions to ensure that the road trip is as safe as possible for your dog.

Crating your Pug while driving

Although you may be tempted to let Puggy ride unrestrained in the car, it's not a safe way for her to travel, no matter how far you're going (see Figure 12-1). In an accident, her small body becomes a projectile with no protection from injury. She can also be thrown into another passenger during a crash.

Figure 12-1: It may look like fun, but it isn't safe for Puggy to ride in a convertible.

©Tony Nunes

So, to be on the safe side, put your Pug in her wire pet carrier when traveling in the car. Wire carrier manufacturers make a variety of sizes and models that are convenient to keep in the car. You can usually find them in pet supply stores or pet supply catalogs. For more information about wire carriers, see Chapter 10.

If you're going on vacation in a motor home and taking Puggy with you, she still needs to ride in her own wire pet carrier (see Figure 12-2). Just because a large vehicle like this has so much room doesn't mean that your dog is any safer roaming around without secure protection.

Figure 12-2:
These Pugs are riding safely and happily in a motor home.

©Elaine Gewirtz

To protect your Pug in her carrier, firmly secure it so it doesn't roll over or slide during driving. In a motor home, you can also build a small ledge on which to secure the carrier, and attach brackets or bungee cords to the wall to hold the carrier in place. Be sure to point any bungee hooks outward and away from the carrier. If you place the hooks inside the carrier, they may damage your Pug's eyes.

Place Puggy's crate in a spot inside the car where the air freely circulates around her. Don't block the sides and top with luggage or packages. She needs room to breathe!

Whenever possible, I like to put my dog's carrier in the middle of my SUV behind the first row of seats. At least if Puggy is in that location and we're rear-ended by another car, Puggy may not be as badly injured as she would if she were traveling in her carrier in the very back.

If you're tight for space in your car, consider getting crates that have doors that swing to one side instead of the other (some crates have doors that open from the left side and others from the right side) or doors in the middle of the long side of the crate. These types of crates may make it easier to get your Pug in and out of the carrier.

If you plan on taking your Pug lots of places in the car, consider purchasing a second carrier that you can leave in the car all the time.

Opting for a seat belt harness or car seat (and getting your Pug to like it)

If you just can't fit Puggy's wire carrier safely into your car, you can always let Puggy go along for the ride wearing a seat belt harness or sitting in a safety car seat. Both of these items are made especially for dogs, are adjustable, and attach to your regular car seat belt. They help restrain Puggy and add protection for her if you have to make a quick turn or stop suddenly.

You can find doggy seat belt harnesses or safety car seats in a pet supply store or a pet supply catalog. Both are fairly inexpensive and can stay in your car all the time. If you're a two-car family and frequently trade off rides for your Pug, consider putting a restraint device in both cars to make things easier for you!

It may take some time before your Pug enjoys the ride with these restraints, but the protection she receives is worth it. Remember that this is a new experience for her. She may struggle to get out of the restraint or try whining or crying before building up to barking to express her displeasure with this new contraption.

To head off her temper tantrum or to prevent her from doing the Pug wiggle out of the restraint, give her a Stay command when you buckle her up. To let her know that she's not allowed to act like an escape artist, reseat Puggy if she tries to get out.

The first few times that you have her in her restraint, you may want to get a volunteer (if possible) to sit next to her while you're driving. When Puggy doesn't wiggle around and remains quiet for even a few minutes, praise your Pug by telling her what a good dog she is and offering her a very small food treat.

If you're just beginning to get Puggy used to her car seat, don't make the first few trips very long ones. Start off slowly with short trips — even little jaunts for quick errands or trips around the block help you train her to behave in the car.

Making sure your Pug behaves on the open road

You want to be able to safely take your Pug with you in the car. Be sure to take the precautions I describe in the following sections so that both of you can enjoy the journey.

Instituting a no-head-out-the-open-window policy

Keep the windows partially closed when Puggy is sitting on the seat in her car seat or harness. Sure, she may want to see what's outside, but if Puggy is sitting tall in her seat, she can still catch a glimpse of things whizzing by. If the car air-conditioning is on, that's all she needs in the air department on a hot day.

If your car isn't air-conditioned and you need to cool the car off, roll down your Pug's window only about a quarter of the way. This is just enough to let some air pass through for circulation but not enough for her to think about sticking her head out. You can roll down the other windows in the car, but not more than about halfway.

Although she may love putting her head out the window, doing so can actually be dangerous to your Pug. The wind pressure can give her an ear infection. Strange particles in the air or bugs can also fly into her eyes and cause damage. In fact, too much wind, no matter what window it comes through, can carry odd particles into the car and right into Puggy's eyes.

Be sure to put your power window locks on when you're riding with your Pug. If she accidentally steps on the lock, she could get her head caught in the window.

Preventing barking and panting

Puggy may love to ride in the car, but she shouldn't love *barking* in the car for any reason while you're behind the wheel!

Loose barking dogs are distracting for the driver. Many accidents are caused by drivers who are paying attention to what their dog is doing rather than to what's happening on the road.

Although you may not mind the occasional protective barking, don't let your Pug carry on. The last thing you want to hear while you're driving is constant barking. To let her know that this isn't acceptable car behavior, give her the verbal command, "No!" or "Quiet!" If she still persists, trying putting some oomph into your verbal command until you get the message across.

Taking along a collar, leash, and ID

You're not the only one who needs identification while away from home. Your Pug also needs some ID when you go out. A tag that shows her city license and city registration number is one form of ID, but it doesn't have your name, address, and phone number. Puggy needs a second tag with your name and your current address and phone number (including your area code) firmly attached to her collar. It's a good idea to have the word *reward* put on the tag, too. Or you can have her tattooed or microchipped with this information. For more information about microchipping, tattooing, and other ways to keep Puggy identified at all times, see Chapter 13.

Always take your Pug's leash along or have her wear it when you go out. If she's sitting in a harness or doggy car seat, the leash should still be attached to her collar. If she's sitting still, it shouldn't become entangled. But don't leave the leash on your Pug when she's riding inside her carrier. She can easily become tangled up in it and possibly strangle herself. Take the leash off before you put her in the carrier but leave it clipped to the front of the carrier. That way, you can find it easily if you need to remove Puggy from her carrier quickly.

Although Pugs frequently pant when they're even a little warm, excessive panting isn't healthy and can also make her overheat. The best way to stop your Pug from panting too much in the car is to figure out why she's panting to begin with. She may be too hot in the car. If you're slightly warm while riding, she's probably even warmer. Try cooling off the inside of the car as much as possible.

Another reason that your Pug may be panting is that she's nervous about being in the car. You can't really stop your Pug from panting if she's nervous, but you may be able to help alleviate the cause of the nervousness. Your dog may simply need to realize that riding in a car isn't scary (unless you're really a very bad driver).

To prevent the panting and reduce your Pug's car-riding anxiety, take her somewhere, even for just a short ride around the block every day or every other day. Eventually, she takes her car trips in stride and cuts down on her panting!

Keeping your Pug cool enough

Because your Pug may be next to a window, you need to watch the amount and intensity of sun that may be shining through the glass. It may be too hot for your Pug, and she can overheat and possibly die from heatstroke. For more information about keeping your Pug cool, see Chapter 8.

No matter what the temperature is outside the car, it's always hotter inside if the car isn't air-conditioned. To keep Puggy cool in the car while you're driving, here are some ideas to try:

✔ Move Puggy's car seat, harness, or pet carrier away from the window into the middle of the car where the sun isn't likely to be hitting it.

✔ Put up a sunshade on the window. Sunshades are small removable screens that you can attach to the window with a suction cup. Parents use the same thing in their cars to protect their babies from getting too much sun. You can find sunshades in a baby store.

✔ Use a portable fan for extra cooling power (see Figure 12-3). These fans attach to the sides of the carrier or can be positioned next to Puggy's carrier.

Figure 12-3:
Keep a fan near your Pug's carrier in hot weather.

©Judi Crowe

Never, ever leave Puggy in a closed car, even for a few minutes, when it's warmer than 75 degrees outside. On a warm day, the temperature inside a closed car can rise to more than 100 degrees. Your car can quickly become an oven and turn deadly for your Pug.

Avoiding carsickness

Your Pug's first car ride may not be the joyous occasion you want it to be. Your Pug may get carsick. Her eyes look glassy, she drools or vomits, and she's generally pretty miserable.

A dog usually gets carsick every time she gets into a car until her system adjusts to the motion. It may take just a few times — or maybe months — before she gets over this feeling. In fact, after she gets carsick the first time, you may have a hard time convincing Puggy that the next ride will be any better, especially if she gets in the car only once a year to visit the veterinarian.

Never fear, though. The following are some things you can do to help your Pug overcome this condition:

- **Conditioning with frequent trips:** Although all that drooling that Puggy does because she's carsick makes a mess, one definite way to help her overcome motion sickness is to keep taking her for rides in the car. The more often she goes for a ride, the sooner her system becomes accustomed to the motion.

  Take your Pug somewhere in the car every day. It doesn't have to be a long trip — a short trip around the block works just fine. If you're really pressed for time, put your Pug inside the car, start the engine, drive out your driveway, and then come right back.

- **Withholding food before leaving:** Refrain from feeding your Pug or giving her lots of water a few hours before you're planning to take her on a car ride. Without food or water in her stomach, she's less likely to vomit, although she sure tries.

- **Facing forward:** If your Pug is riding in a carrier, try positioning the door of the carrier so that it faces forward. This way, you may fool her stomach into thinking that there isn't that much motion going forward. Some dogs are more likely to be carsick if they're looking backward.

  Also, if possible, open the window nearest the carrier about halfway so fresh air blows into Puggy's face.

- **Trying a home remedy:** Although this tip isn't scientific, some Pug owners report success at overcoming carsickness if they give their Pug about a tablespoon of honey an hour before they leave the house. The honey coats and soothes the Pug's stomach.

  Other owners give their Pugs gingersnap cookies before they leave the house. Although neither of these methods is tried and true, one or the other may just help your Pug until she gets over the carsickness.

Leaving on a Jet Plane

The time may come when you want to take Puggy with you when you're flying somewhere. Although all _you_ have to do to fly is buy a ticket, pass through security, and get on the plane, things get a lot more complicated when a dog flies the friendly skies.

Whatever the reason for your airline trip, don't just show up at the airline counter with your dog and expect to jump right into your window seat. (Generally, you should plan on checking your Pug in at the airport two to three hours before your departure.) Airline travel with dogs isn't a spur-of-the-moment thing. The airline industry and individual airlines have conditions and rules that may not be so friendly to dogs who want to spread their air wings.

Before you decide to take Puggy on a plane, find out what the airline's transport rules are and make plans to comply with them before you buy your own ticket. After hearing the regulations, you may decide that you don't want to take Puggy with you on a plane, after all.

Understanding what airlines require

For starters, your Pug needs a separate reservation to travel on the plane. In fact, the airline charges an extra fee for your pet. The amount depends on whether she rides in the passenger area of the plane or down below in the cargo section. (Every airline charges a different fee.)

Generally, you can take a toy dog on the plane with you if she's small enough to fit in a soft carrier and stowed beneath the seat in front of you during take-off and landing. (Be sure to ask the airline you're flying how big the space beneath the seat is.) She can't wander in the aisles, and no, she doesn't get her own movie. Keep in mind, however, that if your Pug puppy is staying with you in the main cabin, she may get fussy, and you may have trouble calming her down on a long flight.

If a Pug is too large to fit in a carry-on bag beneath your seat, she must fly in an airline-approved pet carrier with solid sides in the cargo section beneath the plane. The pet carrier must be properly labeled with your identification and final destination information. It must be tall enough for your Pug to stand up in without hitting her head and wide enough for her to easily turn around in. The carrier needs to have two plastic dishes attached to the inside of the carrier door — one for food and one for water. Some airlines require that a small bag of food be taped to the top of the carrier as well and that some type of padding — a newspaper, blanket, or doggy pad be put inside the crate.

Because Pugs overheat easily, it's also a good idea to secure a portable fan to the front door of her carrier. The airlines appreciate this extra precaution you're taking for your pet.

Dogs in solid pet carriers are checked in as excess baggage and placed in the cargo section of the plane. This section beneath the plane is pressurized and is the same temperature as the cabin. By the way, a change of planes isn't a good idea for dogs riding in the cargo section. Baggage handlers can get busy or forgetful, and there's always a chance that your Pug may not get transferred to the connecting flight in time. Try to take a direct route whenever possible.

Getting a health certificate

Before the airline can accept your dog for transport, a representative must see a recent health certificate supplied by your veterinarian. Your veterinarian is required to examine your Pug in her office before she can fill out the certificate. The exam determines whether your Pug's in good health and if your veterinarian thinks she can make the trip safely.

Check the airline you wish to travel on for the latest rules on how far in advance you can get your health certificate.

Put your health certificate in a safe place — maybe with your airline ticket — so you don't forget to take it to the airport. You can't fudge on this one. If your dog doesn't have a health certificate, she stays home.

Preparing Puggy for planes

Airports are loud and noisy places, and your Pug may feel frightened by all the different sights, sounds, and smells she encounters when getting on and off the plane.

To prepare her for these new experiences, here are some things you can do:

- ✔ If your Pug has never spent the night in a solid-sided carrier before, begin training her at least a few weeks before your flight to get her accustomed to being in there. When she's comfortable in her carrier, she can relax during the trip because it's her familiar comfort zone.

- ✔ If your Pug hasn't visited many noisy places before, take her walking in front of the airport a few times or go for a quick stroll in and out of the terminal.

- ✔ If your Pug has never been inside her carrier while it's being moved, try simulating the experience for a few days before her departure. Put Puggy in the carrier, place it on a cart, and roll it around. She needs to get used to the idea of being moved around because that's what happens at the airport.

- ✔ If Puggy is leaving on an early morning flight, don't feed her for a few hours before departure. Even the calmest Pug will be nervous, and having food in her stomach can make her sick. Feed her a little more the day before she leaves, if you have to.

Factoring in the weather

Before they accept animals for transport, all airlines want to make sure that the weather is not too hot or too cold before they take off and when they land in another city. This precaution is for the dog's safety. Often, planes have to wait on the tarmac before taking off, and the temperature inside the plane and the cargo section isn't controlled during those times.

When you make your reservations, check the airline policy on the weather restriction because airlines frequently change their policies. They don't take dogs if they decide it's too hot or too cold where you're landing. Take this into consideration when you schedule your flight. It may be safer in the long run to take a *red-eye,* or late-night, flight so that you can travel in the coolest part of the day.

Part IV
Raising a Healthy and Active Pug

The 5th Wave   By Rich Tennant

"Something's wrong with the dog. He doesn't look like himself today."

In this part . . .

Chapter 13 is all about how to keep your Pug healthy by maintaining good veterinary care, staying current on vaccines, having her or him spayed or neutered, and making sure he's identified when he goes out. Likewise, in Chapter 14, I explain what inherited diseases and common ailments Pugs can have. Being armed with that information can help you keep Puggy physically and mentally fit. Chapter 15 talks about keeping your Pug active by participating in obedience and agility competitions. And I round out this part with Chapter 16, which talks about how to make your Pug a champion at dog shows.

Chapter 13

Getting Good Medical Care for Your Pug

Right now your Pug may be fine, so it's likely hard to imagine that he'll ever have any health problems. Still, you need to take as many precautions as possible to keep your Pug in rip-snortin' good shape. What's the famous cliché that really makes sense here? An ounce of prevention is worth a pound of cure. If all it takes to make sure that Puggy doesn't get a fatal illness is a little shot once every year or once every two years, it's well worth the effort.

Having a veterinarian whom you can trust and feel comfortable with helps enormously when it comes to making sure that your Pug stays healthy. In this chapter, I tell you how to find a good vet and what to expect when you take your dog there for checkups. In addition, this chapter offers the inside scoop on all the vaccines that your dog needs. I also discuss how to take your Pug's temperature and give him a pill if you have to, and why it's so important to spay or neuter your dog.

Finally, I explain how to put together a first-aid kit that's good to have at home or when you're traveling with your Pug and how to get proper identification for your dog so that he's safe when he's out and about.

Finding a Good Veterinarian

A good veterinarian is your Pug's best buddy (next to you, of course). She is a person who genuinely likes dogs, has their best interests at heart, knows how to recognize a problem, and can fix it as quickly as possible.

A good veterinarian does the following:

- ✔ Treats your dog with confidence and respect.
- ✔ Regards your office visit as a special time and doesn't rush you.
- ✔ Considers any concern you have seriously and explains what's going on in language that you can understand.
- ✔ Takes care of the medical problem to the best of her ability or refers you to a specialist if she can't find the answer.

To locate a doctor for your Pug, check with the following sources to get their recommendations:

- ✔ Other dog or Pug owners in your area
- ✔ Members of your local kennel club
- ✔ Local groomers
- ✔ The American Veterinary Medical Association's Web site at www.avma.org
- ✔ A Pug online message board
- ✔ Your Pug's breeder

When you have a good referral, or even several, and you want to find out more about a veterinarian before you actually need one, schedule a consultation appointment. That appointment allows you to determine if a vet is right for your dog.

During that appointment, you want to ask a few key questions, such as:

- ✔ **What are your veterinary credentials?** It's interesting to know what veterinary school the vet graduated from and maybe why she chose that location to begin with. Hopefully, she didn't get her degree online.
- ✔ **Do you specialize in a particular area of veterinary medicine?** This is good to know if your Pug ever has a particular problem that you need more information about.
- ✔ **How many other Pugs have you cared for?** Ideally, you want your veterinarian to have specific experience with your breed.

✔ **Do you consult with another veterinarian if you encounter a problem you're not familiar with?** Here you're hoping that your veterinarian doesn't take on a problem she may not know too much about and can seek advice.

✔ **Do you perform your own surgeries?** It's comforting to know that your veterinarian can take care of the problem that you've discussed in the office.

✔ **Who monitors the dogs after surgery, and where are they cared for?** There are probably one or more technicians in charge of this area, but you want your veterinarian to be checking in on your dog, too.

✔ **Does your office give tours of the surgical and post-op areas?** Some veterinarians hold an open house for their clients periodically so people can see those areas.

✔ **Do you have your own laboratory in the office, or do you have to send lab tests out to other labs to be read?** It's cheaper and faster if results are analyzed in the office, although some tests do need to be run at out-side laboratories because they require specialized equipment. It's nice to know this ahead of time.

✔ **Do you have any dogs?** It's nice to know that your veterinarian shares his life with a dog, too — maybe it's even a Pug!

✔ **Do you attend veterinary conferences throughout the year?** Such conferences provide the latest information in veterinary medicine and knowing that your veterinarian keeps up with the newest procedures helps your peace of mind.

✔ **How much veterinary or dog experience do you require your staff to have?** When you bring your Pug in to the office, it's reassuring if the staff is comfortable around dogs.

Expect to pay a fee for the veterinarian's time during the consultation appointment.

Visiting the vet for the first time

After you choose a veterinarian, it's time to take Puggy for his first appointment. When you do so, you probably want to take along the following:

✔ **A list of questions you want to ask the veterinarian:** If this is the first time you're seeing this veterinarian, you may want to ask some of the questions mentioned in the previous section. That is, if you haven't held a previous consultation with the vet.

You also want to know if your new Pug looks okay — do his eyes and his skin and coat look healthy? Does the veterinarian recommend feeding a certain type of food? Does she have any training tips for Pugs?

✔ **A record of all the vaccines and wormings your Pug has already had:** Your veterinarian needs this information before he can give your dog any additional vaccines or worming medication. (See the "Vaccinating Your Pug" section, later in the chapter, for more information.) You also want to know when you should bring your dog in for his set of vaccines.

✔ **A recent stool sample:** A stool sample is needed to check Puggy for parasites. Your veterinarian's office may be able to collect one if you forget or are unable to do this, especially if your Pug hasn't already been checked for the presence of parasites.

✔ **A leash:** Veterinary offices require dogs to be on a leash. If you have a puppy that isn't leash trained yet, you can carry him, but be sure to leave the leash attached anyway in case he jumps out of your arms.

Try not to let your Pug walk on the office floor. If he hasn't had all his vaccines, he's susceptible to diseases that other dogs may be transmitting.

✔ **A check, your credit card, or some cash:** Ask before you go which payment methods your veterinarian accepts.

Getting regular checkups

Having a good veterinarian can make all the difference in your Pug's well-being because she knows at a glance if something isn't quite right with your dog. The relationship with your vet starts the first day you bring your puppy in for his first examination and continues every year during his checkup.

Routine things your vet should look for

Pugs need regular checkups, just like people do. Just as your doctor routinely examines your heartbeat, blood pressure, and so on, a vet should always check the following things on your Pug:

✔ **Weight:** Your vet wants to make sure that your puppy continues to gain weight while he's growing. After he's grown, the vet should make sure he maintains a healthy weight.

✔ **Temperature:** A dog's normal body temperature ranges from 100 to 102.5 degrees Fahrenheit.

✔ **Eyes:** The veterinarian checks your Pug for *entropion,* a condition where his eyelashes rub against the surface of his eyes, causing irritation. She also looks for anemia, jaundice, glaucoma, and any discharge or swelling. See Chapter 14 for more info about common Pug eye problems.

✔ **Ears:** The vet checks to make sure that your dog doesn't have an ear infection.

✔ **Mouth:** When your vet examines your dog's gums and teeth, she wants to make sure he doesn't have any impacted teeth, gum problems, or unusual sores.

✔ **Heart and lungs:** Your vet checks your Pug's heart and lungs to make sure they aren't enlarged and that they're free of heart disease and tumors.

✔ **Anal area:** The vet checks for any obstruction or infection, and she may have to clean out Puggy's anal glands. See the section "Cleaning anal glands," later in this chapter.

✔ **Skin and coat:** Your vet should check for any spots of hair loss. This could indicate mange (see Chapter 14 for more on mange).

Report to your veterinarian any medical condition you're concerned about or any odd behavior in your Pug. It may be just the information she needs to detect a problem. Although it sounds like your veterinarian is looking for only bad things, she can also reassure you that your Pug is in tip-top shape.

Other checks the vet should perform

Besides examining your Pug for the routine stuff, your veterinarian looks for signs of other problems, too. If your veterinarian thinks that something doesn't look just right with Puggy, she may recommend the following tests:

✔ Blood test

✔ Electrocardiogram

✔ Lab work

✔ Sonogram

✔ Urine collection

✔ X-rays

Just sit, stay, and wait in the exam room if the vet wants to take your Pug into the laboratory for these procedures. Your dog is likely to squirm away from the doctor and want you to coddle him if you go with him. Your presence makes the procedure more difficult. He'll be back safe and sound in no time.

The office has the results back as soon as possible, and your veterinarian should patiently explain the outcome in language you can understand.

Getting Extra Medical Help

Your regular veterinarian should be able to identify and treat most, if not all, of the medical problems that your Pug ever has. Somewhere down the road, however, you may encounter an illness or condition that's difficult for your veterinarian to pin down, even after she's tried a few different treatments. When she's stumped, she may suggest that you take your Pug to a specialist for further treatment.

Likewise, there may be times when your Pug has a medical problem and your veterinarian isn't in the office (the middle of the night, a holiday, or on the weekend, for example). In these cases, you need to find another veterinarian in a hurry. The following sections discuss both situations and help you decide what to do.

Seeing a specialist

So, what exactly is a veterinary specialist? A *veterinary specialist* is a veterinarian who is board certified by a specialty board approved by the American Veterinary Medical Association (AVMA). To earn that title, she must complete a veterinary school program approved by the AVMA.

Before receiving official certification by the specialty board, a veterinarian must complete extra educational requirements and pass rigorous examinations in her field. A specialist is usually listed something like this: DVM, Diplomate American Board of Veterinary Practitioners, Board Certified in Surgery.

Because these veterinarians see patients with the same problems, they become experts. They zero in on many different kinds of treatments that are available and keep up with the latest developments in their fields of expertise. Veterinarians have private specialty practices in the following areas:

- ✔ Animal behavior
- ✔ Cardiology
- ✔ Dentistry
- ✔ Dermatology
- ✔ Internal medicine
- ✔ Oncology
- ✔ Ophthalmology
- ✔ Orthopedics

The American Veterinary Medical Association (www.avma.org) can furnish you with a list of board-certified specialists. You can also find specialists at veterinary schools and make an appointment for them to see your dog.

If your regular veterinarian took X-rays of your Pug, ask the vet's office to send them to the specialist you've selected or to give the images to you so that you can take them with you to your specialty appointment.

Visiting the ER

If your Pug needs to see a veterinarian when your vet's office is closed, you have to find a good emergency clinic or another veterinarian. I can't tell you how many times I've taken my dogs to the emergency clinic because my regular veterinarian wasn't working on Thanksgiving or at 11 p.m.

Don't wait until an emergency comes up to look for an after-hours veterinarian. You'll be panic stricken because you're afraid that Puggy won't be okay while you're frantically searching the phone book for a doctor. In fact, I recommend keeping the phone number of the nearest ER clinic posted by your phone or up on the fridge where you can quickly find it.

When you have your first meeting with your veterinarian, find out where you should take your dog when the office is closed. Is there an emergency clinic she recommends or another qualified veterinarian?

Vaccinating Your Pug

While puppies are still nursing, they're immune to many diseases. But that immunity gradually begins to wear off by the time puppies reach 5 to 6 weeks old. Until they begin to build their own immunity, they're susceptible to several serious infectious diseases. That's why taking your dog to the veterinarian to have him vaccinated his first year is crucial. The vaccines provide protection against diseases and get the body started on building up its own immunity.

Keep the following things in mind when getting your Pug vaccinated:

- ✔ Give Puggy his regular meal either right before or right after you take him to the veterinarian for his vaccine because he may not want to eat anything when the serum begins working its way through his system.

- ✔ If your dog misses a few meals, has diarrhea, or is vomiting or coughing, don't give him any vaccines. His immune system is already working overtime to fight off these problems, and it can't receive any of the benefits of a vaccine.

- ✔ Keep an eye on your Pug for two to three hours after he receives the vaccine from your veterinarian to make sure that he doesn't have one of the following reactions:

  - Gray gums

  - Hives or red splotches

  - Swollen eyelids

- Excessive itching

- Coughing

- Vomiting

- Diarrhea

- Overall weakness or trembling

If you notice one of these signs, rush your Pug back to the veterinarian immediately.

✔ Keep track of your Pug's vaccines and ask the veterinarian when he needs the next one. Then be sure to keep up with the regular schedule. Once a year, he needs booster shots for these vaccines.

✔ Until Puggy has had all his vaccines, don't take him into public grassy areas where a lot of other dogs are present. Their urine or feces can carry diseases that your dog has no immunity against. After your dog has been vaccinated, however, you want to start socializing him. See Chapter 12 for more information about socializing your Pug.

✔ If you're traveling with your Pug, don't take him to the veterinarian to get his vaccines right before you leave. The stress of the vaccinating experience combined with all the travel hoopla can make your dog more susceptible to illness. He definitely needs to have his vaccines at the right time — just not right before a trip. Schedule the appointment a week or two before you leave.

The following sections detail some common Pug vaccinations.

Distemper

Distemper is a highly contagious and often fatal viral disease that causes neurological damage. Unvaccinated puppies are often the victims, although some older dogs may get it, too.

Watch for some of these symptoms of distemper: diarrhea, vomiting, little or no appetite, coughing, nasal discharge, swollen eyes, fever, convulsions, and lethargy. Early detection and treatment can save the dog, although permanent brain damage may result.

Hepatitis

Both people and dogs can get hepatitis, which is a disease that affects the liver. The form that applies to dogs gets transmitted through a dog's stool, saliva, or urine.

The symptoms of hepatitis are the same as they are in distemper, but dogs with hepatitis are also very thirsty. When a dog contracts this disease, it rapidly spreads throughout the body and can be fatal if it isn't caught in time.

Leptospirosis

Pugs can get leptospirosis if they meet up with wild animals, such as raccoons, squirrels, skunks, and rats who carry it. Dogs can also get lepto if they eat something that's contaminated by animals who are infected. The contamination also remains in water supplies where livestock or rats congregate. Leptospirosis damages the liver and kidneys, and people can catch it from a dog who has it. For more information about leptospirosis, the Centers for Disease Control has a Web site you can access at www.cdc.gov/ncidod/dbmd/diseaseinfo/leptospirosis_g_pet.htm.

Be on the lookout for these symptoms of leptospirosis: bloody diarrhea or urine, fever, overall weakness, vomiting, no appetite, red eyes, excessive thirst, and mouth ulcers.

Consult with your veterinarian before giving this vaccine. It has produced many fatal reactions in puppies and in Toy breeds. More puppies die from the vaccine than they do the disease. Older leptospirosis vaccines don't protect against all the strains of the disease.

Parvovirus

Parvovirus is highly contagious and fatal, and puppies can die within days of contracting it. The stomach lining, bone marrow, and lymph nodes are affected. It's transmitted through contaminated stools, and Pugs can get it from ingesting contaminated stool from their feet.

If a young puppy suddenly becomes listless and doesn't want to eat, he may have parvovirus. Early signs also include vomiting, bloody diarrhea, and fever.

Parainfluenza

Parainfluenza, which is a combination of several different viruses and a bacteria, spreads from dog to dog like wildfire. This condition isn't fatal, but it weakens the dog until it runs its course. Listen for a dry, hacking cough. Your veterinarian can prescribe an antibiotic.

Rabies

Rabies is so fatal to dogs and so dangerous to people who are bitten by dogs who have it that state laws require every dog to receive regular vaccinations to prevent it. The vaccine needs to be repeated once every three years in some states, while other states require that it be given once a year or every other year. Dogs can get it from other animals who have it, and it affects the nervous system.

To detect signs of rabies, watch for radical changes in a dog's disposition. If he suddenly becomes aggressive or too calm, develops stomach pain and a fever, and his facial muscles contort, rush him to your veterinarian immediately.

Bordatella

Bordatella is also known as kennel cough. It's an upper respiratory disease — a hacking, gagging cough — that dogs can get from other dogs who have it. In most cases, it's not fatal or even serious — just irritating to the dog — and it runs its course in a few weeks. You can't do much for a dog after he has it, but a nasal spray vaccine can help prevent a dog from getting it. Young puppies and older dogs, in some cases, can have Bordatella progress into pneumonia, so you should take every precaution not to contract it.

If you're taking your dog to a kennel, or if he's going to dog shows or dog parks where lots of other dogs are present, ask your veterinarian to give him a bordatella vaccine. Your dog needs this vaccine once a year.

Monitoring Puggy's Health at Home

Although I hope Puggy isn't ever sick, if he is, you may have to give him some medication or take his temperature. Don't worry! You can handle these things, and this section can help you.

Giving medication

You may have to give your Pug a pill occasionally, and you can do it in several ways. Your veterinarian lets you know whether the medication must be given on an empty stomach or with food. Many pills can be mixed in with food, but you have to be sure that he eats all the food and takes the pill. If he leaves the pill behind, you have to be more inventive.

For example, try hiding the pill inside a small piece of cheese or within a wad of peanut butter. Make sure that your Pug swallows all the cheese or peanut butter containing the pill. If you need another way to give the pill, ask your veterinarian whether you can grind the pill in a small food grinder before mixing it with food.

If none of these ways works, put the pill inside your Pug's mouth as follows:

1. **Open Puggy's mouth and gently point it upward.**
2. **Carefully insert the pill on the very back of your dog's tongue.**
3. **Hold your dog's muzzle closed for a few seconds and, at the same time, stroke his chin and neck.**
4. **Continue holding his muzzle for a few moments until you see him swallow.**
5. **Tell him he's a great dog and give him a small treat.**

The medication may also come in a liquid form, which makes it easy to mix into your Pug's dog food or with a little bit of cottage cheese.

Taking your Pug's temperature

If you suspect that Puggy is ill and you feel that you should take him to your veterinarian, it helps if you know whether your Pug is running a fever. That way, when you call your veterinarian's office to make an appointment, you can report the temperature. That information lets the office know whether you have an emergency and need to bring your Pug in right away or whether you can come in a bit later.

Taking your dog's temperature sounds more difficult than it is. After you've done it once, you can do it quickly and easily from then on. But, don't worry — it doesn't hurt!

When taking your Pug's temperature, it helps if you have someone to assist you, but if not, you can easily do this yourself.

All you need is a pet ear thermometer or a human digital thermometer. The pet ear thermometer is very easy to use and gives you Puggy's results in one second. You simply insert it inside his ear and hold it there for a moment. The temperature appears on a readout screen.

On the other hand, to take his temperature with a digital thermometer, follow these steps:

1. **Apply some lubricating jelly to the tip of the thermometer.**

2. **With one arm, hold Puggy firmly beneath and across his abdomen.**

3. **Use your other hand to insert the thermometer into your Pug's rectum.**

4. **Wait a few moments.**

   The thermometer beeps when the job is done.

5. **Give Puggy a treat and tell him he's a good dog because he stood still for you.**

A dog's normal body temperature ranges from 100 to 102.5 degrees Fahrenheit, although many small dogs, including Pugs, have a temperature in the higher range.

Many different factors could prompt a high temperature in your Pug, including exercise, excitement, hot weather, or disease.

Checking anal glands

If you notice your Pug scooting his bottom along the carpet, it means that his anal glands are uncomfortable. The anal glands are two small scent glands, which lie on either side of the anus. Normally, they empty on their own every time your dog defecates.

Continually check the glands to see if they're swollen. Your veterinarian can clean them by expressing the glands and may prescribe an antibiotic to clear the infection. You can also clean the glands, but you have to ask your veterinarian or groomer to show you how to express them. It's a smelly operation, so be prepared to hold your nose! You can do the job in the bathtub with or without bathing him.

Another (easier) way to empty the glands is to try giving your Pug a tablespoon of canned pumpkin once a day in his food for one to three days. The roughage in the pumpkin may do the trick without your having to manually clean them.

Putting Together a First-Aid Kit

You never know when your Pug will have an emergency and you need some first-aid items. The following list shows you how to assemble a first-aid kit that you can keep at home or take along when you take your Pug on the road.

Be sure to keep the kit in a location you can get to easily, such as an unlocked drawer or cupboard. The kit should also be portable so you can bring it to your Pug. Keep the kit tightly closed so everything inside stays clean and dry. Either a plastic container with a tight-fitting lid or a fishing tackle box works great for this purpose.

The following list explains what you want to assemble for the first-aid kit:

- **Your veterinarian's phone number or the phone number of a veterinarian in the city you're visiting:** In an emergency, you may not remember where you've listed the number.

- **Phone number of the after-hours emergency clinic:** It helps to have it handy if you need it.

- **ASPCA Animal Poison Control Center's phone number:** 888-426-4435.

- **Three large plastic garbage bags:** These can protect your car upholstery and household furnishings from blood, urine, and feces.

- **Digital thermometer:** In case you have to take Puggy's temperature.

- **Rubbing alcohol:** To clean the thermometer prior to using it and again afterward.

- **Small flashlight:** In case of a power outage or if there's not enough light to see a problem spot that your Pug may have.

- **Hydrogen peroxide:** For cleaning wounds and wiping away blood.

- **Antibiotic ointment:** To use in a wound after it's been cleaned.

- **Sterile cotton balls, rolled cotton, or cotton strips:** These items help with ear cleaning or wiping out a wound.

- **Ear cleaner:** This product can be part of routine care.

- **Sterile gauze pads:** To stop bleeding and cover wounds.

- **Nonstick adhesive tape or Vet wrap:** These are more comfortable than ordinary tape that sticks to hair. These keep gauze bandages in place.

- **Small scissors:** To cut the bandages.

- **Benadryl:** Yep, this is the same human medication used in case of bee stings and spider bites. You can use it on your Pug if he's scratching or sneezing uncontrollably. Be sure to consult with your veterinarian before giving it, though.

- **Anti-diarrhea liquid:** But if the diarrhea lasts more than a day, see your vet.

- **Clean washcloth, dishcloth, or towels:** To wash any wounds.

Getting Fixed — Definitely!

Maybe you think you'd like a puppy from your Pug. But the fact is that dogs have litters, so you're left with several puppies to find good homes for. Having a litter is a huge responsibility that not everyone can handle. Unless you're showing your dog and are a conscientious reputable breeder, I suggest that all Pugs be spayed or neutered so they don't make puppies.

Female Pugs get *spayed,* and male Pugs get *neutered.* The terminology is different based on the dog's gender, but both words refer to the same thing — sterilizing your dog.

Way too many puppies are born every year whom no one wants. By spaying or neutering your Pug, you help alleviate this problem. These puppies wind up in shelters that are bursting at the seams because they have to take care of more dogs than they have room for. The result? In some places, dogs who aren't adopted within a few days must be killed.

A second reason to sterilize your dog is that it's healthier. Females have less risk of developing breast cancer, especially if they're spayed before the first time they have a heat cycle, which is around 6 months of age. Males who are neutered are protected from prostate and cancer problems later in life. (Males need to be neutered by the time they're 1 year old.)

Another reason to sterilize your male Pug is that it makes him a calmer pet who isn't always thinking about where his next date is coming from. If you're worried that sterilizing your male may make him sluggish, let me set your mind at ease. Without all those raging hormones surging through his body, he can focus on whatever job you choose to give him and can concentrate on behaving himself.

Another reason to spay your female Pug is that an unspayed female is fertile, also known as *being in season,* for about 21 days, twice a year. During this time, she drips blood all over the house. Who needs this? Only an experienced reputable breeder.

Identifying Your Pug

Having your Pug properly identified is the best way to protect him in case he becomes separated from you. Unfortunately, your Pug can't keep his ID in a pants pocket or a handbag. It has to be firmly attached to the dog.

Using a tag

The easiest way to let everyone know who your Pug is, is to attach a tag with your address and phone number on it to your dog's collar. Many different kinds of tags in all different shapes, sizes, and colors are available. You can find imprinted tags in pet supply stores, over the Internet, and through mail-order catalogs that sell dog supplies.

Check the imprint on the tag to make sure that it hasn't worn thin and become too difficult to read. If you move or change your phone number, don't forget to update the tag. Also, check the collar to make sure that it hasn't stretched out of shape or that the snap or buckle isn't broken.

After your Pug has his rabies vaccine, you can get his license through your local county animal control department. That office can also give you an ID tag with your dog's county registration number imprinted on it. Your Pug then has two tags and two ways for you to track him down.

Microchipping

A microchip is a permanent identification that goes with your Pug wherever he goes. Each microchip has a unique code that identifies the dog's owner. The microchip is about the size of a raw grain of rice and is implanted by a veterinarian into the top of Puggy's shoulder blades. Microchipping is a pain-less procedure that's perfectly safe and lasts forever.

When a scanner is passed over your Pug's shoulders, the dog's ID number automatically appears in the readout. Most shelters and veterinarians have a microchip scanner, which makes it easy to locate the owner.

Even if your dog is microchipped, use a collar and tag on your Pug as a backup plan.

Tattooing — but not at a parlor

Another way to identify your Pug is to have him tattooed. No, I'm not saying you should take him to some sleazy, creepy place to have "I Love My Owner" tattooed inside a large red heart on his shoulder. Tattooing is a permanent and fairly painless way of keeping a number on your dog so that you can identify him if he gets lost.

You can choose where you want the number tattooed on your Pug, but most people choose the inside of the thigh or the back leg. You can also choose any number that you can remember. A popular choice is your dog's American Kennel Club registration number.

If your Pug gets lost, and I hope that never happens, someone can look at that number and contact the AKC to find out who Puggy belongs to. Hopefully, he's registered with the American Kennel Club.

Chapter 14

Dealing with Signs of Sickness

- -

In This Chapter

▶ Demystifying inherited diseases

▶ Spotting skin problems

▶ Getting rid of parasites

▶ Dealing with emergencies

▶ Handling common ailments

- -

It would be great if nothing bad ever happened to your sweet little Pug, but that's not realistic. Sometimes even with the best of care, your Pug may come down with a health problem or two. In this chapter, I talk about the various diseases your dog can inherit and how to get rid of common parasites.

At least with nasty pests, you can take precautions to prevent the problem. But with emergencies, you have to act quickly and rush Puggy to the veterinarian, so I also explain when you need to do that. And sometimes your Pug just needs first aid and a little TLC, and I discuss those instances, as well.

Recognizing Inherited Diseases

Generally, Pugs are healthy dogs. But just like people, dogs can inherit diseases from their relatives. Defective genes can be passed from generation to generation, with some diseases being more common than others.

Being aware of what the health problems are can help you be on the lookout for them. Armed with the information in the following sections, you can seek medical help for your Puggy right away or know what you can do to possibly prevent a health problem.

Head- or brain-related conditions

If you look at a Pug's head, you see that she has a flat, smooshed-in face with a pushed-in nose. Although a Pug's head is generally regarded as being one of the Pug's most recognizable (and cutest) features, it's also responsible for many of a Pug's health problems.

Idiopathic epilepsy

Idiopathic epilepsy is a problem not only for Pugs but 35 or more other dog breeds, too. This disorder, which causes repeated seizures, is one of the most common diseases of the nervous system. The seizures aren't due to any other problem and just seem to crop up out of the blue.

When a Pug has a seizure caused by epilepsy, her entire body may become rigid, and she has uncontrolled jerking and head shaking. She may also look like she's shivering and having trouble standing up. Snapping at the air or foaming at the mouth may be other symptoms. Diagnosing the disease is a challenge for veterinarians because these signs may also signal other disorders.

Veterinarians often try to manage or minimize seizures by giving a Pug *anti-convulsant drugs* (medication that helps stop her from having convulsions), which she has to take for the rest of her life.

Pug Dog Encephalitis (PDE)

Pug encephalitis is a specific type of brain inflammation that progresses quickly until it's fatal. Fortunately, it's a fairly rare disease. Veterinary researchers don't know what causes this disease, although they believe it may be inherited, but that has yet to be proven. The disease strikes both males and females equally.

The disease doesn't occur very often, but when it does, it usually strikes young adult Pugs (though a few 4-month-old puppies have been diagnosed with Pug encephalitis).

The first sign that a Pug has encephalitis is neck pain before the onset of seizures. Behavior changes, such as pressing the head against stationary objects and continually turning in circles in one direction, are the next signs. Puggy may become lethargic, depressed, and even blind. Unfortunately, there's no treatment for encephalitis after it begins. Pugs can linger with symptoms of PDE for a few weeks, but they have a reduced quality of life.

Eye diseases

Four eye problems commonly plague Pugs — keratoconjunctivitis sicca (KCS), pigmentary keratitis (PK), entropion, and cataracts.

Researching Pug health

Over the years, veterinary researchers have worked very hard to find the answers to eliminating the hereditary defects that Pugs and other breeds have. A complete solution can't happen overnight, however. Some genetic problems can't be bred out 100 percent, but reputable conscientious breeders do make every effort to work toward eliminating defects in their own breeding program.

Many breeders donate funds to support research and to share information about their own pedigrees and health. The Pug Dog Club of America

(PDCA) is also eager to identify and provide funds for research on health issues that affect the breed. Club members have collected DNA samples of healthy Pugs so that researchers in the future may be able to design genetic tests that show whether a Pug is a carrier or is free of specific diseases.

KCS and PK are common eye diseases in Pugs, and they cause diminished sight or blindness. Pugs as young as 4 months can develop these eye problems, although they typically happen in young to middle-aged dogs.

Keratoconjunctivitis sicca

Your Pug could have *keratoconjunctivitis sicca,* or dry eye, for many reasons — a drug reaction, an autoimmune problem, a virus, or it's just present at birth. With dry eye, the tear ducts are blocked, and when the Pug sleeps, the eye doesn't close all the way, which causes the cornea to dry out.

A Pug with KCS has dull eyes with a thick, stringy discharge. Infection soon sets in, and the mucous membrane covering the eyeball becomes red and inflamed. KCS begins slowly, and you may not even notice it until it gets worse or your veterinarian happens to find it during a routine physical.

Unfortunately, there is no cure for KCS, but treatment is available (see the next section for details).

Pigmentary keratitis

When dark spots begin to spread across the eye's surface, it causes an inflammatory condition of the cornea called *pigmentary keratitis* (PK). PK happens as a result of KCS.

Neither KCS nor PK can be cured, but they can be arrested, with some eyesight restored. The drug *cyclosporine* seems to stimulate tear production, and some veterinary ophthalmologists prescribe steroids. In a severe case, a surgery that peels off the pigmented layers of the eye may help restore eyesight completely.

Once a week, look closely at your Pug's eyes. You shouldn't see any cloudy or dark layers across the cornea. But if you do, take Puggy to your veterinarian as soon as possible so that he or she can prescribe medical therapy. The sooner a Pug receives treatment, the sooner her eyesight may be saved. In fact, Pug owners should have their Pugs' eyes tested every year by a veterinary ophthalmologist or their regular veterinarian.

Entropion

Entropion occurs when a Pug's eyelid naturally rolls inward toward the eye instead of away from it. As a result, the dog's eyelid hairs and eyelashes rub up against the cornea, injuring the thin layer of tears that protects the cornea. They scratch the cornea itself, causing irritation and possible blindness.

Entropion is an inherited eye defect that can be fixed. However, early detection is important. If you catch it early enough, it can be corrected by minor surgery or treated with medication. If entropion is left untreated, it leads to blindness.

The early signs of entropion include the following:

- ✔ Squinting
- ✔ Stained hair below your Pug's eyes
- ✔ Excessive tearing

Cataracts

A *cataract* is a white or yellowish spot of any size on the lens of the eye that impairs your Pug's vision. A dog can either be born with a cataract or acquire it, if she has diabetes. Many adult dogs with cataracts adapt well to gradual vision loss and don't show that they're bothered too much by it as long as everything at home is kept in the same place and they know where the obstacles are. Puppies have more of a problem with cataracts, as they are visually handicapped.

Cataracts can be removed with surgery. A new clear plastic lens replaces the defective eye lens, and vision returns to normal.

Hip, leg, and knee problems

Pugs and many Toy breeds are susceptible to having bone and joint diseases in their lower limbs. These diseases, which I discuss in the following sections, can be due to hereditary factors, although physical stress on the joints or trauma can aggravate a condition.

Hip dysplasia

Hip dysplasia is a crippling defect that occurs when the head of the thigh bone doesn't fit well into the socket in the hip. The not-quite-right fit causes slippage of the head of the thigh bone and joint inflammation. Eventually, a dog with hip dysplasia becomes arthritic.

When a dog has symptoms of hip dysplasia, she may limp or put more weight on one leg than on another, although no one knows when a Pug with dysplasia will begin limping. Environmental factors, such as how many calories a dog eats, the type of exercise she gets, and the weather, determine how severe the pain is. Because every dog reacts to the pain differently, some dysplastic dogs with severe arthritis are very active, and you'd never guess they have discomfort, while others who are only mildly affected are severely lame.

Overfeeding your young Pug while she's still growing may increase the chances that Puggy will develop hip dysplasia. See Chapter 7 for more information about proper feeding of your Pug.

A few breeders get X-rays taken of the male and female they're considering breeding together to make sure their hips are not dysplastic. Although parent dogs with normal hips may produce offspring with hip dysplasia, the chances of that happening are slim.

The Orthopedic Foundation for Animals (OFA) maintains a registry of all dogs whose X-ray results have been submitted for their evaluation. Puppies have to be 2 years old before hip X-rays reveal the defect. The hips are rated excellent, good, or fair. You can check the OFA Web site at www.offa.org to see if any of your Pug's relatives have had their hips X-rayed and if the results are recorded.

If your Pug is limping, take her to your veterinarian, who can X-ray her hips. Surgery can be performed to correct the problem if it's serious enough.

Patellar luxation

Patellar luxation, or dislocated kneecaps, is a common problem in Pugs and in many other small and Toy breeds. It's also known as *slipped stifles, loose kneecaps,* or *luxating patellas.* Pug puppies as young as 5 to 8 weeks can have patellar luxation, but it also occurs in older dogs.

Dogs' knees are in the middle of their back legs, and the kneecap is in front of the knee. The kneecap is a flat, flexible bone that slides up and down on a groove that's located in the long upper bone of the thigh bone. This groove gives the leg flexibility so that the knee can either straighten out or bend. If the groove isn't deep enough, the patella can't easily slide up and down, so it pops up and out of place.

Patellar luxation is an inherited problem. A veterinarian can detect the problem after feeling the dog's kneecaps and taking an X-ray. Four different levels of the defect exist:

- ✔ **Grade 1 luxations:** These are the least severe, and the dog seldom has any problems.

- ✔ **Grade 2 luxations:** These may cause the knee to lock up, and the dog occasionally skips a step but doesn't have any pain.

- ✔ **Grade 3 luxations:** At this point, the Pug's kneecap shifts to the inside and is pushed back into place, but it doesn't stay there. The Pug may or may not be lame, but her gait doesn't look normal because she doesn't fully extend her legs and keeps them flexed. Surgery is recommended.

- ✔ **Grade 4 luxations:** This rating means the dog has some serious skeletal changes. At this stage, the Pug may limp severely. Surgery can correct the problem.

Owners can't do much to prevent patellar luxations from happening, although with grades 1 or 2, keeping the Pug at a normal weight may reduce joint trauma and pressure on the kneecaps.

Veterinarians can examine dogs for patellar luxation and send the results on to the Orthopedic Foundation for Animals, which maintains a registry of this information. Dogs must be at least12 months old before the results of the exam can be certified.

Legg-Calve-Perthes

Many Toy breeds besides Pugs have Legg-Calve-Perthes (LCP) disease, an inherited skeletal disorder of the hip joints. This disorder causes the head of the thigh bone to begin disintegrating over time. Pugs usually experience this disorder as youngsters, between the ages of 6 months and 1 year. It's very painful and makes Puggy limp. If left untreated, arthritis sets in.

Unlike hip dysplasia, which causes arthritis in both the socket and thigh bone, LCP causes degeneration — total destruction — of the thigh bone, with the socket untouched. LCP usually affects only one side but may affect both hips.

Your veterinarian can take X-rays to confirm the diagnosis and perform surgery to repair the problem.

Identifying Pug Skin Problems

No breed is ever completely free of skin problems, and the Pug is no different. But with the proper diagnosis, care, and treatment, the problems can usually be managed or eliminated.

If your Pug has an unpleasant body odor and you see her scratching herself excessively, chewing her paws, or constantly licking areas of her body, she likely has a skin problem.

The first step in treating your Pug's skin condition is to take her to your veterinarian for an evaluation. The vet can diagnose the problem and probably suggest ways to treat it, including medication, a medicated shampoo, or a change in your Pug's diet. Your veterinarian may also refer you to a veterinary dermatology specialist who can pinpoint the problem.

Skin problems that make your dog hypersensitive to substances in the environment can be inherited. On the other hand, dogs who don't inherit this tendency can probably withstand environmental elements without having coat problems. The environmental factors that cause some Pugs to develop skin problems include allergies to flea bites, dust or mold pollens, or even hot, humid weather. If your Pug has an allergy, her immune system reacts by releasing substances that make her skin itch and look red or greasy. Pugs can scratch themselves so much that the hair on their coats can actually fall out.

To find out what kind of skin problem your Pug has and how to treat it, take Puggy to a veterinary dermatologist who may decide that testing for the specific causes of the problem is a good idea. Some of the tests or procedures that your doctor may choose to do include:

✔ Examining the crust of an infected area to look for yeast overgrowth

✔ Growing a culture of the hair to look for ringworm

✔ Injecting various substances into the dog's skin to see if any of them cause a reaction

✔ Performing a skin biopsy on a tumor to determine whether it's benign or malignant

✔ Plucking hairs and examining them under a microscope to look for evidence of a fungal infection

✔ Running blood tests or a urinalysis to determine if there is thyroid disease, which may cause a skin problem

✔ Scraping the skin to check for mites

These tests narrow down the causes so your veterinarian can prescribe treatment. Treatments can include the following:

✔ Allergy shots

✔ Antibiotics

✔ Antifungal medication

✔ Antihistamines

✔ Dietary supplements

✔ Steroids

✔ Shampoos and dips

Allergies

Some Pugs come down with allergies according to what season it is. During one time of the year, they can get itchy and sometimes chew their feet. The problem expands throughout the whole year. After testing, a veterinary dermatologist can prescribe antihistamines, steroids, and special shampoos. Allergy shots may help, too. Pugs don't usually have food allergies, but your veterinarian may suggest that you try feeding her a hypoallergenic diet.

Demodectic mange

Pug puppies and some adults are prone to mange. (It's known to run in families sometimes.) *Demodectic mange* is an invasion of canine mites on the skin. If a Pug has a strong immune system, the system fights off these mites. If the Pug's immune system is somewhat weak, these mites multiply and remain as long as possible on the Pug's skin.

With demodectic mange, your dog loses hair, develops skin eruptions, and has secondary bacterial infections that make her itch. On the surface, this mange gives the coat a moth-eaten appearance, and a Pug can look bald, in spots. Puppies as young as 4 months can come down with a case of demodectic mange, although this skin problem can occur as late as 18 months.

If you see small spots on your Pug's face or body that have thin hair or no hair at all, take your dog to the veterinarian for an examination as soon as possible. Your veterinarian can diagnose it with a deep skin scraping. It's not contagious, but your vet may want to prescribe an oral medication or a medicated dip that you can bathe your dog in to kill the mites.

Although some cases of demodectic mange clear up by themselves, other cases can become a serious problem. If you see these bald spots crop up early enough, you can save your Pug's coat from going bald.

Staph infections

Staph looks like pimples or lesions on a Pug's skin. The hair follicles are infected, and the pimples can look like hives with the hair sticking up on the bumps. Where there isn't any hair, the lesions resemble ringworm (see the next section for details about ringworm). Oral antibiotics and a medicated shampoo can clear up a staph infection.

Ringworm

Ringworm is a fungus that grows on the skin. Ringworm begins in warm, humid weather and is transmitted to other dogs and people. It starts by invading the outer layers of the skin, nails, and hair, and subsists on the protein from shedding skin cells. It can go into remission 1 to 3 months after it begins.

Ringworm has a very distinctive look to it — a circle that's ½ inch to 2 inches in diameter with patchy hair loss. The whole area appears scabby. If you notice something like this on your Pug, ask your veterinarian to examine it. He can prescribe a topical or oral antifungal medication for your dog.

To help get rid of ringworm, clean your floors with a mild bleach solution or other household disinfectant, professionally clean your upholstered furniture if your dog was sitting on it, and dispose of your dog's bedding. Without disinfecting your environment, the problem may spread to both humans and other animals.

Yeast infections

If your Pug is very itchy, has an odor, and has blackened, thickened skin, she may be suffering from a yeast infection. Pugs who had a staph infection and were treated with antibiotics are prone to getting yeast infections. The drugs kill off the bacteria, and then the yeast moves in.

Puggy can have yeast infections in her armpits, feet, and under her neck. If she has a yeast infection in her ears, you smell something foul, and her ears have a heavy wax buildup. Your veterinarian can diagnose the problem by doing skin scrapings and ear swabs. Your vet can also give you special anti-yeast medications and medicated shampoos to rid Puggy of yeast.

Eliminating Parasites

It may not be pleasant to think about, but Pugs can get parasites — those nasty little freeloading organisms that sponge off your dog and weaken her system. Are they fun? No. Are they preventable? Sometimes. The good news is that there are some ways to ward them off and keep Puggy pest-free.

Preventing fleas and ticks

If you're lucky enough to live in a desert climate like Las Vegas that's hot and dry, you don't have to worry about your Pug getting fleas. Everywhere else, particularly in the hot, humid southern states like Florida, and also in California, fleas have a party and live it up on dogs every day of the year.

When Pugs have fleas, they scratch and scratch to get rid of them and end up tearing at their own hair, leaving red blotches on the skin. These blotches are wet and painful to Puggy, and all the hair around those areas eventually falls out. The problem usually crops up quickly on the head and neck, and along the lower back and thighs. Within hours of being bitten by a flea, a Pug loses hair.

Flea problems only get worse because the little devils multiply faster than you can say, "Puggy's got an itch!" To wipe them out, you need to mount a triple threat attack by treating the dog, her bedding, and the entire household, including the yard. If your Pug goes for car rides, you have to eliminate fleas there, too. Fleas live in the carpet, grass, or bedding and hop off and on your dog whenever they want a meal. They lay eggs, which hatch quickly, and grow up to feast on Puggy as soon as they mature.

One way to get rid of fleas permanently is to interrupt the flea life cycle. Ask your veterinarian to give you a monthly prescription flea tablet for Puggy. The good news is that this medication sterilizes the fleas so they can't reproduce. The bad news is that the fleas and any eggs they laid hang around for another two or three weeks until they die. You can also apply a few drops of an adulticide flea treatment between Puggy's shoulder blades year-round. This kills the fleas that hop on your Pug before they're able to take a bite.

On the same day that you kill fleas on Puggy, be sure to wash all Puggy's bedding and clean any upholstered furniture she usually sits on, vacuum all carpet and floor areas, and spray the yard with a flea insecticide.

Ticks are another story. They like wooded areas, or even tall grass and leafy plants, and they love to leap onto dogs' bodies and embed themselves into their skin. Ticks can give Puggy severe diseases, such as Lyme disease.

Avoid letting your Pug go near areas that may be tick-infested. If you do, run your fingers over her entire body, including her ears, head, and toes, to search for ticks. If you find any, be sure to remove the head carefully with tweezers, rubber gloves, or a tissue. A tick doesn't care if it bites a dog or a human to cause infection.

Warding off heartworms

Of all the internal parasites, heartworms are the deadliest. Mosquito bites can transmit heartworm disease, which is fatal, if not treated. Talk to your veterinarian about the presence of heartworms in the area where you live and if he feels that it's necessary to give heartworm prevention to your Pug. Some veterinarians recommend heartworm prevention in the summer months when more mosquitoes are out.

Although it helps to keep Puggy out of mosquito-ridden areas, you should also give her a daily or monthly medication to prevent heartworms. Before beginning any medication to prevent heartworms, your veterinarian should perform a blood test to determine if heartworms are already present. If so, he should prescribe a different medication.

Getting rid of other types of worms

Your Pug may also have to deal with roundworms, whipworms, tapeworms, or hookworms. These worms cause different symptoms in your Pug, ranging from mild discomfort to death.

Roundworms

These are the most common parasites, and they look like long strands of white spaghetti. Yuck! They show up in the feces of young puppies who get them from a contaminated environment or from their mother. Puppies can get very sick if they have lots of them, although if adults get roundworms, they can tolerate them.

A puppy with roundworms has a dull coat and a swollen belly, but she looks skinny. Look for diarrhea, vomiting, coughing, or pneumonia, and contact your veterinarian immediately if you think she has roundworms. Your veterinarian can prescribe a deworming medication for you to give Puggy. To keep roundworm infection out of your backyard, pick up feces promptly and deposit them in a sealed container.

Whipworms

Your Pug can get these parasites when she eats something that's been contaminated with whipworm eggs. Too many whipworms in your Pug's system can show up as anemia, diarrhea, and weight loss. Be sure to clean up fecal matter in the yard regularly to avoid contamination.

Tapeworms

If you ever see small, white segments that look like rice around your Pug's anus, these are dried-out tapeworms. When a dog takes a nip at an infected flea, she ingests the tapeworm egg. Once inside the dog's body, the tapeworm egg hatches. Rodents and dead animals have tapeworms, so don't ever let Puggy eat these things if she finds them.

Dogs with tapeworms usually have diarrhea, little or no appetite, and a dull coat. Your veterinarian can prescribe a deworming product.

Hookworms

Just like their name, these internal parasites are shaped like hooks about a quarter to a half-inch long. Grown dogs get them by stepping on contaminated feces or soil. Signs of hookworms in young puppies are anemia and bloody or black diarrhea, and the parasites can be fatal to puppies.

If you suspect that your Pug has a type of worm, collect a fresh fecal sample and take it to your veterinarian. He can detect which worm is causing the problem and prescribe a deworming treatment to get rid of it.

Guarding against Giardia

Picture this scene. You're taking Puggy for a walk when suddenly you meet a friend on the street whom you haven't seen in a while. The two of you start talking, and while she's waiting, Puggy begins sniffing the ground and licking water from a puddle. About a week later, she has mucous diarrhea that won't go away and has lost weight. The culprit? Your Pug is infected with *Giardia,* a single-celled organism that she's picked up from the fecal-contaminated water she drank on your walk. She can also get Giardia by licking another dog's stool that's contaminated with it.

Your veterinarian can prescribe a course of treatment that will ease Puggy's discomfort.

Coping with coccidia

Pugs can also get *coccidia,* another one-celled organism, by eating stools that contain it. I know, I know, that's pretty gross! Puppies who live in crowded situations such as pet shops, kennels, commercial breeders, and animal shelters have a higher chance of getting coccidia through contaminated food or water. A dog with coccidia may have some of these signs:

- Bloating
- Bloody stool
- Straining during elimination
- Vomiting
- Weight loss

Coccidia can be prevented by picking up and disposing of stools promptly and cleaning the kennel area with a strong ammonium hydroxide solution. Your veterinarian can diagnose coccidia quickly and treat it with sulfa drugs.

Handling Emergencies

Sometimes you can't tell whether a medical problem is an emergency or something that will just go away on its own. When in doubt, call your veterinarian. If it's a true emergency, the people at the vet's office may be able to give you some suggestions on what you can do to help Puggy in the meantime, especially if you have to move her.

If Puggy has any of the conditions I discuss in the following sections, transport her to the veterinarian immediately:

Poisoning

Pugs are curious creatures, so it's not surprising if your dog investigates things that aren't good for her. Because she's small, just a small amount of a toxic substance can be fatal.

Go through your home, yard, and garage to make sure that the following products are locked away or stored up high, where your Pug can't reach them:

- ✔ Alcohol

- ✔ Automotive products (antifreeze is lethal)

- ✔ Cleaning products (toilet-bowl cleaner is lethal)

- ✔ Cold pills, allergy medication, antidepressants, and vitamins

- ✔ Flea and tick products

- ✔ Garden pesticides

- ✔ Human pain-relieving medications, such as aspirin

- ✔ Rat and mouse poison

- ✔ Tobacco products

Also remember to keep the lid on the trash cans and keep all spoiled foods out of your Pug's reach. And although you can't do much to prevent a snake, a scorpion, or a spider from biting Puggy, these creatures have poisonous venom that can be deadly.

If you think your dog has ingested a poisonous substance or has received a poisonous bite, watch for signs of vomiting, bloody diarrhea, or tremors. She may also have breathing difficulties, excessive salivation, or a nosebleed. If she has any of these, transport her to a veterinarian immediately.

If you have any questions about poisoning, call the American Society for the Prevention of Cruelty to Animals (ASPCA) Animal Poison Control Center at 888-426-4435. This nonprofit 24/7 number operates 365 days a year. Depending on the problem, there may be a $45 consultation fee you can charge to your credit card. After hearing what the problem is, the center can provide information over the phone, fax you instructions on how you can help your dog at home, or tell you whether you need to take your Pug to your veterinarian immediately.

Seizures

No doubt about it: A seizure is frightening the first time you see it. It starts when your dog gets a strange look in her eyes, and then her legs begin jerking uncontrollably, or her head begins shaking. The dog is unable to walk and can't respond to anything you say to her. She also may collapse.

What do you do? Unfortunately, there isn't much you can do while she's having a seizure, but stay close by and comfort her and make sure that she doesn't fall and hurt herself. Dogs don't swallow their tongues, so you don't have to worry about that. The seizure itself may last only a few seconds, but it may seem more like hours to you because your Pug seems to be in pain.

Keep your hands away from your dog's mouth when she's having a seizure. She could bite you without meaning to.

When the seizure ends, let her recuperate and take her outdoors. She may need to relieve herself. Call your veterinarian immediately and take Puggy for an examination.

Although one seizure isn't life-threatening, repeated seizures can be fatal. Your veterinarian can advise you.

Steady bleeding

It's easier said than done, but if your dog is bleeding a lot, don't panic! Get a clean dishtowel, hold it firmly against the wound for 30 seconds, and then wrap it around the wound. If Puggy is thrashing around, attach a leash to her collar so you can guide her movement more easily. Transport her to your veterinarian as quickly as possible.

Overheating

Pugs are especially prone to becoming overheated or getting heatstroke, which can be fatal. If the temperature climbs above Puggy's own natural body temperature at about 101 degrees Fahrenheit, she may get heatstroke. High humidity and temperatures in the mid-80s are also dangerous conditions.

To keep your Pug cool, stand her on top of some wet towels or inside a pool of cool water. If she likes ice chips, give her a few of those. You can also rub the inside of her gums or the inside of her thigh with ice chips. You can also use your car's air-conditioning or a portable fan to cool Puggy off in a hurry.

Dealing with Common Pug Problems

Not all health problems that Puggy has are dire emergencies. In this section, I address some everyday ailments that your Pug may experience.

Bordatella (kennel cough)

At least once in Puggy's life, she'll cough. Unless it's nonstop, it's not a big deal. But keep in mind that Pugs are prone to *reverse sneezing* where they forcefully suck in air. Although it seems like they're gasping or choking, they're really just clearing their sinus or nasal passages and quiet down after a few minutes.

Don't confuse this with repeated bouts of coughing and gasping, which could mean that Puggy has *bordatella,* or kennel cough, a highly contagious respiratory disease that dogs get from other dogs at kennels or dog shows. Bordatella isn't usually serious, but your veterinarian can prescribe cough suppressants to calm it.

If you're taking Puggy to a kennel, or she's going to be around a lot of dogs, be sure she has a bordatella vaccine once every six months. The kennel requires proof that this has been done before it accepts her. I talk about the bordatella vaccine more in Chapter 13.

Diarrhea

One or two loose stools don't mean that Puggy has a serious case of diarrhea. In fact, if they're followed by a normal bowel movement and she seems okay otherwise, she's probably just fine. Sometimes loose stools just happen.

However, more than one or two may require a change in diet to quiet her bowels. They're probably in an uproar because she's eating a different food, the water source is different, she's had too much to eat, or she's nervous.

Call your veterinarian and report your Pug's symptoms. He may suggest that you bring in a stool sample to be analyzed and then bring your Pug in for an exam. In the meantime, you can do the following:

- Discontinue feeding Puggy her regular kibble.
- Give her small amounts of cottage cheese and rice to eat.
- Make sure that she continues to drink water so that she doesn't become dehydrated.
- Give her some over-the-counter antidiarrhea medication recommended by your veterinarian.

Vomiting

If Puggy has no symptoms, other than one or two bouts of vomiting, it's probably not too serious. In fact, all Pugs may vomit occasionally in their lifetimes. It can happen for the following reasons:

✔ Gulping too much water

✔ Chewing sharp blades of grass that irritate the throat lining

✔ Eating something that disagrees with her

If your dog is vomiting, you can take some steps to help her. When feeding times come around, skip her regular food and let her stomach rest for 24 hours without any food. Then give her a very small meal of boiled rice and boiled chicken. If that stays down after one or two meals, add in her regular food by the third meal. If that food doesn't stay down, call your veterinarian immediately.

If Puggy is less than 1 year old or older than 8 or 9 years and she can't keep any food or water down, contact your veterinarian right away. Persistent vomiting means that your Pug has a severe disease, especially when she has other signs, such as lethargy, pain, fever, and loss of appetite.

Chapter 15

Keeping Your Pug Busy

In This Chapter

▶ Encouraging your Pug to try new things

▶ Introducing obedience and agility competitions

▶ Becoming a therapy dog

▶ Getting your Pug together with the kids for some quality time

*H*ow exciting! Your Pug has caught on to your routine and knows how to mind his p's and q's around the house. Now's the perfect time for you to introduce him to some more challenging activities, such as obedience training, agility tests, or visiting hospital-bound patients. Participating in these activities gives your Pug some important jobs to do and the chance to flex his brainpower. In this chapter, I talk about a few activities that you (and even the kids) can get involved in with your Pug.

Motivating Your Pug

If you think that you have to do a lot of fast-talking to convince your Pug to get involved in some new activities, guess again. Pugs are always ready for a good time. They love a challenge and eagerly approach new adventures with curiosity and wonder. Your Pug's desire to gain new skills increases when he sees that you're upbeat and happy about the experience. He picks up on your being pleased and wants to make you happy.

Handing out food rewards and giving your Pug plenty of verbal praise always help when you get started with any new training. What's verbal praise? When your Pug hears you say in a happy voice, "What a good boy!" or "That a way, fella!" Plus, when he realizes that he gets something yummy when he does what you want, he'll do whatever he can to get another one.

Becoming a Good Citizen

You know that your Pug acts like a good dog around the house, but if you're wondering how well he can behave around strangers in public, prepare him to take the Canine Good Citizen (CGC) test. Sponsored by the American Kennel Club, the CGC test evaluates how well a dog can master certain elements of good behavior and how he may handle situations that he may encounter in real life. With only a small amount of training that you can do at home, any dog can pass this test.

To be dubbed a Canine Good Citizen, dogs must show that they can do the following with their leash on:

- **Accept a friendly stranger:** Your Pug needs to allow a friendly stranger to walk up to you, begin a conversation, and shake your hand. Your Pug must stay close to you and not try to protect you or shy away.

- **Sit politely for petting:** Your Pug must allow a friendly stranger to pet his head and body. You can talk to your dog throughout the exercise, but he can't act shy, aggressive, or resentful.

- **Sit politely for grooming:** In this test, your Pug demonstrates that he can be easily examined and handled by a stranger. The evaluator lightly brushes or combs your Pug and lightly examines the ears and gently picks up each front foot.

- **Walk on a loose leash:** Here, you demonstrate control of your Pug. You don't want him to pull you on the leash. Your dog is on one side of you as you go for a short walk. You must make one left turn, one right turn, one about turn, one stop during the middle of the test, and another stop at the end.

- **Walk through a crowd:** This test shows that your Pug can walk through a crowd under control. You and your Pug must pass close to at least three people, and although your dog can show some interest in the strangers, he must continue to walk with you without being shy or too exuberant. You can praise your dog, but he can't pull on the leash.

- **Sit and lie down on command, staying in place:** Your Pug has to show that he knows the basic commands to sit and lie down. Then you have to tell your dog to stay before you walk down a 20-foot line away from your Pug and then turn around and come back.

- **Come when called:** Puggy has to come when you call him. You walk 10 feet away from him, turn to face him, and then call him. He must come when called.

- **React appropriately to another dog:** This test involves a second handler with another dog on a leash 10 yards away. You and the other handler stop and shake hands, talk a few minutes, and then walk past each other for 5 yards. Both dogs should be slightly interested in one another but must stay next to their handlers' sides without acting shy or aggressive.

✔ **React well to distraction:** In this test, your Pug shows how confident he can be around distractions. The evaluator sets up some distractions, such as dropping a chair or having a jogger run in front of the dog. Your Pug can show some interest and be somewhat startled but shouldn't panic, try to run away, show aggression, or bark.

✔ **Behave during supervised separation:** Here, Puggy must remain with a trusted person. The owner goes out of sight for three minutes. Your Pug doesn't have to stay in place, but he shouldn't bark, howl, whine continually, pace, or act very nervous.

Many Pugs pass this test with flying colors, but don't worry if your Pug doesn't pass the first time. He can always take it again another day. Many training clubs and kennel clubs offer classes to help you prepare Puggy to pass this test. You have to be patient and practice a little every day, but the results are worth it.

Obeying Commands Competitively

If you enjoyed teaching your Pug how to Sit and Stay (I discuss such basic commands in Chapter 11), consider participating in obedience competitions. The American Kennel Club began holding obedience competitions in 1936, and the exercises are basically the same today.

Every dog who enters can qualify for a title if he is properly trained and the handler doesn't make too many mistakes! In obedience, your Pug must complete exercises and earn a score that's at least 50 percent of the possible points (ranging from 20 to 40) and get a total score of at least 170 out of a possible 200. Each time your dog gets that magic 170 qualifying score, he gets a *leg* toward his title. Three legs earned at three different shows and Puggy becomes an obedience-titled dog!

These competitions can be a lot of fun for both you and your Pug. You can hone your training skills while teaching your Pug some practical behaviors that he can use throughout his lifetime (see Figure 15-1).

In preparation for competing, you need to take your Pug to classes. But don't worry because you can find a lot of obedience classes and instructors to train with. Sure, this instruction takes a lot of time and patience, but when you're building a bond with your Pug, it's worth it. For more information on finding classes and trainers, see Chapter 11.

There are three levels of titles, and each is more difficult than the one before it. The levels are divided into A and B at a trial; A classes are for beginners whose dogs have never received a title, and the B classes are for handlers who have put a title on a dog before.

Figure 15-1:
This well-behaved
Pug
watches his
owner for
the signal
to stand.

©Meg Callea

Earning a basic obedience title

The basic obedience title is the Companion Dog, or CD. The first level for the CD — Novice — means that your Pug can demonstrate the skills required of a good canine companion. The dog has to heel both on and off leash at different speeds, come when called, stay (still and quietly!) with a group of other dogs when told, and stand for a simple physical exam.

The American Kennel Club awards titles after a dog has successfully passed the requirements set for them. So, just as a doctor tacks an MD after his or her name, your Pug can add this distinction to his name, as well. Just imagine calling your dog Ranger's Perfect Wrinkle, CD. Sounds funny, but you can do it!

Dogs in AKC shows compete against themselves, not against other dogs.

Moving on to advanced degrees

After your Pug has earned his CD title, he can progress to advanced degrees — Companion Dog Excellent (CDX), Utility Dog (UD), and Utility Dog Excellent (UDX).

The second level, Open, is the Companion Dog Excellent (CDX) title. Here your Pug must do many of the same exercises as in Novice, but off leash and for longer periods. Additionally, he has to complete jumping and retrieving tasks. The final level is the Utility Dog (UD) title. In addition to more difficult exercises, the dog also must perform scent-discrimination tasks.

The best of the best dogs can go on for even more titles. Utility Dogs who place in Open B or Utility B classes earn points toward an Obedience Trial Champion (OTCH) title. Utility Dogs who continue to compete and earn legs in both Open B and Utility B at 10 shows receive the title Utility Dog Excellent (UDX).

Ready, Set, Go: Getting Agile in Agility

According to the American Kennel Club, agility is the fastest growing dog sport in the United States (fetch is a close second). But why is agility so popular? The answer's pretty simple: Agility is fun and exciting for dogs and their owners, and it provides an opportunity for them to participate in an activity together.

At an agility trial, dogs run, jump, and crawl through a fast-paced obstacle course. Working without a leash, you (the owner) run alongside your Pug or position yourself beside obstacles on the course and guide your dog through his paces (see Figure 15-2).

Each dog and handler team takes a turn on the course by themselves, and their performance is timed. The fastest times are eligible for a placement — first, second, third, or fourth.

An agility title follows the dog's registered name. These are the obstacles that Puggy must complete to earn an agility title:

- **Open tunnel:** Your Pug runs as fast as possible to the entrance of the tunnel from any angle and quickly runs through it.

- **Closed tunnel:** The dog runs to another tunnel at any angle and pushes through the chute at the other end.

- **Pause table:** Your Pug jumps onto a table and quickly sits or lies down when you give the command. He has to hold it five seconds and then spring from the table when the handler gives the next command.

- **Weave poles:** Your Pug must weave between a series of poles, going from side to side.

- **Dog wall:** The dog races up, across, and down a plank.

- **Seesaw:** Your Pug must maintain his balance on a seesaw.

- **Tire jump:** Puggy leaps through a tire.

- **A-frame:** Your Pug quickly runs up the panel of an A-frame obstacle, scrambles over the apex, and runs down, being sure to touch specific squares on the plank.

- **Jumps:** The dog jumps over a bar, panel, and a double or triple jump without knocking the bar or board down.

- **Broad jump:** Puggy leaps over the broad jump.

Dogs of all sizes and shapes can run an agility course. Officials raise or lower the equipment, depending on the size of the dog.

If you have a Pug who needs a dose of extra confidence, agility gives him just what he needs. When he realizes that he can climb the A-frame or go over a seesaw all by himself, he'll be very proud.

Starting off slowly

You and your Pug won't be running the course at your first session. Instead, you walk through the course once and introduce the obstacles to your Pug one at a time until he feels comfortable enough to run around and through them.

Figure 15-2: This Pug loves jumping and clearing the bar with room to spare.

©Meg Callea

Before beginning agility training, make sure that your Pug doesn't have any leg or foot injuries. Because he'll be running and jumping around the course, any injury he already has can only get worse. You don't have to take him to the veterinarian to be checked out unless you think your Pug has a foot problem.

In competition, the obstacles listed earlier are arranged in various patterns that are set by the judge. These patterns are always different from trial to trial. The difficulty of each course depends on what title you're going for. The beginning titles, which your Pug can receive fairly easily, are Novice Agility (NA) and Open Agility (OA).

The Novice class proves that the dog can complete the exercises on the equipment within a reasonable amount of time. In Open, the course gets more difficult with a few more twists and turns, but the exercises are the same as the Novice class. Passing the Open title requires split-second timing and teamwork between the handler and dog.

Advancing to the fancy stuff

After your Pug masters the basic agility course, he can graduate to the more difficult courses and obstacles and earn advanced titles: Agility Excellent (AX), Master Agility Excellent (MX), and Master Agility Champion (MACH). Of course, these courses take more time and patience to master. But what better way is there for your Pug to get out and have a blast?

Becoming a Therapy Pug

When people are hospitalized or move to assisted-living centers, they often have to leave their pets behind. But more and more health facilities today allow friendly, well-behaved dogs to visit patients. Besides cheering up residents, these special dog visits provide soothing company. For many patients, a visit from a friendly dog brings back wonderful memories of when they and their own dog lived in their own home.

Because a Pug is small and friendly, has an even disposition, and can take the strange sights, smells, and sounds of institutional settings in stride, he's a great candidate for a therapy dog. As a therapy dog, he'll be making hospital rounds visiting children and adults who are ill.

Being a therapy dog is a volunteer job, although your Pug needs some training before he can regularly see patients. You can find many pet therapy organizations with certified instructors throughout the United States who help prepare dog and owner teams for therapy work. Both male and female and purebred and mixed-breed Pugs are welcomed into programs.

Although every therapy organization has slightly different requirements for its visitors, many groups require dogs to have passed the American Kennel Club's Canine Good Citizen (CGC) test (see the section "Becoming a Good Citizen," earlier in the chapter, for more information). They also want dog and owner teams to visit with more experienced teams before they go into rooms on their own.

A Match Made in Heaven: Activities for Kids and Pugs

Pugs and kids are a natural match because both love to have a good time. In fact, something as simple as spending time together is a popular activity for Pugs and kids. Pugs are very content to be held, and they can wait patiently if their juvenile owner is busy (see Figure 15-3).

Figure 15-3: These Pugs enjoy hanging out with their young companion.

©Meg Callea

Pugs also make good listeners (see Figure 15-4) because they're never critical. No wonder children like them, huh?

But if you're looking for organized activities for the kids to do with your Pug, don't worry. You have plenty to choose from, including the two that I describe in the following sections.

REMEMBER

Be sure to take your child to observe these activities first before signing her up. She may not want to get involved in structured dog activities, wanting instead to play with your Pug at home to her heart's content.

Figure 15-4:
Pugs do anything to stay with their playmates — even listen to piano practice.

©Judi Crowe

Junior Showmanship

The American Kennel Club has special competitions for children ages 10 to 18, called Junior Showmanship. Here, children can show their Pugs in purebred dog shows. Unlike in adult dog shows, these junior dogs aren't judged on how they look. In junior competition, judges evaluate the children's skills at handling their dogs and working as a team, as shown in Figure 15-5. (For more information about adult dog shows, turn to Chapter 16.)

Pugs make excellent Junior Showmanship dogs. They're small enough for children to handle easily, they're willing to please their little owners by listening to and following directions, and they get along well with other dogs during competition.

Sure, preparing a Pug and his juvenile owner for Junior Showmanship takes some training, but both of them receive rewards for their efforts. Your Pug has a chance to show off what a good companion he can be, and your child can demonstrate how well he handles and cares for the dog.

Figure 15-5:
This youngster and her Pug are pretty proud of winning Best Junior Handler at an AKC show. What teamwork!

©Tony Nunes

Obedience, agility, therapy, and 4-H

If showing your dog to a championship in Junior Showmanship isn't up your child's alley, she can train your Pug to compete in obedience and agility trials and compete alongside adults when she's at least 8 years old.

She can also train Puggy to be a therapy dog. Can you imagine the joy on a bedridden patient's face when a child walks into her room with a Pug she can cuddle? Pugs also make excellent 4-H companions. In 4-H, children find out how to groom and train their dogs and how to exhibit them in competition.

Chapter 16

There's No Business Like (Dog) Show Business

. . . .

In This Chapter

▶ Seeing how dog shows operate

▶ Considering the pros and cons of showing your dog

▶ Training Puggy to be a show dog or getting help from a pro

▶ Traveling to the shows

. . . .

Maybe you've seen dog shows on television and can easily imagine your dog being a part of that scene. If you're wondering what having a show dog involves, this chapter fills you in.

First you train, and then you begin going to dog shows where, besides spending some quality time with Puggy, you also have the chance to see some of the best representatives of more than a hundred other breeds. In addition, going to dog shows gives you the opportunity to find out more about your dog's health, ancestry, and temperament. Breeders are more than willing to give advice and share information.

When you get your dog involved in competing against other Pugs, a whole new world opens up for you. I give you a snapshot of the experience in the next few pages.

Appreciating the Sport of Dog Showing

Dog shows were first held to choose breeding stock. Today's competitions also give special dogs a chance to earn the title of *champion*, or *Ch*.

What kind of Pug deserves to add Ch in front of her name? A Pug who's been specifically bred to look and act pretty much like her ancestors did in China centuries ago. Responsible show breeders devote many years to producing healthy and well-adjusted dogs who are good representatives of their breed. (In case you were wondering, yes, puppies can enter dog shows, beginning when they're 6 months old.)

To succeed in the show ring, your Pug must tolerate all the hoopla at a dog show — crowds, noise, people who want to pet your dog, and the rigors of travel. It's not just about being a pretty dog.

Comparing your Pug to the AKC standard

When you go to a show, you hear the phrase breed standard. The *breed standard* is the American Kennel Club's (AKC) standard for the Pug, which is a written description of all the attributes and physical features that a Pug should have. The standard also mentions how Puggy should gait in the show ring and points out that her personality should be even-tempered. A show Pug needs to be stable, playful, outgoing, and eager to show off her charm to the judges. See Chapter 3 for a full explanation of the breed standard.

Before you decide to enter your dog in a show, you want to evaluate her against the AKC standard. In fact, if you bought her from a breeder, it's a good idea to consult with your breeder, as well. Although you may have purchased a show-quality Pug puppy, dogs don't always grow up to look the way, even experienced breeders think they will. Mother Nature's just funny that way, I guess.

Sometimes a dog who starts out as a dynamite show prospect at 8 weeks of age develops an undesirable characteristic, such as light-colored or small eyes, which makes Puggy look more like a pet-quality dog. Hopefully your breeder has bred and owned many champions over the years and should be able to help you compare your mature Pug to the breed standard.

Even if you didn't buy your Pug from a breeder, you should still have her evaluated by one before you consider showing her. For names of reputable breeders, contact the AKC's breeder referral. You can find info on that service in Chapter 19.

If your breeder can't help you determine whether your Pug is show material, try asking Pug breeders whom you meet at dog shows. Although no dog is born perfect, you want your show Pug to come as close to the AKC standard as possible and measure up to adding that Ch to the front of her name.

Understanding how dogs are evaluated

For a dog to receive the title of champion from the American Kennel Club, she must compete against other dogs of the same breed and win a total of 15 points.

One through five points can be awarded at each show, and there is one judge who evaluates each dog. Two of your wins, called *majors,* must be worth three, four, or five points under two different judges. These points are awarded based on the number of dogs who are competing that day. The more dogs that enter, the more points. The number of dogs required for points varies with the breed, sex, and geographical location of the show. Each year the AKC makes up the schedule of points.

In the show ring, the judge evaluates all the dogs in the same breed to see how closely they resemble the AKC standard. In order for the judge to evaluate their bodies quickly, dogs must be trained to do the following:

- ✔ Walk and run on your left side without pulling you on the leash
- ✔ Stand and stay still

The hands-on examination is quick and includes the dog's teeth, head, and body. If a dog growls or bites the judge, she may be disqualified from showing.

This competition is subjective, which means that every judge may see your Pug differently. Pug beauty is in the eye of the beholder (or, in this case, the judge), and what one judge likes a lot about your dog, another judge on a different day may not.

Showing in a subjective competition may be confusing, especially when you're first starting out. With a different judge at every show, you may see a dog win one day and then lose the next. In fact, there's no written score, and the judge never tells you what he likes or doesn't like about your dog. The judge's job is to interpret the breed standard to the best of his ability. As a result, he may place more emphasis on some characteristics. It's your job to evaluate your own dog and see how well she conforms to the AKC standard.

Generally, however, a good dog is a good dog overall no matter who looks at it. A Pug can become a champion if she meets the following requirements:

- ✔ She fits the standard and has few or no undesirable characteristics.
- ✔ She's in good condition at the proper weight.
- ✔ She's happy, has a good attitude, and likes showing off in the ring.
- ✔ She's well-trained for the show ring.
- ✔ She's expertly presented to the judge.

The longer you watch Pugs at dog shows, the more you can discover about the dog game and what it takes to win.

After evaluating each entry, the judge chooses the following:

- ✔ Best male
- ✔ Best female
- ✔ Runner-up or reserve winner for each sex
- ✔ Best Pug overall, called Best of Breed
- ✔ Best of breed runner-up who's the opposite sex

Later in the day, the best of breed of every breed goes back into the ring to compete again against other dogs in the same group. Here are the seven groups:

- ✔ Sporting
- ✔ Hound
- ✔ Working
- ✔ Terrier
- ✔ Toy
- ✔ Non-Sporting
- ✔ Herding

Another judge evaluates the dogs in these groups and chooses a winner and three runners-up. For the last round of the show, each first-place winner in each group goes back into the ring to compete for the coveted Best in Show title. There's only one winner here.

If you really want your Pug to become a champion, don't take the results of the show personally. The judge doesn't know how much you love your dog, and that doesn't influence his decision. He just picks the best dog in the ring on that day.

Recognizing What's Involved in Showing Your Dog

If you know that you have a Pug with show potential, you may be wondering how much time and expense it takes for your Pug to earn her championship. Make no mistake, dog showing is a serious hobby. And, like all hobbies, it requires a good deal of time and money. If you become a good handler and your dog meets the AKC standard and likes showing, you can earn your dog's championship in a few months.

Although competing does take a commitment, I can tell you that it's well worth the effort. For example, the time you spend grooming and training your dog (not to mention traveling back and forth to dog shows) gives you a chance to build a bond with Puggy that can last a lifetime. Furthermore, while you're on the road with your Pug and hanging around the show ring, you have a chance to meet plenty of new people. Finding new friends who share your affinity for Pugs is another bonus of showing your dog.

If the folks you meet at a show have been showing longer than you have, they're bound to give you some good hints and tips about showing and training your Pug for the ring and how to keep her healthy.

However, I'd be remiss if I didn't also tell you about the following downsides to showing your dog:

- If you don't have a Pug with very good conformation, you may have a hard time getting that Ch designation.

- Showing can get expensive, depending on how involved you get in the sport. If you choose to train your dog yourself, you have to buy some special equipment because dog shows are held both indoors and outdoors and you want to protect Puggy and yourself from the elements.

  Conversely, you have to pay for the services of a professional trainer if you choose to go that route. See the section "Deciding Who Will Show Your Pug" for more info on both options.

  In addition, you need to fill out an entry form and submit it with the correct fee (usually $20 to $30) several weeks before the show. You can't enter a dog show on the spur of the moment. Each show has an entry deadline, and after that time, you're out of luck, no matter what excuse you give! (To find a list of all the AKC shows throughout the United States, check out the Events Calendar, published by the *AKC Gazette.*)

- Most shows are held on the weekends, so you need to be free to travel (and have a dependable car).

- Although rewarding, training your dog can sometimes be a challenge, which means you need a healthy dose of patience.

- Even the best dogs lose on occasion, so be ready to lose gracefully. No one likes a crybaby (I'm talking about you, not your dog).

If you're worried that Puggy can't be a loveable pet if she's a show dog, never fear. Other than not being spayed or neutered, show dogs act just like pets at home and should be treated the same way. You can still take them on outings, let them sleep on the bed or the couch with you, and give them plenty of kisses. Your Pug is your pet at home and a show dog in the big ring.

Deciding Who Will Show Your Pug

The next decision you have to make is whether you want to retain the services of a professional dog handler who can train your Pug and take her into the show ring for you or whether you want to do the job yourself. This section takes a look at both choices so that you can decide which works best for your situation.

Hiring a professional

You can find many qualified professional handlers in every area of the United States who earn their living showing dogs. The best handlers do this full-time, have a kennel to house the dogs before they go to a show, and own safe vehicles with adequate heating and air-conditioning. They also belong to the Professional Handlers Association of America and are certified by the AKC's Handler Program.

These talented men and women have spent years working around dogs and know how to groom, train, and show them off to their very best. Assuming a dog is good show material, a reputable handler can usually earn your Pug's Ch in about half the time it takes you to do the same job as a new exhibitor. Handlers do charge clients for this service, and the fees range from $75 to $100 per show plus travel expenses, depending on the distance covered. They may also charge a boarding fee, which ranges from $10 to $20 a day.

For a list of professional handlers in your area, contact the American Kennel Club through the Internet or regular mail. See Chapter 19 for specific contact information.

Climbing into the ring yourself

If you decide that you'd like to try showing your dog yourself, congratulations! Not counting the car, your initial cost to get started can range from $300 and up, depending on what you select. Here are some items that you need to get started:

- **Reliable car:** Your vehicle should be in good running order and have a good air-conditioning and heating system. You certainly don't want to break down far from home with a dog to care for. If you have a medium or large dog, the vehicle should have enough room for a dog crate (wire pet carrier).

- **Grooming supplies:** You need a grooming table so that you don't have to bend over to groom your Pug. You also need to train Puggy to stand still on a grooming table because at a dog show, that's where the judge examines your Pug (see Figure 16-1). Other grooming must-haves include nail clippers, brushes, a shedding blade, and dog shampoo. See Chapter 9 for more specifics about grooming.

Figure 16-1:
This Pug has been trained by her owner to stand still on a table at the dog show so that the judge can see her closely.

©Judi Crowe

✔ **Two show leashes and collars:** Take two leashes just in case one gets lost or breaks.

✔ **Suitable dog show attire:** You can't just show your dog in the same footwear and clothes you wear to wash the car or lounge on the beach. Here's what you need:

- **Comfortable, sturdy shoes:** You want to be sure that you can easily walk or run in them and that they stay on your feet and don't make noise.

  If you're showing indoors, the noise of shoes slapping on the floor bothers some dogs and distracts them from doing their best.

- **Business-type clothing:** Men should wear a sports jacket, dress shirt, tie, and slacks, and women need dress slacks or a skirt or dress for women. You should have an easily accessible pocket on the right side that you can use to store dog treats while you're in the ring.

- **Protective rain clothing:** If the show you're attending is outdoors, it's always a good idea to bring your rain gear along. You never know when Mother Nature's going to surprise you and your Pug.

✔ **Wire pet carrier:** While you're waiting to go into the ring at the show, your dog may need a quiet, secure place to rest. A wire pet carrier is just the ticket. If it's very hot or cold at the show, your Pug can go inside her carrier and cool off or warm up prior to showing.

✔ **Cart to transport the carrier at the shows:** When you arrive at the show, you can walk your Pug to the ring on her leash, but the carrier still has to go, too. Use a sturdy cart (they sell them at dog shows) to roll the carrier and your supplies.

✔ **Sunshade or a small tent in hot weather to keep your dog cool and prevent her from getting sunstroke:** You can use the same equipment in rainy weather. Because shows are held both indoors and outdoors, you need this equipment for protection.

✔ **A battery-powered fan and a few bags of ice in a cooler:** These items help keep Puggy cool and comfy and ward off the threat of heatstroke at the show.

✔ **Water from home and a travel water bucket or bowl:** Your dog may be thirsty at the show, so bring water from home. That way, you don't run the risk of her system becoming upset from drinking water she's not used to. For more information about bringing water with you, see Chapter 7.

✔ **Small food treats:** Giving your dog some small food treats while you're in the ring rewards her for a job well done.

You can always start out on your own and hire a handler to take over the job down the road, if you want, but you certainly can do the job yourself.

Finding classes and trainers

To prepare you and your dog for the show ring, you need to sign up for conformation classes. Here you can find other people showing their own dogs and instructors who also show their own dogs. It's a great way for you to give your dog lots of practice before the real shows.

Locating conformation classes close to home is fairly easy. First, contact the American Kennel Club. Someone there can refer you to dog show superintendents who are in charge of shows in your area. They know where all the classes are being held.

You can also ask your breeder, veterinarian, or other dog owners who show their dogs for names of trainers who teach good conformation classes. It's a good idea to get the names of a few trainers and go to a few different classes so that you can expose your dog to a variety of dogs and simulated show practice. Your local kennel club also is able to tell you where to find good classes.

In the class, you find out the following:

✔ How a show is conducted and all the rules

✔ The kind of collar and leash to use in the show ring

✔ How to position the collar and how to hold and use the leash correctly

✔ How to train your dog to stand still, or *stack,* on a grooming table so that the judge can easily examine your Pug and check her body and teeth

✔ How to teach your Pug to get along with other show dogs without wanting to play all the time

✔ How to let your Pug show off at the right time

If you're uncomfortable with the teacher for any reason — either you don't like the methods she uses or the way she interacts with your dog — then find a new class and instructor. Don't stop training altogether just because you may not agree with the instructor.

Plan on spending several weeks to a few months preparing your Pug to begin competing. Some people just need a little more time to learn a new skill and to connect with their dogs about the training.

Doing a trial run

When you feel that you've mastered the class instruction, take Puggy to a few *matches,* or practice shows. They're conducted like a real all-breed dog show — there's a judge and a ring just like you find at a regular show, but they don't count toward a championship title and they're a little more casual. You don't have to dress up for them, and often the judge can help you. Matches are also cheaper to enter — usually around $5, instead of the $25 for a regular show. For a list of matches in your area, contact your dog show superintendent.

Taking Your Pug to Shows

Traveling with a dog requires some special planning. In Chapter 12, I give you my recommendations about what to take on an ordinary car trip. However, when you're going to a dog show, I suggest traveling as light as possible. You'll be nervous enough as it is, so the fewer things to have to remember, the better.

Besides some of the things that I list in the section, "Climbing into the ring yourself" earlier in the chapter, you should take along some basics for your and Puggy's safety and comfort:

✔ **Dog food for Puggy:** If you're going to be away overnight, bring your dog's meals along.

✔ **A few extra towels:** You can wet them down to help cool Puggy off or use them to clean muddy paws.

✔ **An extra dog mat:** This item comes in handy for Puggy's carrier in case she dirties the first one.

> ✔ **Some clean-up bags:** It's your responsibility to clean up after your dog. Shows are pretty strict about this rule, so make sure that you're prepared.
>
> ✔ **Your veterinarian's phone number in case of an emergency:** Also have the name and phone number of a veterinarian at your final destination.

Striving for a championship title means travel time. Because you'll be on the road a lot with Puggy, she should have proper identification, in case she gets lost or stolen. For more information on different ways to identify your Pug, see Chapter 13.

Keeping It All in Perspective

Although you love your Pug to pieces, when you start showing her, you may realize that other Pugs out there are better show prospects. That's okay. If you really want a show dog, you can always purchase another Pug puppy from a show breeder. Or you may decide that conformation showing just isn't for you.

Perhaps you and Puggy are better suited for obedience or agility competitions (see Chapter 15 for more on these competitions). That's okay, too. The type of competition doesn't matter. What does matter is that you enjoy the time you spend with your Pug, regardless of the activity.

Part V
The Part of Tens

In this part . . .

I can't let you get to the end of this book without some final quick and useful hints to use with your Pug. So in this part, I offer a list of ten do's and don'ts to help you have quality Pug time. In addition, I give you ten reasons why you shouldn't consider breeding your Pug. Finally, I round out the book with a list of ten resources where you can go for even more Pug info.

Chapter 17

Ten Do's and Don'ts of Living with a Pug

. . . .

In This Chapter
▶ Keeping your Pug happy and healthy
▶ Avoiding bad habits Pugs can fall into

. . . .

Looking for more information on things you should or should not be doing with your Pug? This chapter offers a list of my top ten favorite things. The first five suggestions are the do's, and the second five are the don'ts.

Do Feed Your Pug Properly

A good diet can help your Pug maintain a quality lifestyle and good health. You can't give him a better present than this. Many premium foods are on the market, or you can opt for a homemade diet that has all the same vitamins and minerals as the commercially prepared foods. Good nutrition goes a long way to a long and happy life. For more information on feeding a good Pug diet, see Chapter 7.

Do Train Your Pug to Be a Good Companion

Every Pug needs some training, but training Pugs doesn't take much effort because a little goes a long way with this breed. If you just spend a little time each week working on training at home or taking him to a few classes, you're rewarded with a Pug who is a pleasure to have around. Anyone who comes to visit will appreciate meeting a well-behaved dog. For more information about training your Pug, see Chapter 10.

Do Keep Your Pug Well Groomed

Yes, Pugs do shed, but keeping your dog's coat clean and brushed can help reduce the shedding a little. Although Pugs don't require much grooming, regular bathing and brushing once every three weeks makes Puggy feel and look better. I also recommend cleaning out your Pug's wrinkles every day. And keep those nails trimmed once a week, too. He can walk better if he doesn't have to rock backward just trying to maintain his balance. For more information about grooming, see Chapter 9.

Do Keep Your Pug Active

An active Pug is a healthy and a happy Pug. Although he doesn't need to have a lot of exercise, some exercise is good for him . . . and for you. Get out for a walk a few times a week, take him swimming, or even throw a ball for him to chase. These activities help keep your Pug limber and maintain muscle tone. For more information about exercising your Pug, see Chapter 8.

Do Be Aware of Potential Health Problems

As the old saying goes, forewarned is forearmed. If you know what health problems Pugs can have, you're in a better position to prevent your Pug from succumbing to them. For more information about Pug health, see Chapter 14.

Or if he does have a health problem, having some background knowledge about common Pug health concerns allows you to deal with it and seek medical help as soon as possible. If you need to find more information about finding a veterinarian, getting vaccinations, and spaying and neutering, see Chapter 13.

Don't Let Your Pug Get Overweight

Being overweight is the number one problem that many Pugs have. It can shorten their lives and be the cause of many illnesses. Sure, he may look sad when he gazes up at you, wanting more food, but stop and think what's really good for him — his health. Just say no to extra meals or get in the habit of giving him some cut up pieces of people-food veggies to fill the hunger you think he has. Chances are that if you're feeding him a premium-quality food in the right amounts, he doesn't need anything extra, at all.

Don't Spoil Your Dog

Toy dogs sure know how to get their way with humans. All Pugs have to do is cuddle up to you and wag that cute little curly tail back and forth. And bingo, they've made you give them what they want. Besides, once you see those big googly eyes staring up at you, how can you resist? Still, don't let your Pug run the household. You're the one in charge, so don't go falling for any of that cute stuff!

Here's where Puggy may need to spend some private time away from you. Use Puggy's pet carrier to reinforce that you're the boss. Another way to get the message across that you're the leader is for you to go through the door before he does. Believe me, he'll still like you in the morning, even if you enforce a few rules.

Don't Let Unruly Children Bother Him

Your job is to protect your Pug from visiting children who aren't treating him the way you think they should. Instruct kids what to do and what not to do around your Pug and supervise, supervise, supervise. If you feel for any reason that they're mistreating your Pug, step in and discontinue the play. If Puggy could talk, he'd tell you the same thing.

Don't Neglect Your Pug

After the honeymoon period of having a Pug wears off, you're still going to have your dog for a long time. Keep your life with your dog interesting by taking him along on outings with you. Try to find things the two of you can do together, such as agility competitions or therapy, and make him a part of your life. Not only is this good for him, but you benefit from having a companion, too.

Don't Forget to Kiss, Hug, and Pet Your Pug

Pugs need love, that's for sure. Some need your attention all the time — every time you sit down, they expect to be petted. Or they follow you around from room to room, anticipating that you can stop on the way to give them a hug. Although this may be more love than you want to give every day, give your Pug the attention he deserves.

Talk to him, take him for a walk, go for a ride, or whatever, but do something every day with him. That way, he may not insist on constant hands-on attention. Of course, if you like doing this, enjoy every minute of adoring your Pug.

Chapter 18

Ten Reasons Not to Breed Your Pug

*Y*ou love your Pug with all your heart and soul. Why, then, would you want to put her life in danger by breeding her?

The truth is that breeding pups is a much bigger job than many people think. In fact, the job is better left to experienced breeders who've dedicated their lives to safeguarding the breed. If you're one of these people, I certainly don't want to discourage you. But if you're contemplating breeding because you think it's fun, skip it! In fact, this chapter offers ten reasons why you should pass on the mother dog experience.

It Creates More Homeless Pugs

Ask any animal shelter workers, and they can tell you that way too many Pugs are homeless. Why? Too many puppies are being bred by backyard breeders who can't find homes for all the pups they breed. These are people who place their pups with anyone who can pay for them, not necessarily the people who can give them good homes. Soon these people lose interest or have a dog problem they don't want to take the time to solve, so they abandon the dog.

It Doesn't Yield Another Pug Just Like the Mother

If you think you want to breed because you love your Pug so much that you want another just like her, guess what — it won't happen. Like people, no two dogs are alike.

It Can Be Very Expensive

If you think that you can make some extra money by selling puppies, guess again. You can't, especially if you have unexpected veterinary expenses, such as a Cesarean section (which is very expensive), or health problems with the puppies. The routine veterinary bills for the mother before she delivers and care of the puppies afterward can be costly enough.

It Doesn't Teach the Kids about the Birds and the Bees

If you want the kids to experience the miracle of birth, choose another miracle to give them. Children are usually bored or scared by the experience and have no interest in the process.

It Isn't Fun

If you simply think breeding a litter sounds like fun, it's not. The reality is that you could lose your beloved Pug during delivery and have to hand-feed the puppies around the clock. That's hardly fun.

Your Pug May Not Be Healthy Enough to Be Bred

Only the best can produce the best. Although your Pug may be very cute and lovable, you don't want to pass on any undesirable traits to her kids, do you? Ask yourself whether your Pug has any health issues, including skin problems

or being overweight (more than 26 pounds). Does she ever snap at anyone?
Does she have other undesirable characteristics that prevent her from becoming an AKC champion? (See Chapter 16 for more on becoming a champion
Pug.) If so, by breeding her, you'd be making inferior puppies, not good ones.

Reputable show breeders routinely test their dogs to make sure that they
won't be passing down any inherited diseases. Without having these expensive tests, you have no way of knowing what deadly diseases your Pug puppies may have.

It Risks Your Pug's Life

Just because you breed your Pug doesn't guarantee that she can successfully
deliver a healthy litter of puppies. After she becomes pregnant, anything can
happen to her. She can get an infection, run a high fever, and have complications. The worst thing is that you could end up losing your loving Pug. Would
a litter of puppies be worth that cost to you?

It's a Major Time Commitment

How many sleepless nights or days off from work can you deal with? While
your Pug is recuperating from delivery, the mother and puppies are still susceptible to lots of health problems. For example, you have to be on a constant vigil to monitor how much the mother and pups eat and drink, whether
they're urinating and defecating okay, and whether the mother is nursing the
puppies enough. You also have to check regularly to make sure that the
mother doesn't accidentally roll over and crush the pups.

And another big question to ask yourself is: Do you know enough to recognize a health problem when you see it, and if so, can you do something about
it before it's too late?

Parting with the Puppies May Be Too Emotional

If you spend 10 weeks of your life caring for your pups night and day, don't
expect it to be easy for you to say goodbye to them when the time comes for
them to go to their homes. On the day they're supposed to leave, picture
yourself with these puppies for the last time. How will you feel? Do you have
the heart to do this? If not, I recommend spaying your female.

Finding Good Homes for the Puppies May Be Hard

What's a good home? It's people who commit to keeping a pup forever and providing good nutrition, regular veterinary care, emergency services, proper training and housing, and lots and lots of love. Finding homes like this for every puppy in the litter takes as much time and patience as rearing the litter does, if not more.

You'll be searching for these people — who are, in all likelihood, total strangers to you — and you have to answer all their questions and be available when they're able to come and see the puppies. Then you have to ask them enough tough questions to feel satisfied that they're the right people for the job. If they're not, you have to start the process all over again.

Bear in mind that you don't have much time to find homes for the pups. Puppies don't start moving around much until they're 5 weeks old, and ideally, they need to go to their new homes when they're between 8 and 10 weeks old.

Taking the Puppies Back After They're Grown Isn't an Option

Maybe you want to have just one litter because you have friends or family members who think your Pug is so wonderful that they want one of her puppies. Keep in mind, however, that they may change their minds when the time actually comes to take home a Pug puppy. When they do, you're responsible for keeping the puppies you can't place.

Reputable breeders offer a health guarantee and a take-back policy. Can you honor an agreement that you'll take the puppy back and return a portion of their money or give them a free replacement if the puppy develops a crippling hereditary condition within 24 months? If pups do come back, do you have the space and money to keep so many dogs? If the answer is no, plan on spaying your Pug.

Chapter 19

Ten Resources for Pug Lovers

*I*f you're looking for more information about your Pug, you've come to the right place. Maybe you want to network with other Pug owners, share training information, or find out about common Pug health issues. This chapter provides a list of organizations and resources you can consult.

Pugs.com

This Web site (`www.pugs.com`) provides information about Pugs and their health, care, and training. It also offers information about finding a Pug. The site is very extensive; in fact, its owners have 25 years of experience with the breed.

Pugs.org (The Pug Dog Club of America)

This is the Web site of the Pug Dog Club of America, the national Pug breed club (`www.pugs.org`). It provides sources for finding a breeder, choosing puppies, joining the club, researching Pug health, and understanding dog shows. It also gives information on H.O.P.E., its Pug rescue organization.

The American Kennel Club

The American Kennel Club (AKC) is concerned with every breed of purebred dogs; it provides information and listings about shows, clubs, rules for conformation, obedience, agility, and other companion competitions.

You can contact the American Kennel Club by mail at 5580 Centerview Drive, Raleigh, NC 27606 or online at www.akc.org. For questions about purebred Pug registrations, call 919-233-9767 or e-mail info@akc.org.

Pug Rescue Organizations

You can find an alphabetical listing of all the Pug rescue organizations throughout the United States on www.frankthepug.org/rescues.htm. If you want to adopt a rescue Pug, this Web site is the best place to start looking. You can also e-mail the site, at bmegel@adelphia.net.

American Veterinary Medical Association

The American Veterinary Medical Association (AVMA) provides a wealth of medical information, such as how to select a pet, and tells you about pet health and other veterinary news on its Web site, www.avma.org. The site even has a section just for children about pet care and pet health.

If your dog needs more veterinary care than your own vet can give, you may need to look for an AVMA-recognized veterinary specialist in your area. The AVMA Web site can help you locate one. It provides listings of all the veterinary specialty organizations, such as the American College of Veterinary Ophthalmologists, the American College of Veterinary Behaviorists, or the American College of Veterinary Dermatology.

Delta Society

The Delta Society's Web site (www.deltasociety.org) provides information about its Pet Partner Program. The program screens and trains volunteers and their pets to visit hospitals, nursing homes, rehabilitation centers, schools, and other facilities. It links volunteers with facilities that request visiting pets in their own community. Write to the Delta Society at 580 Naches Ave. SW, Suite 101, Renton, WA 98055-2297. You can also contact this group by phone, 425-226-7357; fax, 425-235-1076; or e-mail, info@deltasociety.org.

The Association of Pet Dog Trainers

The Association of Pet Dog Trainers (APDT) is concerned with positive training methods for dogs and general education about training. It also provides a list of dog trainers in every state and local area. Contact the group at Association of Pet Dog Trainers, P.O. Box 1781, Hobbs, NM 88241; phone, 800-PET-DOGS (800-738-3647); fax, 856-439-0525; e-mail, information@apdt.com; Web site, www.apdt.com.

North American Dog Agility Council

Established in 1993, the North American Dog Agility Council (NADAC) provides information on agility clubs and competition. For more information, write to the North American Dog Agility Council, Inc. 11522 South Hwy 3, Cataldo, ID 83810, or access its Web site at www.nadac.com. The NADAC also sanctions agility trials.

The United States Dog Agility Association

The United States Dog Agility Association (USDAA) puts on agility trials throughout the United States. It also provides information on agility clubs and competition. You can contact the USDAA at P.O. Box 850955, Richardson, TX 75085-0955; phone, 972-487-2200; fax, 972-272-4404; or online at www.usdaa.com.

The Association for Pet Loss and Bereavement

The Association for Pet Loss and Bereavement (APLB) acknowledges that losing a pet can be painful. This group is experienced in counseling people after they have lost their pets. Members are counselors who have also lost a pet. Contact them at P.O. Box 106, Brooklyn, NY 11230; phone, 718-382-0690; e-mail, aplb@aplb.org; or online at www.aplb.org.

Pug Talk Magazine

If you're looking for a magazine about Pugs, this is it. The magazine has 80 pages of photos and articles on Pug health, training, humor, and day-to-day living. Available by subscription, the magazine comes out six times a year. To find out more about the magazine, check out www.pugtalk.com or e-mail tupelo@wctc.net.

Index

FOR DUMMIES®

The easy way to get more done and have more fun

PERSONAL FINANCE

Personal Finance FOR DUMMIES
0-7645-5231-7

Investing FOR DUMMIES
0-7645-2431-3

Home Buying FOR DUMMIES
0-7645-5331-3

Also available:

Estate Planning For Dummies
(0-7645-5501-4)

401(k)s For Dummies
(0-7645-5468-9)

Frugal Living For Dummies
(0-7645-5403-4)

Microsoft Money "X" For Dummies
(0-7645-1689-2)

Mutual Funds For Dummies
(0-7645-5329-1)

Personal Bankruptcy For Dummies
(0-7645-5498-0)

Quicken "X" For Dummies
(0-7645-1666-3)

Stock Investing For Dummies
(0-7645-5411-5)

Taxes For Dummies 2003
(0-7645-5475-1)

BUSINESS & CAREERS

Accounting FOR DUMMIES
0-7645-5314-3

Grant Writing FOR DUMMIES
0-7645-5307-0

Resumes FOR DUMMIES
0-7645-5471-9

Also available:

Business Plans Kit For Dummies
(0-7645-5365-8)

Consulting For Dummies
(0-7645-5034-9)

Cool Careers For Dummies
(0-7645-5345-3)

Human Resources Kit For Dummies
(0-7645-5131-0)

Managing For Dummies
(1-5688-4858-7)

QuickBooks All-in-One Desk Reference For Dummies
(0-7645-1963-8)

Selling For Dummies
(0-7645-5363-1)

Small Business Kit For Dummies
(0-7645-5093-4)

Starting an eBay Business For Dummies
(0-7645-1547-0)

HEALTH, SPORTS & FITNESS

Fitness FOR DUMMIES
0-7645-5167-1

Golf FOR DUMMIES
0-7645-5146-9

Diabetes FOR DUMMIES
0-7645-5154-X

Also available:

Controlling Cholesterol For Dummies
(0-7645-5440-9)

Dieting For Dummies
(0-7645-5126-4)

High Blood Pressure For Dummies
(0-7645-5424-7)

Martial Arts For Dummies
(0-7645-5358-5)

Menopause For Dummies
(0-7645-5458-1)

Nutrition For Dummies
(0-7645-5180-9)

Power Yoga For Dummies
(0-7645-5342-9)

Thyroid For Dummies
(0-7645-5385-2)

Weight Training For Dummies
(0-7645-5168-X)

Yoga For Dummies
(0-7645-5117-5)

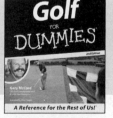

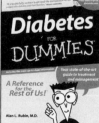

Available wherever books are sold.
Go to www.dummies.com or call 1-877-762-2974 to order direct.

WILEY

FOR DUMMIES®

A world of resources to help you grow

HOME, GARDEN & HOBBIES

Feng Shui FOR DUMMIES
A Reference for the Rest of Us!
0-7645-5295-3

Gardening FOR DUMMIES
A Reference for the Rest of Us!
0-7645-5130-2

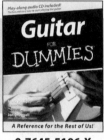

Guitar FOR DUMMIES
A Reference for the Rest of Us!
0-7645-5106-X

Also available:

Auto Repair For Dummies
(0-7645-5089-6)

Chess For Dummies
(0-7645-5003-9)

Home Maintenance For
Dummies
(0-7645-5215-5)

Organizing For Dummies
(0-7645-5300-3)

Piano For Dummies
(0-7645-5105-1)

Poker For Dummies
(0-7645-5232-5)

Quilting For Dummies
(0-7645-5118-3)

Rock Guitar For Dummies
(0-7645-5356-9)

Roses For Dummies
(0-7645-5202-3)

Sewing For Dummies
(0-7645-5137-X)

FOOD & WINE

Cooking FOR DUMMIES
A Reference for the Rest of Us!
0-7645-5250-3

Cookies FOR DUMMIES
A Reference for the Rest of Us!
0-7645-5390-9

Wine FOR DUMMIES
A Reference for the Rest of Us!
0-7645-5114-0

Also available:

Bartending For Dummies
(0-7645-5051-9)

Chinese Cooking For
Dummies
(0-7645-5247-3)

Christmas Cooking For
Dummies
(0-7645-5407-7)

Diabetes Cookbook For
Dummies
(0-7645-5230-9)

Grilling For Dummies
(0-7645-5076-4)

Low-Fat Cooking For
Dummies
(0-7645-5035-7)

Slow Cookers For Dummies
(0-7645-5240-6)

TRAVEL

Italy FOR DUMMIES
A Travel Guide for the Rest of Us!
0-7645-5453-0

Hawaii FOR DUMMIES
A Travel Guide for the Rest of Us!
0-7645-5438-7

Las Vegas FOR DUMMIES
A Travel Guide for the Rest of Us!
0-7645-5448-4

Also available:

America's National Parks For
Dummies
(0-7645-6204-5)

Caribbean For Dummies
(0-7645-5445-X)

Cruise Vacations For
Dummies 2003
(0-7645-5459-X)

Europe For Dummies
(0-7645-5456-5)

Ireland For Dummies
(0-7645-6199-5)

France For Dummies
(0-7645-6292-4)

London For Dummies
(0-7645-5416-6)

Mexico's Beach Resorts For
Dummies
(0-7645-6262-2)

Paris For Dummies
(0-7645-5494-8)

RV Vacations For Dummies
(0-7645-5443-3)

Walt Disney World & Orlando
For Dummies
(0-7645-5444-1)

Available wherever books are sold. Go to www.dummies.com or call 1-877-762-2974 to order direct.

FOR DUMMIES®

Plain-English solutions for everyday challenges

COMPUTER BASICS

PCs FOR DUMMIES

0-7645-0838-5

The Flat-Screen iMac FOR DUMMIES

0-7645-1663-9

Windows XP ALL-IN-ONE DESK REFERENCE FOR DUMMIES

0-7645-1548-9

Also available:

PCs All-in-One Desk
Reference For Dummies
(0-7645-0791-5)
Pocket PC For Dummies
(0-7645-1640-X)
Treo and Visor For Dummies
(0-7645-1673-6)
Troubleshooting Your PC For
Dummies
(0-7645-1669-8)

Upgrading & Fixing PCs For
Dummies
(0-7645-1665-5)
Windows XP For Dummies
(0-7645-0893-8)
Windows XP For Dummies
Quick Reference
(0-7645-0897-0)

BUSINESS SOFTWARE

Excel 2002 FOR DUMMIES

0-7645-0822-9

Word 2002 FOR DUMMIES

0-7645-0839-3

Office XP 9 IN 1 DESK REFERENCE FOR DUMMIES

0-7645-0819-9

Also available:

Excel Data Analysis For
Dummies
(0-7645-1661-2)
Excel 2002 All-in-One Desk
Reference For Dummies
(0-7645-1794-5)
Excel 2002 For Dummies
Quick Reference
(0-7645-0829-6)
GoldMine "X" For Dummies
(0-7645-0845-8)

Microsoft CRM For Dummies
(0-7645-1698-1)
Microsoft Project 2002 For
Dummies
(0-7645-1628-0)
Office XP For Dummies
(0-7645-0830-X)
Outlook 2002 For Dummies
(0-7645-0828-8)

Get smart! Visit www.dummies.com

- **Find listings of even more *For Dummies* titles**
- **Browse online articles**
- **Sign up for Dummies eTips™**
- **Check out *For Dummies* fitness videos and other products**
- **Order from our online bookstore**

Available wherever books are sold. Go to www.dummies.com or call 1-877-762-2974 to order direct.

FOR DUMMIES®

Helping you expand your horizons and realize your potential

INTERNET

The Internet FOR DUMMIES
0-7645-0894-6

The Internet ALL-IN-ONE DESK REFERENCE FOR DUMMIES
0-7645-1659-0

eBay FOR DUMMIES
0-7645-1642-6

Also available:

America Online 7.0 For Dummies
(0-7645-1624-8)

Genealogy Online For Dummies
(0-7645-0807-5)

The Internet All-in-One Desk Reference For Dummies
(0-7645-1659-0)

Internet Explorer 6 For Dummies
(0-7645-1344-3)

The Internet For Dummies Quick Reference
(0-7645-1645-0)

Internet Privacy For Dummies
(0-7645-0846-6)

Researching Online For Dummies
(0-7645-0546-7)

Starting an Online Business For Dummies
(0-7645-1655-8)

DIGITAL MEDIA

Digital Photography FOR DUMMIES
0-7645-1664-7

Photoshop Elements 2 FOR DUMMIES
0-7645-1675-2

Digital Video FOR DUMMIES
0-7645-0806-7

Also available:

CD and DVD Recording For Dummies
(0-7645-1627-2)

Digital Photography All-in-One Desk Reference For Dummies
(0-7645-1800-3)

Digital Photography For Dummies Quick Reference
(0-7645-0750-8)

Home Recording for Musicians For Dummies
(0-7645-1634-5)

MP3 For Dummies
(0-7645-0858-X)

Paint Shop Pro "X" For Dummies
(0-7645-2440-2)

Photo Retouching & Restoration For Dummies
(0-7645-1662-0)

Scanners For Dummies
(0-7645-0783-4)

GRAPHICS

PowerPoint 2002 FOR DUMMIES
0-7645-0817-2

Photoshop 7 FOR DUMMIES
0-7645-1651-5

Macromedia Flash MX FOR DUMMIES
0-7645-0895-4

Also available:

Adobe Acrobat 5 PDF For Dummies
(0-7645-1652-3)

Fireworks 4 For Dummies
(0-7645-0804-0)

Illustrator 10 For Dummies
(0-7645-3636-2)

QuarkXPress 5 For Dummies
(0-7645-0643-9)

Visio 2000 For Dummies
(0-7645-0635-8)

Available wherever books are sold. Go to www.dummies.com or call 1-877-762-2974 to order direct.

FOR DUMMIES®

The advice and explanations you need to succeed

SELF-HELP, SPIRITUALITY & RELIGION

  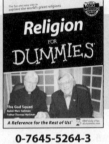

Sex For Dummies
0-7645-5302-X

Parenting For Dummies
0-7645-5418-2

Religion For Dummies
0-7645-5264-3

Also available:

The Bible For Dummies
(0-7645-5296-1)

Buddhism For Dummies
(0-7645-5359-3)

Christian Prayer For Dummies
(0-7645-5500-6)

Dating For Dummies
(0-7645-5072-1)

Judaism For Dummies
(0-7645-5299-6)

Potty Training For Dummies
(0-7645-5417-4)

Pregnancy For Dummies
(0-7645-5074-8)

Rekindling Romance For Dummies
(0-7645-5303-8)

Spirituality For Dummies
(0-7645-5298-8)

Weddings For Dummies
(0-7645-5055-1)

PETS

Puppies For Dummies
0-7645-5255-4

Dog Training For Dummies
0-7645-5286-4

Cats For Dummies
0-7645-5275-9

Also available:

Labrador Retrievers For Dummies
(0-7645-5281-3)

Aquariums For Dummies
(0-7645-5156-6)

Birds For Dummies
(0-7645-5139-6)

Dogs For Dummies
(0-7645-5274-0)

Ferrets For Dummies
(0-7645-5259-7)

German Shepherds For Dummies
(0-7645-5280-5)

Golden Retrievers For Dummies
(0-7645-5267-8)

Horses For Dummies
(0-7645-5138-8)

Jack Russell Terriers For Dummies
(0-7645-5268-6)

Puppies Raising & Training Diary For Dummies
(0-7645-0876-8)

EDUCATION & TEST PREPARATION

 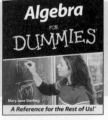 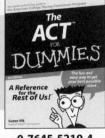

Spanish For Dummies
0-7645-5194-9

Algebra For Dummies
0-7645-5325-9

The ACT For Dummies
0-7645-5210-4

Also available:

Chemistry For Dummies
(0-7645-5430-1)

English Grammar For Dummies
(0-7645-5322-4)

French For Dummies
(0-7645-5193-0)

The GMAT For Dummies
(0-7645-5251-1)

Inglés Para Dummies
(0-7645-5427-1)

Italian For Dummies
(0-7645-5196-5)

Research Papers For Dummies
(0-7645-5426-3)

The SAT I For Dummies
(0-7645-5472-7)

U.S. History For Dummies
(0-7645-5249-X)

World History For Dummies
(0-7645-5242-2)

Available wherever books are sold. Go to www.dummies.com or call 1-877-762-2974 to order direct.

FOR DUMMIES®

We take the mystery out of complicated subjects

WEB DEVELOPMENT

Creating Web Pages For Dummies
0-7645-1643-4

HTML 4 For Dummies
0-7645-0723-0

Dreamweaver MX For Dummies
0-7645-1630-2

Also available:

ASP.NET For Dummies
(0-7645-0866-0)

Building a Web Site For Dummies
(0-7645-0720-6)

ColdFusion "MX" For Dummies (0-7645-1672-8)

Creating Web Pages All-in-One Desk Reference For Dummies
(0-7645-1542-X)

FrontPage 2002 For Dummies
(0-7645-0821-0)

HTML 4 For Dummies Quick Reference
(0-7645-0721-4)

Macromedia Studio "MX" All-in-One Desk Reference For Dummies
(0-7645-1799-6)

Web Design For Dummies
(0-7645-0823-7)

PROGRAMMING & DATABASES

C++ For Dummies
0-7645-0746-X

XML For Dummies
0-7645-1657-4

Access 2002 For Dummies
0-7645-0818-0

Also available:

Beginning Programming For Dummies
(0-7645-0835-0)

Crystal Reports "X" For Dummies
(0-7645-1641-8)

Java & XML For Dummies
(0-7645-1658-2)

Java 2 For Dummies
(0-7645-0765-6)

JavaScript For Dummies
(0-7645-0633-1)

Oracle9i For Dummies
(0-7645-0880-6)

Perl For Dummies
(0-7645-0776-1)

PHP and MySQL For Dummies
(0-7645-1650-7)

SQL For Dummies
(0-7645-0737-0)

VisualBasic .NET For Dummies
(0-7645-0867-9)

Visual Studio .NET All-in-One Desk Reference For Dummies
(0-7645-1626-4)

LINUX, NETWORKING & CERTIFICATION

 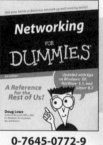

Red Hat Linux 7.3 For Dummies
0-7645-1545-4

Networking For Dummies
0-7645-0772-9

A+ Certification For Dummies
0-7645-0812-1

Also available:

CCNP All-in-one Certification For Dummies
(0-7645-1648-5)

Cisco Networking For Dummies
(0-7645-1668-X)

CISSP For Dummies
(0-7645-1670-1)

CIW Foundations For Dummies with CD-ROM
(0-7645-1635-3)

Firewalls For Dummies
(0-7645-0884-9)

Home Networking For Dummies
(0-7645-0857-1)

Red Hat Linux All-in-One Desk Reference For Dummies
(0-7645-2442-9)

TCP/IP For Dummies
(0-7645-1760-0)

UNIX For Dummies
(0-7645-0419-3)

Available wherever books are sold.
Go to www.dummies.com or call 1-877-762-2974 to order direct.

 **WILEY**